ANNUITY
Principles and Products

LOMA (Life Office Management Association, Inc.) is an international association founded in 1924. LOMA is committed to a business partnership with its worldwide members in the insurance and financial services industry to improve their management and operations through quality employee development, research, information sharing, and related products and services. Among LOMA's activities is the sponsorship of the FLMI Education Program—an educational program intended primarily for home office and branch office employees.

The *Associate, Annuity Products and Administration (AAPA) Program* is designed for people who work with all areas of annuities—including product development, marketing/sales, administration, customer service, systems, investments, accounting, and legal/compliance—as well as regulators. To earn the AAPA designation, a student must complete all required courses as outlined in LOMA's most current *Education and Training Catalog*. Upon successful completion of all required courses, the student receives a diploma awarded by LOMA and is entitled to use the letters *AAPA* after his/her name.

Statement of Purpose:
LOMA Educational Programs Testing and Designations

Examinations described in the LOMA *Education and Training Catalog* are designed solely to measure whether students have successfully completed the relevant assigned curriculum, and the attainment of the AAPA and other LOMA designations indicates only that all examinations in the given curriculum have been successfully completed. In no way shall a student's completion of a given LOMA course or attainment of the AAPA or other LOMA designation be construed to mean that LOMA in any way certifies that student's competence, training, or ability to perform any given task. LOMA's examinations are to be used solely for general educational purposes, and no other use of the examinations or programs is authorized or intended by LOMA. Furthermore, it is in no way the intention of the LOMA curriculum and examinations staff to describe the standard of appropriate conduct in any field of the insurance and financial services industry, and LOMA expressly repudiates any attempt to so use the curriculum and examinations. Any such assessment of student competence or industry standards of conduct should instead be based on independent professional inquiry and the advice of competent professional counsel.

ANNUITY
Principles and Products

John P. Burger, FLMI, ACS

Kristen L. Falk, FLMI ACS, AIAA, AAPA, AIRC, ARA

Patsy Leeuwenburg, Ph.D., FLMI, ACS, ALHC, AIAA, ARA, AIRC, PAHM

LOMA
Atlanta, Georgia
www.loma.org

Associate, Annuity Products and Administration
Education Program

Information in this text may have been changed
or updated since its publication date.
For current updates, visit www.loma.org.

Second Edition

Authors:	John P. Burger, FLMI, ACS
	Kristen L. Falk, FLMI, ACS, AIAA, AAPA, AIRC, ARA
	Patsy Leeuwenburg, Ph.D., FLMI, ACS, ALHC, AIAA, ARA, AIRC, PAHM
Manuscript Editor:	Mark Adel, FLMI, PCS, AIRC, PAHM
Exam Editor:	Melanie Green, FLMI, ACS, AIAA
Project Manager:	Jena L. Kennedy, FLMI, ACS, AIAA, ALHC, HIA, MHP, PAHM, CLU
Production Manager:	Stephen J. Bollinger, ACS
Copyeditor:	Steve Tunnell
Indexer:	Mary Rauch
Typesetters:	Allison Ayers
	Stephen J. Bollinger, ACS
	Mary Rusch
	Kathleen Ryan, FLMI, PCS, AIRC, AIAA, ARA, PAHM
Production Coordinator:	Amy Souwan
Print Buyer:	Audrey H. Gregory, ACS
Permissions Coordinator:	Iris F. Hartley, FLMI, ALHC
Administrative Support:	Aurelia Kennedy-Hemphill
	Mary Rusch
Cover Designers:	Stephen J. Bollinger, ACS
	Kathleen Ryan, FLMI, PCS, AIRC, AIAA, ARA, PAHM

Copyright © 2004 LOMA (Life Office Management Association, Inc.) *All rights reserved.*

11 10 09 08 07 06 05 04   10 9 8 7 6 5 4 3 2 1

This text, or any part thereof, may not be reproduced or transmitted in any form or by any means, electronic or mechanical, including photocopying, recording, storage in an information retrieval system, or otherwise, without the prior written permission of the publisher.

While a great deal of care has been taken to provide accurate, current, and authoritative information in regard to the subject matter covered in this book, the ideas, suggestions, general principles, conclusions, and any other information presented here are for general educational purposes only. This text is sold with the understanding that it is neither designed nor intended to provide the reader with legal, accounting, investment, marketing, or other types of professional business management advice. If legal advice or other expert assistance is required, the services of a competent professional should be sought.

Library of Congress Cataloging-in-Publication Data

Burger, John P.
   Annuity principles and products / John P. Burger, Kristen L. Falk, Patsy Leeuwenburg. — 2nd ed.
     p. cm.
  "Associate Annuity Products and Administration, Education Program."
  Includes index.
  ISBN 1-57974-194-0
   1. Annuities. I. Falk, Kristen L. II. Leeuwenburg, Patsy, 1948- III. Associate Annuity Products and Administration Program. IV. Title.

HG8790.B87 2004
368.3'7—dc22

ISBN 1-57974-194-0
Printed in Canada

Contents

Preface ix

CHAPTER 1: Annuity Basics 1
Key Figures in an Annuity Purchase 3
    Contract Owner 4
    Insurer 5
    Annuitant 5
    Payee 6
    Beneficiary 6
Types of Annuities 7
    Immediate and Deferred Annuities 7
    Single-Premium and Flexible-Premium Annuities 9
    Fixed and Variable Annuities 10
    Individual and Group Annuities 11
    Qualified and Nonqualified Annuities 12
The Annuities Market 12
    Changing Demographics 12
    Changing Retirement Income Needs 14
    Concerns About Current Retirement Savings Programs ... 15
    Savings and Money-Management Features of Annuities ... 16

CHAPTER 2: The Annuity Contract 19
Formation of the Annuity Contract 21
    The Completed Annuity Application 21
    The Initial Premium 23
    Contract Provisions 23
    Entire Contract Provision 23
Administration of Annuities During the Accumulation Period 26
    Crediting Earnings 26
    Fees and Charges 28
    Payment of Death Benefits 32
Distributions 33
    Nonannuitized Payout Options 33
    Annuitized Payout Options 35
    Payout Options for Variable Annuities 37
    Calculating Annuity Payments 39

CHAPTER 3: Fixed Annuities 43
Traditional Fixed Annuities 45
    Principal Guarantees 45
    Interest Rate Guarantees 45
    Payout Guarantees 46
    Inflation Erosion 48

Equity-Indexed Annuities 48
   Principal Guarantees 48
   Interest Rate Guarantees 49
   Vesting Rights 52
Market Value Adjusted Annuities 52
   Investment Options 53
   Market Value Adjustments 53
Future of the Fixed Annuity Market 54

CHAPTER 4: Variable Annuities 57
Investment Risk and Return 59
Subaccount Investments 59
   Asset Classes 61
   Asset Allocation 63
   Subaccount Values 64
   Contract Values 66
Special Services 66
   Automatic Dollar Cost Averaging 68
   Transfers Between Subaccounts 69
   Automatic Rebalancing 69
Guaranteed Living Benefits 70
Guaranteed Death Benefits 71

CHAPTER 5: Investment Basics 73
Investment Principles 75
   Risk and Return 75
   Time Value of Money 80
   Dollar Cost Averaging 81
   Diversification and Asset Allocation 82
Investment Features of Variable Annuities
and Other Financial Products 83
   Investment Security 83
   Access to Funds 83
   Tax Advantages 85
   Payout Options 88

CHAPTER 6: Individual and Group Annuities 91
Individual Annuities 93
   Saving for Retirement 93
   Managing Lump Sum Distributions 96
   Funding Education 99
Group Annuities 100
   Qualified Retirement Plans in the United States 101
   Registered Retirement Plans in Canada 109
   Nonqualified Retirement Plans 110

CHAPTER 7: Taxation of Annuities 113
U.S. Income Taxes 116
    Income Taxes on Annuity Premiums 116
    Income Taxes on Annuity Earnings 117
    Income Taxes on Annuity Benefit Payments 117
    Income Taxes on Withdrawals 120
    Income Taxes on Loans 121
U.S. Penalty Taxes 123
U.S. Estate Taxes 125
Other U.S. Taxes on Annuities 126
    Exchanges 126
    Rollovers 127
Canadian Taxation of Annuities 127

CHAPTER 8: Regulation of the Annuity Industry ... 129
U.S. State Regulation 131
    Solvency Regulation 133
    Market Conduct Regulation 134
U.S. Federal Regulation 140
    Securities Regulation 141
Canadian Provincial Regulation 146
    Solvency Regulation 146
    Market Conduct Regulation 146
Canadian Federal Regulation 147

CHAPTER 9: Marketing and Distributing Annuities 149
Market Selection 151
Product Development 153
    Product Planning 153
    Comprehensive Business Analysis 155
    Product Technical Design 155
    Product Implementation 156
    Sales Monitoring and Product Review 158
Financial Design 158
Product Promotion 160
    Personal Selling 160
    Advertising 161
    Sales Promotion and Marketing Materials 161
    Publicity 163
Product Distribution 163
    Personal Selling Distribution Systems 165
    Financial Institutions Distribution Systems 170
    Direct Response Distribution Systems 172

CHAPTER 10: The Future of Annuities ... 177
Economic Changes ... 179
- Market Volatility ... 179
- Corporate Changes ... 180

Demographic Changes ... 181
- Aging of the Population ... 181
- Changing Employment Profile ... 182
- Slower Wage and Earnings Growth ... 182

Regulatory Changes ... 182
- Industry Consolidation ... 183
- Tax Reforms ... 184
- Reclassification of Annuities ... 186

Social Security Changes ... 186
- Tax Increases ... 186
- Benefit Reductions ... 187
- Program Privatization ... 188

Industry Response ... 189
- New Fixed Annuity Products ... 189
- New Equity-Indexed Annuity Products ... 189
- New Variable Annuity Products ... 191
- Financial Services ... 192

Glossary ... 197
Index ... 225

Preface

The purpose of *Annuity Principles and Products, Second Edition,* is to provide an overview of the annuities industry, with a special emphasis on basic concepts and annuity products. This book has been designed for students who are preparing for LOMA's AAPA 273 examination in the Associate, Annuity Products and Administration (AAPA) designation program. The examination is based exclusively on the assigned textual materials, including information in the body of the text and in the Insights and Figures in each chapter. To ensure that you are studying from the correct textbook and study aid, check the current LOMA *Education and Training Catalog* for a description of the texts assigned for the AAPA 273 examination.

Several features have been included in each chapter to help you organize your studies, reinforce your understanding of the materials, and prepare for the examination. As we describe each of these features, we offer suggestions for studying the material.

Learning Objectives. The first page of each chapter contains a list of learning objectives to help you focus your studies. Before reading each chapter, review these learning objectives. Then, as you read the chapter, look for material that will help you meet the learning objectives.

Key Terms. The text assumes that you have no previous experience with annuities, so basic terms and concepts are defined and explained. Important terminology is highlighted in ***italic, boldface type*** when the term is first used and then defined and explained. Key terms and definitions are repeated in the margins alongside or near the text discussion. All key terms are included in a list at the end of each chapter and in a comprehensive glossary at the end of the book. Each glossary entry identifies in brackets the number of the chapter in which the term is defined. As you read each chapter, pay special attention to the key terms.

Insights and Figures. Insights and Figures appear throughout the text and are designed to amplify the text's descriptions of certain topics. These Insights and Figures should help you better understand how annuities operate and how they function in the context of the insurance and financial services industry. Insights and Figures may contain information that is tested on the AAPA 273 examination.

Test Preparation Guide. Besides this book, LOMA's *Test Preparation Guide for AAPA 273, Annuity Principles and Products, Second Edition,* (Atlanta: LOMA, 2003) is assigned reading for students preparing to take the AAPA 273 examination. Used along with this textbook, the Test Preparation Guide will help you master the course material. Included in the Guide are practice exam questions, a full-scale sample examination, and answers to all the questions.

LOMA recommends that you use the Test Preparation Guide for this course. **Studies indicate that students who use LOMA study aids consistently perform significantly better on LOMA examinations than other students.**

Acknowledgments

Annuity Principles and Products is the result of the joint efforts of professionals from insurance and financial services industry companies and LOMA staff. Members of LOMA's Equity Products and Annuity Committee (EPAC) were involved with the project from its inception. They helped to shape the AAPA program, commented on the initial outline for the first edition of this text, and provided the authors with valuable material and industry perspectives. Many of the members of the committee also graciously volunteered considerable amounts of their time to review textbook chapters. Michael Jensen, Associate, Operations Management, LOMA, facilitated communication with the committee and provided valuable assistance. On behalf of LOMA and its membership, the authors would like to express our thanks to these individuals who generously gave their time and energy and shared their expertise for the development of this textbook.

Textbook Review Panels

Annuity Principles and Products underwent extensive review by industry experts during both the initial development process and subsequent revision. The source materials, invaluable suggestions, and critical evaluations supplied by LOMA's text reviewers were essential to the book's accuracy and completeness.

The authors of the first edition received valuable input from the following reviewers: Paula Boswell Beier, FLMI, ACS; Paige C. Clark; Constance A. Doern, FLMI; Carol Ann Detlef, CLU, FLMI; Sandra Fox; Elizabeth Gottfried, FLMI, ACS; Michael R. Hood; Barbara A. O'Rourke, ACS; Audrey Paulsen; Diana Scheel, FLMI, ACS, CLU, ChFC; Teresa Shumila, FLMI, ACS; David J. Tobin, CPA, FLMI; Linda T. Weinstein, FLMI, ACS, CEBS; Dan Werner, FLMI, CLU, ChFC. Much of the work done by these reviewers for the first edition of the text continues into the second edition.

The second edition of the text underwent similar review by industry experts. The following individuals served as reviewers for the second edition of the text:

- Ryan E. Baxter, ACS, AAPA, *Business Automation Specialist*, Manulife Financial

- Marc E. Cavadel, J.D., FLMI, ACS, PCS, AAPA, AIAA, AIRC, ARA, ACP, CCP, *Assistant Vice President - Annuity Compliance* Protective Life Insurance Company

- Julie A. Churchwell, FLMI, ACS, PCS, *Training & Development Coordinator - Individual Division*, Ameritas Life Insurance Corporation

- Kitty Coulon, *Senior Finance Analyst*, State Farm Insurance Company

- William R. Keller, Jr., CLU, FLMI, *Director, Annuity Products Group*, AIG VALIC

- Jeff Kulesus, FLMI, AAPA, ACS, AIAA, AIRC, ARA. ASF, CSF, LUTC, *Assistant Vice President, Policy Forms & Compliance*, Jefferson Pilot Financial Insurance Companies

- Kevin D. Looney, FLMI, AAPA, ACS, *Director, Annuity Customer Service*, MassMutual Insurance Company

- Lynn A. Milewski, FLMI, ACS, *Director, Annuity Administration & Compliance, Annuity and Accumulation Products Department*, Northwestern Mutual

- Steven A. Rohrig, MBA, CRPS, AAPA, *Individual Retirement Plans Consultant, Advanced Sales*, Mutual of Omaha Insurance Company

- Christine Washington, AAPA, *IRA/Annuity Administrator*, ING Institutional Markets

- Dan Werner, FLMI, CLU, ChFC, *Assistant Director, Product and Distribution Compliance*, Principal Life Insurance Company

Additional assistance during the review process was provided by

- Mitchell Swanda, CFP, AAPA, *Financial Planner*, USAA Financial Planning Services

- James H. Potter, CLU, ChFC, *Sales Support Specialist, Annuity and Accumulation Products Department*, Northwestern Mutual

- Gerald J. Simonich, *Manager, Annuity and Accumulation Products Department*, Northwestern Mutual

LOMA Staff/Consultants

As is the case with all textbooks developed by LOMA, *Annuity Principles and Products, Second Edition,* required the dedicated teamwork of a number of LOMA staff members and consultants. LOMA texts, including *Intro to Annuities, Life and Health Insurance Marketing,* and *Regulatory Compliance: Insurance and Annuity Products,* proved to be valuable background materials for the authors. Mark Adel, FLMI, PCS, AIRC, PAHM, Senior Associate, Education & Training, served as manuscript editor for the project and Melanie Green, FLMI, ACS, AIAA, Senior Associate, Education & Training, served as examinations editor. Steve Tunnell copyedited the text. All of these LOMA reviewers made valuable suggestions. Aurelia Kennedy-Hemphill, Administrative Assistant, Education & Training, provided administrative support for the project. Stephen J. Bollinger, ACS, managed the typesetting, design, and production of the book. Iris F. Hartley, FLMI, ALHC, obtained the permissions for use of copyrighted materials. Audrey H. Gregory, ACS, made all printing arrangements.

Special thanks go to Jena L. Kennedy, FLMI, ACS, AIAA, ALHC, HIA, MHP, PAHM, CLU, Assistant Vice President, Education & Training, who championed the project from its onset and supervised the second edition, making many improvements to the text in the process. Thanks also go to Katherine C. Milligan, FLMI, ACS, ALHC, 2nd Vice President, Education & Training and William H. Rabel, Ph.D., FLMI, CLU, Senior Vice President, Education & Training for their support and encouragement.

John P. Burger, FLMI, ACS
Kristen L. Falk, FLMI, ACS, AIAA, AAPA, AIRC, ARA
1999
Patsy Leeuwenburg, Ph.D., FLMI, ACS, ALHC, AIAA, ARA, AIRC, PAHM
Atlanta, Georgia
2003

Annuity Principles and Products

CHAPTER 1

Annuity Basics

After studying this chapter, you should be able to

- Identify the key figures in an annuity purchase
- Describe the major types of annuities
- Describe some of the factors that have led to the increased popularity of annuities

During the past twenty years, annuity contracts have played an increasingly important role in financial and retirement planning in the United States. An ***annuity contract*** is a legally enforceable written agreement between an insurance company and a contract owner under which the insurer promises to make a series of periodic payments to a named

Key Figures in an Annuity Purchase
Contract Owner
Insurer
Annuitant
Payee
Beneficiary

Types of Annuities
Immediate and Deferred Annuities
Single-Premium and Flexible-Premium Annuities
Fixed and Variable Annuities
Individual and Group Annuities
Qualified and Nonqualified Annuities

The Annuities Market
Changing Demographics
Changing Retirement Income Needs
Concerns About Current Retirement Savings Programs
Savings and Money-Management Features of Annuities

Chapter 1 — Annuity Basics

person in exchange for a premium or a series of premiums. One of the most important functions of annuities is to provide a continuous stream of retirement income. Because annuities receive favorable treatment under U.S. tax regulations, they also provide a means of accumulating and protecting wealth prior to retirement.

In the past, only insurance companies were allowed to sell annuities and other insurance products. Regulatory barriers protected insurers against competition from other financial services companies and from companies in other industries. Today, many of the regulatory barriers between business sectors have been removed, and annuities can be sold by banks, stockbrokers, and direct response distributors as well as by insurance companies. Insurers, however, are still the only companies allowed to issue (that is, design, develop, underwrite, and administer) annuities.

This text provides a broad overview of annuity products and principles. In this chapter, we introduce some important annuity basics. We start with a description of the key figures in an annuity purchase and the major types of annuity products. Then we describe some of the factors contributing to the growth of the annuity market. Keep in mind that this chapter is intended to provide a broad overview of annuity principles and products.

In the chapters that follow, we discuss the formation and administration of annuity contracts, describe fixed and variable annuities, describe how variable annuities can be used as investments, discuss the role of individual and group annuities in retirement savings plans, and explain how annuities are taxed, regulated, and marketed in the United States and Canada. We end with a look at some of the trends that are likely to impact annuity products in the future.

Key Figures in an Annuity Purchase

An annuity purchase creates a contract between the **contract owner**—the person who applies for and purchases the annuity—and the **insurer** that issues and administers the annuity. The contract owner and the insurer are considered to be parties to the annuity contract and have certain rights and responsibilities under the contract. Financial services providers that sell but do not issue annuities function as distributors and are therefore not parties to the contract.

---

annuity contract.
A legally enforceable written agreement between an insurance company and a contract owner under which the insurer promises to make a series of periodic payments to a named person in exchange for a premium or a series of premiums.

contract owner.
The person who applies for and purchases an annuity.

4 | Annuity Principles and Products

An annuity purchase also involves a variety of other key individuals or entities including the

- *annuitant*—the person whose lifetime is used to measure the length of time annuitized payments (that is, lifetime payments) are payable under the annuity contract
- *payee*—the person or legal entity who receives the annuity payments
- *beneficiary*—the person or legal entity who receives the annuity death benefits, if applicable

The following example describes a hypothetical annuity purchase. We will refer to this example as we describe the roles and responsibilities of the contracting parties and other key figures.

> In 1990, Rhonda Jackson, age 50, paid $50,000 to Long Life Insurance Company for the purchase of an annuity. She elected to begin receiving annuity payments on her 65th birthday, about 15 years from the date of purchase, and to continue receiving payments each month for the rest of her life. When Ms. Jackson reaches her 65th birthday, Long Life will use the value of her annuity and her expected remaining lifetime to calculate the dollar amount of the annuity payments that Ms. Jackson will receive each month. If Ms. Jackson dies before her 65th birthday—when the annuity payments are scheduled to begin—Long Life will pay a specified death benefit to Ms. Jackson's sister, Linda Burns.

Contract Owner

As defined earlier, the contract owner is the person or entity that applies for and purchases an annuity. In our example, Ms. Jackson is the contract owner. The contract owner can be a real person or an entity such as a trust, a partnership, or a corporation. A contract owner that is not a person is often called a **non-natural owner**. Although most annuities are owned by one person or entity, ownership of an annuity can be shared by two or more persons or entities. A person or entity who shares ownership of an annuity with the contract owner is known as a **joint owner**. In some types of joint ownership, decisions about the contract require the approval of both the contract owner and the joint owner.

The contract owner is granted certain rights under the annuity contract. For example, the contract owner has the right to select the annuitant and payee and to designate the beneficiary. In our example, Ms. Jackson named herself as both the annuitant and the payee and designated her sister as the beneficiary. The contract owner also determines when annuity payments will begin, how often they will be paid, and how long they will last. Ms. Jackson elected to receive monthly annuity

---

annuitant.
The person whose lifetime is used to measure the length of time annuitized payments are payable under an annuity contract.

payee.
The person or legal entity who receives the annuity payments.

beneficiary.
The person or legal entity who receives annuity death benefits, if applicable.

non-natural owner.
An entity, such as a trust, partnership, or corporation, that owns an annuity contract.

joint owner.
A person who shares ownership of an annuity with the contract owner.

payments beginning on her 65th birthday and continuing until her death. Depending on the type of annuity, the contract owner may also have the right to

- Cancel the contract and receive a refund (minus any applicable charges) before payments begin
- Add money to or withdraw money from the annuity
- Change the beneficiary and annuitant
- Change the ownership of the contract
- Assign the annuity contract to another person or entity.

We will discuss the contract provisions that grant these rights to the contract owner in Chapter 2.

Insurer

In exchange for the contract owner's completed annuity application and initial premium, the insurer promises to perform certain functions. For example, the insurer promises to make annuity payments according to the terms of the contract. The insurer also promises to pay the beneficiary any death benefits, if applicable. As long as the contract remains in force, the insurer is obligated to fulfill these promises. In the example above, Long Life's obligations under the contract are to make scheduled monthly annuity payments to Ms. Jackson and, if Ms. Jackson dies before the annuity payments begin, to pay a death benefit to Ms. Burns.

Annuitant

As you will see later in the text, certain types of annuities provide annuity payments based on a specified annuitant's life expectancy. Therefore, the annuitant must be a natural person—not a legal entity such as a trust or corporation. Most often, the contract owner and the annuitant are the same person, as they are in our example. Occasionally, however, a contract owner may name someone other than himself as the annuitant. If the annuitant is someone other than the contract owner, the annuitant is not considered a party to the contract and generally has no rights under the contract.

A contract owner also may purchase an annuity that names more than one annuitant. If the contract owner names two or more annuitants whose life expectancies are considered together when determining annuitized payments, each annuitant is considered to be a ***joint annuitant***. Unless the contract owner names a separate payee, the annuitant is the payee and joint annuitants share the annuity payments according to the terms of the contract. If a contract owner names one person as a primary

joint annuitant.
A second person, in addition to the primary annuitant, whose life is used to measure the length of time annuitized payments are payable.

contingent annuitant.
A person who becomes the annuitant of an annuity contract if the primary annuitant dies before annuity payments begin or during the payout period.

annuitant and then names a second person to serve as the annuitant if the primary annuitant dies before annuity payments begin or during the payout period, that second person is known as a **contingent annuitant.** Both the annuitant's and the joint annuitant's or contingent annuitant's ages and life expectancies are used to determine the length of time annuity payments will be made.

Payee

The payee designated in an annuity contract can be a natural person or a legal entity. The payee has the right to receive annuity benefit payments according to the terms of the contract. Unless the payee is also the contract owner, the payee generally has no other rights under the contract.

Most often, the contract owner, the annuitant, and the payee are the same person, as they are in our example. Occasionally, however, contract owners may name someone other than themselves to receive annuity payments. This situation is described below.

> Sangeeta Sharma supports her disabled brother, Ravi, who is confined to a nursing home. Sangeeta has enough money to pay for Ravi's care, but she is concerned about what would happen to Ravi if she were to die before he does. To ensure that Ravi's nursing home care will be paid for as long as he lives, Sangeeta purchased an annuity that immediately begins providing the monthly payments to the nursing home and will continue to make payments to the nursing home until Ravi dies. As the purchaser, Sangeeta is the contract owner. Ravi, whose lifetime is used to determine the length of time annuity payments will be made, is the annuitant. The nursing home that receives the annuity payments is the payee.

The contract owner also can designate a second person as a joint payee or contingent payee. A joint payee shares annuity payments with the primary payee. A contingent payee receives payments only if the primary payee dies before all of the payments specified by the contract have been made.

Beneficiary

If the contract owner dies before annuity payments begin, the insurer is obligated by the terms of most annuity contracts to pay death benefits to a named annuity beneficiary. Under certain circumstances, a death benefit also may be payable to a beneficiary after annuity payments begin. The contract owner can name any natural person or legal entity as beneficiary. In our first example, Ms. Jackson named her sister as beneficiary of her annuity, but she could have named her husband, a child, a trust, or even her estate. The annuity beneficiary has no rights under the annuity contract except to receive the death benefit, and, in most cases, the contract owner may change the beneficiary designation on the annuity contract at any time. If a spouse is named as beneficiary, the spouse's consent may be required for a beneficiary change.

Types of Annuities

Annuities can be divided into the following classes according to their structure and operation:

- Immediate and deferred annuities
- Single-premium and flexible-premium annuities
- Fixed and variable annuities
- Individual and group annuities
- Qualified and nonqualified annuities

The following sections provide an overview of each of these major classes.

Immediate and Deferred Annuities

Annuities are classified as either immediate annuities or deferred annuities, depending on when the insurer begins making periodic annuity payments. Under the terms of an ***immediate annuity***, payments generally are scheduled to begin one annuity period after the date on which the annuity is purchased. The ***annuity period*** is the time span between each of the payments in the series of periodic annuity payments. The annuity period is typically one year or one month, but other payment options, such as quarterly or semi-annually also are available.

To illustrate how the annuity period affects the timing of annuity payments, consider a contract owner who purchases an immediate annuity on March 1, 2004. If the annuity has an annual annuity period, the insurer will begin making annuity payments on March 1, 2005. If the annuity has a monthly annuity period, the insurer will begin making annuity payments on April 1, 2004.

Because payments under an immediate annuity are scheduled to begin no more than one year after purchase, immediate annuities typically are purchased with a single premium payment. They often are used to convert a lump-sum payment into an income stream, making them attractive vehicles for providing retirement income.

immediate annuity.
An annuity contract under which annuity payments generally begin one annuity period after the date on which the annuity is purchased.

annuity period.
The time span between each of the payments in the series of periodic annuity payments.

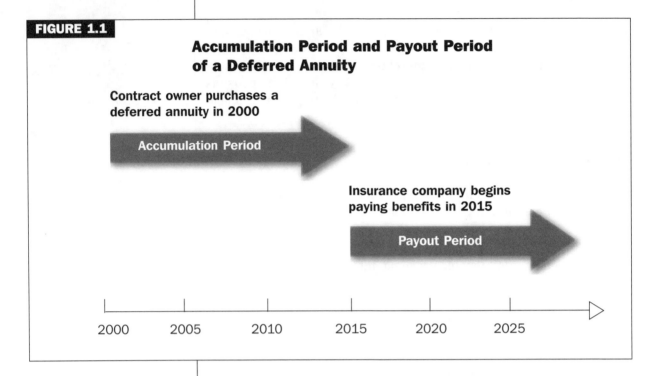

FIGURE 1.1 — Accumulation Period and Payout Period of a Deferred Annuity

deferred annuity.
An annuity contract under which periodic annuity payments generally begin more than one annuity period after the date on which the annuity is purchased.

accumulation period.
The time period between the date the contract owner purchases a deferred annuity and the date that annuity benefit payments begin.

payout period.
The time during which annuity benefit payments are made.

A *deferred annuity* is an annuity under which periodic annuity payments generally are scheduled to begin more than one annuity period after the date on which the annuity was purchased. The annuity described in our first example is a deferred annuity. Although a deferred annuity contract typically specifies the date on which payments are scheduled to begin, the contract owner usually can change this date before the first annuity payment is made, subject to any restrictions in the contract.

The time period between the date the contract owner purchases a deferred annuity and the date that annuity benefit payments begin is known as the *accumulation period*. Because annuity payments for an immediate annuity begin no more than one annuity period after purchase, immediate annuities have no accumulation period. The period during which annuity benefit payments are made is known as the *payout period*. Figure 1.1 illustrates the accumulation period and payout period for a deferred annuity.

Deferred annuities can be purchased with a single premium or with a series of periodic premiums. Note that every annuity purchased with the payment of periodic premiums is by definition a deferred annuity. Figure 1.2 compares the key features of immediate and deferred annuities.

Single-Premium and Flexible-Premium Annuities

When a contract owner purchases an immediate annuity, he typically pays for the contract with a single lump-sum premium. A deferred

FIGURE 1.2

A Comparison of Immediate and Deferred Annuities

Key Feature	Immediate Annuity	Deferred Annuity
Premium	Purchased with a single premium	Can be purchased with a single premium or a series of premiums
Accumulation Period	None; benefit payments usually begin no more than one year after the annuity is purchased	Usually lasts for years but is at least one annuity period
Purpose	To convert a lump sum into an income stream	To accumulate funds until a future point in time

annuity can be purchased with a single lump-sum premium or a series of periodic premiums. Although the decision regarding how premiums are paid does not affect the function of the annuity, it does affect the length of time that the insurer holds the premium payments. Under most circumstances, the longer the insurer holds a given premium, the greater the earnings generated by that premium will be.

An annuity that is purchased by the payment of one lump-sum premium is called a **single-premium annuity**. As we mentioned in the last section, a single-premium annuity can be either an immediate annuity or a deferred annuity. Under a **single-premium immediate annuity (SPIA)**, the insurer uses the premium to provide annuity payments one annuity period after the annuity is purchased. SPIAs can be used as retirement vehicles, to fund life insurance or long-term care insurance premiums, to spread out lottery payments and personal injury settlement payments, and to achieve a variety of estate planning objectives. Under a **single-premium deferred annuity (SPDA)**, the lump-sum premium is held by the insurer and payments are deferred until some future date specified by the contract owner. Because annuity payments for an SPDA usually do not begin until at least one year after purchase, most insurers will accept additional premiums, known as **window premiums**, for an SPDA during the first contract year.

Deferred annuities also can be purchased with a series of periodic premiums paid over a stated period of time. Most deferred annuities purchased with periodic premium payments are classified as flexible-premium annuities. Under a **flexible-premium annuity**, neither the

single-premium annuity.
An annuity contract that is purchased by the payment of one lump-sum premium.

single-premium immediate annuity (SPIA).
An annuity contract purchased with a single premium payment that begins paying annuity benefits one annuity period after the annuity is purchased.

single-premium deferred annuity (SPDA).
An annuity contract under which the lump-sum premium used to purchase the annuity is held by the insurer and payments are deferred until some future date specified by the contract owner.

window premiums.
Additional premiums paid during the first contract year of a single-premium deferred annuity.

flexible-premium annuity.
An annuity contract purchased with periodic premium payments in an amount that falls between a stated minimum and a stated maximum.

fixed-premium annuity.
An annuity contract that requires the contract owner to pay premiums of a fixed amount at specified, regular intervals.

fixed annuity.
An annuity contract under which the insurer guarantees the minimum interest rate that will be applied to premium payments and the minimum annuity payment that will be made for each dollar of the annuity's accumulated value at the end of the accumulation period.

accumulated value.
The net amount paid for an annuity plus interest earned, less the amount of any withdrawals or fees.

general account.
The general fund of assets invested to support an insurer's traditional, nonvariable insurance products.

equity-indexed annuity.
An annuity that offers certain principal and earnings guarantees, but also offers the possibility of additional earnings by linking the contract to a published index.

index.
A statistical measurement system that tracks the performance of a group of similar investments.

timing nor the amount of each premium payment is specified in the contract; the only requirement is that any premium amount paid during the specified accumulation period must fall between a stated minimum and a stated maximum. For example, a flexible-premium annuity might allow the contract owner to pay any premium amount between $250 and $10,000 annually during a ten-year period. The contract owner can pay premiums each year during the specified period, or decide not to pay any premium in a given year. The amount of any premium the contract owner pays, however, must fall between $250 and $10,000. Occasionally, insurers issue deferred annuities that require the contract owner to pay premiums of a fixed amount at specified, regular intervals. This type of annuity is called a ***fixed-premium annuity***.

Fixed and Variable Annuities

Annuities also can be classified as fixed or variable according to the types of guarantees they offer and how annuity premiums are invested. A ***fixed annuity*** is an annuity under which the insurer guarantees the minimum interest rate that will be applied to premium payments and the minimum annuity payment that will be made for each dollar of the annuity's accumulated value at the end of the accumulation period. The ***accumulated value*** is the net amount paid for the annuity plus interest earned, less the amount of any withdrawals or fees. Fixed annuity premiums are deposited in the insurer's ***general account***, which is the general fund of assets invested to support the insurer's traditional, nonvariable insurance products. Because a fixed annuity provides guarantees from the insurer to the contract owner, it is considered to be a more conservative financial product than a variable annuity.

In recent years, hybrid products such as equity-indexed annuities and market value adjusted annuities have been introduced into the fixed annuity market. An ***equity-indexed annuity*** is an annuity that offers certain principal and earnings guarantees, but that also offers the possibility of additional earnings by linking the contract to a published index. An ***index*** is a statistical measurement system that tracks the performance of a group of similar investments. A ***market value adjusted (MVA) annuity*** is an annuity that offers multiple guarantee periods and multiple fixed rates. Rather than being "locked in" to fixed earnings for the life of the contract, contract owners can move or withdraw premium deposits to take advantage of prevailing market rates. In order to be issued as fixed annuities, equity-indexed and MVA annuities must meet certain regulatory guidelines. Market-based annuities that do not meet these regulatory requirements are considered variable products and must be registered as securities. We will describe fixed annuities in more detail in Chapter 3.

A ***variable annuity*** is an annuity under which the amount of the contract's accumulated value and the amount of the periodic annuity benefit payments fluctuate in accordance with the performance of a specified pool of investments. Variable annuities offer few, if any, guarantees. Instead, contract owners retain the risk associated with their investments. Variable annuity premiums are deposited in a separate account and used to purchase investments in one or more subaccounts. The **separate account** is an investment account maintained apart from an insurer's general account to help manage the funds placed in variable insurance products such as variable annuities. In Canada, the separate account is known as a **segregated account.** A **subaccount** is one of several investment funds in the separate account. Different subaccounts offer different risk and return options.

Variable subaccounts are similar in operation to mutual funds. A **mutual fund** is an account established by an investment company that combines the money of many people and invests it in a variety of financial instruments. Mutual fund shares often are divided into separate share classes based on the type of fee, or "load," that is charged on investments in the accounts. An account that charges a fee for purchasing shares in the account and requires the entire amount of the charge to be paid up front is called a **front-end loaded account.** An account that charges a fee when shares are sold is called a **back-end loaded account.**

Variable annuities are sometimes divided into similar classes based on similar features. The traditional variable annuity is referred to as a B-share annuity because it resembles back-end loaded Class B mutual funds. As insurance companies attempt to keep pace with changing market conditions, newer share-based annuities also have begun to appear. These newer forms include A-share annuities, C-share annuities, and L-share annuities.

It is important to note that even though variable annuities are similar to mutual fund investments and may have the same or similar names, variable annuity subaccounts and mutual funds are always separate investment entities and are treated differently for tax purposes. We will describe the features of variable annuities in more detail in Chapter 4.

Individual and Group Annuities

Insurers sell annuities on both an individual and a group basis. If a person purchases an individual annuity, that person is the owner of the contract. Under a group annuity contract, an employer or group sponsor purchases the contract for the benefit of group members and the employer or group sponsor is the contract owner. Individuals covered under the contract receive certificates describing the annuity benefits provided by the plan, but they are not parties to the group contract. We will discuss both group and individual annuities in greater detail in Chapter 6.

market value adjusted (MVA) annuity.
An annuity that offers multiple guarantee periods and multiple fixed rates; market value adjusted annuities that meet certain regulatory guidelines can be issued as fixed annuities.

variable annuity.
An annuity contract under which the amount of the contract's accumulated value and the amount of the periodic annuity benefit payments fluctuate in accordance with the performance of a specified pool of investments.

separate account.
An investment account maintained apart from an insurer's general account to help manage the funds placed in variable insurance products such as variable annuities. In Canada, the separate account is known as a segregated account.

subaccount.
One of several investment funds in an insurer's separate account; different subaccounts offer different risk and return options.

mutual fund.
An account established by an investment company that combines the money of many people and invests it in a variety of financial instruments.

front-end loaded account.
An investment account that charges a fee for purchasing shares in the account and requires the entire amount of the charge to be paid up front.

back-end loaded account.
An investment account that charges a fee when shares are sold.

tax-qualified plan.
An employer-sponsored retirement plan that satisfies Internal Revenue Code and Employee Retirement Income Security Act (ERISA) requirements and, as a result, provides certain favorable tax treatments for both the employer and the participating employees.

qualified annuity.
An annuity purchased to accumulate or distribute funds from a tax-qualified plan.

nonqualified annuity.
An annuity that does not qualify to receive favorable tax treatment.

Qualified and Nonqualified Annuities

An annuity is classified as "qualified" or "nonqualified" depending on whether it is included in an employee benefit plan that meets complex legal requirements contained in the U.S. Internal Revenue Code and the Employee Retirement Income Security Act (ERISA).

An employer-sponsored retirement plan that satisfies Internal Revenue Code and ERISA requirements and, as a result, provides certain favorable tax treatments for both the employer and the participating employees, is known as a ***tax-qualified plan***. An annuity purchased to accumulate or distribute funds from a tax-qualified plan is known as a ***qualified annuity***. Qualified annuities are exempt from current income taxation during the accumulation period.

All individual annuities and group annuities that are not part of tax-qualified plans are referred to as nonqualified annuities. A ***nonqualified annuity*** has fewer limitations than a qualified annuity on the amount that can be invested, but it also has fewer tax advantages. We will discuss the taxation of annuities in more detail in Chapter 7.

The Annuities Market

Now that you know some of the basics of annuities, we turn our attention to some of the factors that have contributed to the growing interest in annuities as retirement funding vehicles. These factors, which are summarized in Figure 1.3, include (1) changes in population demographics, (2) increased awareness of changes in income needs during retirement, (3) growing concerns about the viability of current retirement savings programs, and (4) the savings and money-management features of annuity products.

Changing Demographics

A look at United States Census information gathered over the last 20 years reveals that the population is growing older and wealthier. These increases in age and affluence have a significant impact on the demand for annuities and other retirement savings products.

Aging Population

In 1980, the median age in the United States was 30.0 years. By 1990, it had increased to 32.8 years and by 1999, it had reached 35.5 years. By 2010, it is expected to be 37.4 years.[1] Life expectancies also are increasing. Census information published in 2000 reported that over 34 million Americans are currently age 65 or older. Approximately 68,000 of these are age 100 or over.[2]

Chapter 1 — Annuity Basics   13

FIGURE 1.3

Factors Contributing to Public Interest in Annuities

Population demographics
- Increasing age/life expectancy
- Increasing affluence

Retirement income needs
- Increasing health care needs
- Changes in economic status
- Changes in family structure

Concerns about current programs
- Viability of Social Security
- Weakening of employer-sponsored pension/retirement plans
- Inadequacy of personal savings

Annuity features
- Savings incentives
- Cash management options

As a result of upward shifts in age distribution and longevity, increasing numbers of people are entering retirement each year and remaining retired for longer periods. For many of these people, annuities offer protection against the very real possibility that they will outlive the resources they have set aside for retirement.

Increasing Affluence

For years, U.S. households have been divided into low-income households, middle-income households, and high-income households. Recently, a fourth economic category—the affluent market—has emerged. The affluent market is defined in terms of total liquid household assets, which include property, investments, and other assets as well as income earned from employment, and consists of the following three subgroups:

- **The mass affluent**, which consists of individuals with total liquid household assets worth $100,000 to $1 million

- **High-net-worth individuals**, which include individuals with total liquid household assets of between $1 million and $25 million

- **Ultra-high-net-worth individuals**, which include individuals with total liquid household assets of $25 million or more[3]

Researchers predict that by 2004, 15 million U.S. households will have a net worth of $1 million or more.[4] For America's wealthy, annuities offer a way to (1) preserve wealth, (2) protect assets from excessive taxation, and (3) accumulate additional wealth.[5]

Changing Retirement Income Needs

During pre-retirement years, financial planning efforts tend to focus on accumulating and preserving funds to meet future financial needs. During retirement, attention shifts to determining how to use retirement income to meet actual financial needs. In many cases, actual needs are different from planned needs, creating mismatches between planned and actual uses of funds.

Changes in retirement income needs typically arise from events that cannot be predicted. These events most often involve (1) changes in health status, (2) changes in economic status, and (3) changes in family structure.

Changes in Health Status

As people age, they become increasingly susceptible to illness and disability. As a result, their health care needs—especially for prescription drugs, acute care, and long-term care—increase. Many elderly also lose functional ability, making it necessary for them to seek assistance with daily activities. At the same time, retirement brings a transition from employer-sponsored health care coverage to government-sponsored coverage, such as Medicare and Medicaid, or individual coverage. The adequacy of coverage provided by government programs is a concern for many retirees. For example, under current law, Medicare pays only 50–55 percent of health care costs. Although legislation has been proposed to increase coverage of prescription drugs and long-term care, current government programs typically offer limited, if any coverage. In addition, Medicare benefits generally are not available to retirees younger than age 65. To fill these gaps in benefits and eligibility, retirees generally must rely on individual coverage, including Medicare supplements. Unfortunately, the cost of such coverage can be prohibitive for many retirees and availability may be limited.

Changes in Economic Status

Most retirees experience at least some change in economic status as they move from the work force into retirement. Although annuities and other retirement plans have gone a long way toward smoothing the transition and improving the general economic status of seniors in the United States, mismatches often exist between financial needs and financial resources.

For example, retirees typically have a pressing need during retirement for a steady stream of income to cover the everyday costs of living. However, many retirement plans pay benefits in a lump sum, rather than in installments, making it necessary for the retiree to manage or reinvest large sums of money. Without some form of planning, retirees can easily overspend and exhaust their funds or underspend and make less than optimal use of their assets. Benefits paid in fixed installments—such as those provided through Social Security, tax-qualified retirement plans, and some annuities—reduce the need for fund management and private investment, but they do not account for increasing financial needs over time and can result in a loss of purchasing power during periods of inflation.

Retirees also need income to cover expenses that are not part of everyday living, including illnesses or accidents, family emergencies, and taxes. Although these expenses may be foreseeable in general terms, their actual timing and impact on resources are difficult to predict.

Changes in Family Structure

Changes in retirement income needs also are triggered by changes in family structure. For example, the loss of income and support caused by death of a spouse or divorce can result in immediate changes in lifestyle and responsibilities for the remaining spouse. In some cases, it can result in significant economic decline and surviving spouses may be unable to maintain the same standard of living they had as couples. Decreases in household size—caused when children marry and relocate—can affect the availability of home care and the need for outside assistance. Increases in household size—created by the need to assimilate children, grandchildren, or parents into the household—can affect the amount of assistance needed by other family members.

Concerns About Current Retirement Savings Programs

Traditionally, retirees in the United States have relied on three sources for retirement income: Social Security, employer-sponsored pension plans, and personal savings. Today, many people question the ability of these sources to provide a reliable income stream during retirement.

During the last several years, the U.S. Congress has engaged in an ongoing debate over the ability of Social Security to provide its current level of benefits to future retirees. The general public and retirement planning experts also are concerned. Recent studies show that 80 percent of Gen Xers—those men and women born between 1965 and 1975—feel that they will have to look beyond Social Security to provide retirement funds,[6] and as many as 52 percent of the nearly 80 million Baby Boomers born between 1946 and 1964 worry about having sufficient funds at retirement.[7]

The economic impact of recent events such as the terrorist attacks on the United States and the highly publicized failures of large corporations have caused retirement experts, employees, and employers to become equally concerned about the availability and adequacy of employer-sponsored retirement plans. More and more companies are reducing their plan options or eliminating existing plans altogether. Others are switching from defined benefit plans, which guarantee a specified benefit for life, to defined contribution plans, which specify contribution amounts but do not guarantee benefit amounts. In a defined contribution plan, the benefit depends on the amount accumulated during an employee's working years. For employers, these changes represent economic savings. For employees, they represent lost security and increased risk.

For many Americans, personal savings plans offer even fewer guarantees and greater risk. Although the average income in the United States is higher than in most other industrialized countries, the savings rate generally is lower. The consequence of poor saving patterns during employment is likely to be inadequate income during retirement.

Savings and Money-Management Features of Annuities

As you have seen, lengthening retirement periods, greater wealth, changing income needs, and deepening concerns over current retirement plans have increased interest in saving money and managing cash flow. Annuities offer a way to accomplish both of these goals.

Annuities provide powerful economic and behavioral incentives to save money. For example, under most traditional savings and investment programs, the risk of people living long enough to deplete the entire amount of their savings before they meet their financial obligations is borne entirely by each individual. With an annuity, at least some of the financial risk of "living too long" is transferred to an insurer. In addition, annuity contracts typically encourage contract owners to keep dedicated retirement funds intact by imposing penalties on early withdrawals. These contract penalties are reinforced by significant tax penalties for early withdrawals. The payment options available in annuity contracts help retirees conserve resources by providing a steady, predictable cash flow and encouraging financial restraint.

Annuities also provide a variety of features designed to provide funds to offset unexpected events. In the past decade, insurers have made the following enhancements to their annuity products, providing guarantees as well as greater choice and flexibility:

- Guaranteed death benefits (for return of premium)
- Earning protection benefits (second death benefit designed to pay taxes)
- Liquidity enhancements (shorter surrender periods, free-outs, waiver of surrender charges for nursing home confinement)
- Expanded lines of fixed and variable annuity products
- Guaranteed living benefits (guarantee on principal, guaranteed minimum income, guaranteed minimum withdrawals, long-term care benefits)
- Fund allocation programs (dollar cost averaging, interest averaging, systematic withdrawals)

These savings incentives, money-management features, and guarantees make today's annuity products an appealing and a convenient way for future retirees to address their long-term financial planning needs.

Key Terms

annuity contract

contract owner

annuitant

payee

beneficiary

non-natural owner

joint owner

joint annuitant

contingent annuitant

immediate annuity

annuity period

deferred annuity

accumulation period

payout period

single-premium annuity

single-premium immediate annuity (SPIA)

single-premium deferred annuity (SPDA)

window premiums

flexible-premium annuity

fixed-premium annuity

fixed annuity

accumulated value

general account

equity-indexed annuity

index

market value adjusted (MVA) annuity

variable annuity

separate account

segregated account

subaccount

mutual fund

front-end loaded account

back-end loaded account

tax-qualified plan

qualified annuity

nonqualified annuity

Endnotes

1. U.S. Census Bureau, "*Statistical Abstract of the United States*: *2001*" http://www.census.gov/prod/2002pubs/01statab/pop.pdf (23 September 2002).

2. Ibid.

3. Jim Connolly, "Huge Trove of Assets Has Providers Ready to Get in the Ring," *National Underwriter*, Life & Health/Financial Services ed. (21 May 2001): 11.

4. Knight Ridder Business News, "Financial Service Firms Put Emphasis on Serving Wealthy, "*Dallas Morning News* via NewsEdge Corporation: 7 October 2001, http://www.newsedge.com (9 October 2001).

5. Jim Connolly, "The Wealthy Are Seeking Advice," *National Underwriter*, Life & Health/Financial Services ed. (7 May 2001): 7.

6. "Who Wants to be a Millionaire? These Days, It Seems Like Most of Us Do," *Business Wire* (6 July 2000).

7. Allstate Insurance Company, "Second Annual Allstate 'Retirement Reality Check' Survey Reveals Baby Boomers' Financial Worries Increasing," http://www.allstate.com/media/newsheadlines/pr_2002/(29 July 2003).

Annuity Principles and Products

CHAPTER 2

The Annuity Contract

After studying this chapter, you should be able to

- Describe the elements necessary for the formation of an annuity contract
- Describe the major provisions that are included in all types of individual annuity contracts
- Discuss the activities that affect the operation of an annuity contract during the accumulation period
- Describe the various distribution options available during an annuity contract's payout period

Annuity Principles and Products

OUTLINE

Formation of the Annuity Contract
The Completed Annuity Application
The Initial Premium
Contract Provisions

Administration of Annuities During the Accumulation Period
Crediting Earnings
Fees and Charges
Payment of Death Benefits

Distributions
Nonannuitized Payout Options
Annuitized Payout Options
Payout Options for Variable Annuities
Calculating Annuity Benefit Payments

In Chapter 1, we discussed the roles and responsibilities of the key figures in an annuity purchase and described the major types of annuities. In this chapter, we describe the features and functions of the annuity contract itself and how annuities are administered.

We begin the chapter with a discussion of how an annuity contract is formed and the general provisions that govern the rights and responsibilities of the contracting parties. We then describe how insurers administer annuities during the accumulation period and the payout period. Keep in mind that each insurance company will have a unique contract for each annuity product and that each contract will have a unique set of provisions. Keep in mind, too, that although many of the provisions described in this chapter are required by law in most states to be included in annuity contracts, the names and exact wording of these provisions may vary from state to state.

Formation of the Annuity Contract

As you recall from Chapter 1, an annuity contract is a legally enforceable written agreement between an insurance company and a contract owner under which the insurer promises to make a series of periodic payments to a named person in exchange for a premium or a series of premiums. The contract is formed when the insurer accepts a completed application and the initial premium for the annuity from the applicant and issues the annuity. When the annuity is issued, the applicant becomes the contract owner.

The Completed Annuity Application

The purchase of an annuity requires the applicant to provide the insurer with certain factual information related to (1) the contract owner, the annuitant, and other key figures who will play a part in the contract and (2) the options to be included in the contract. Applicants can supply this information to the insurer in the form of a written application or they can transmit the information electronically.

Personal Information Provided by the Applicant

Applicants for individual annuities typically provide basic personal information about themselves on the application, including their name, address, phone number, and social security or tax identification number. If the applicant is also the annuitant, applications also require information about the applicant's age and gender. The insurer uses this information to verify the applicant's identity and competency to enter into a contract. Employers or group sponsors who apply for group annuities on behalf of group members supply information about the company or group, such as size and number of members, as well as personal information about individual group members who will be covered under the group contract.

Most annuity applications also require the applicant to provide information about other key figures in an annuity contract. For example, applicants must provide information about the annuitant's current age and sex. In the case of group annuity contracts, group members rather than the group sponsor provide this information. The current age of the annuitant is needed to

- Verify that the annuitant satisfies the contract's age requirements (annuity contracts generally specify a maximum issue age of between 70 and 85 years for an annuitant)
- Calculate the length of the accumulation period (for a deferred annuity)
- Estimate the payment amount and the length of the payout period (for annuities that provide lifetime benefits)

The gender of the annuitant is important because life expectancies vary by gender. Women generally live longer than men of the same age and are expected to receive annuity payments for a longer time period. Insurers also use the age and gender of the annuitant for identification purposes.

When insurers estimate the number and amount of payments to be made during the payout period of an annuity contract that provides lifetime benefits, they use mortality tables to determine how long the annuitant is expected to live. Annuity mortality tables project both the death rate in a particular age and gender group and the number of people who will survive each year—and thus receive annuity payments. In the past, insurers structured life insurance policies to mature at age 95. Longer life expectancies are now pushing maturity ages up, and increasing numbers of policies now include "to age 100" or "lifetime" maturity features. Insurers also are using extended lifetime limits to determine annuity benefit periods.[1]

Individual annuity applicants or group plan participants also designate the payee and beneficiary on the application and provide any identifying information needed for administrative purposes.

Contract Options

In addition to providing information about key figures, annuity applicants or group members supply information about various contract options. For example, applicants typically indicate the

- Timing of subsequent premium payments, if any (monthly, quarterly, semiannually, or annually)

- Way in which subsequent premium payments, if any, will be made (by cash, check, or automatic deposit)
- Length of the annuity period (one month, three months, six months, or one year)
- Date on which annuity benefit payments will begin (within one annuity period or at some specified future date)

Applicants also provide product-specific information. For example, applicants purchasing immediate annuities generally must specify how they wish benefits to be distributed. For deferred annuities, this decision is delayed until the contract matures. Applicants purchasing traditional fixed annuities must select the **contract duration**—a specified time period during which the insurer will pay a specified interest rate on premiums. The contract duration typically is one, three, or five years, and insurers offer different interest rates for different periods. Applicants purchasing variable annuities must choose the subaccounts into which their premiums are to be deposited. We will discuss specific contract options in more detail in later chapters.

contract duration. A specified time period during which the insurer will pay a specified interest rate on premiums for a fixed annuity.

The Initial Premium

Like completion of the application, payment of the initial premium is a requirement for the formation of an annuity contract. In most cases, the applicant submits the initial premium for the contract along with the completed application. For an immediate annuity or any other form of single-premium annuity, the initial premium is the only premium. If the annuity is a flexible-premium annuity or fixed-premium annuity, the initial premium will be the first of a series of premium payments over a specified period of time.

Contract Provisions

The annuity contract includes various provisions that govern the rights and duties of the contracting parties. Many of the provisions included in individual annuity contracts are the same as those included in individual life insurance policies, although their form may differ slightly. The provisions included in group annuity contracts parallel those included in group life insurance policies. The provisions described in the following sections generally are included in all types of individual annuity contracts. Other contract provisions, such as those described in Figure 2.1, apply only to certain types of annuities.

Entire Contract Provision

The **entire contract provision** states that only those documents attached to or appearing in the contract are part of the contract. This

entire contract provision. A provision in an annuity contract which states that only those documents attached to or appearing in the contract are part of the contract.

FIGURE 2.1

Contract Provisions Included in Specific Types of Annuities

Provisions Included in Deferred Annuity Contracts

- **Beneficiary provision:** gives the contract owner the right to name the beneficiary who will receive any survivor benefits payable if the contract owner dies before annuity benefit payments begin.

- **Withdrawal provision:** gives the contract owner the right to withdraw part of the annuity's accumulated value during the accumulation period.

- **Surrender provision:** gives the contract owner the right to surrender the annuity for its cash surrender value during the accumulation period.

- **Nonforfeiture provision**: states the benefit amounts that the insurer will pay if the contract owner stops making premium payments or surrenders the contract. The nonforfeiture provision also states that if the annuity contract provides for settlement in a lump sum, then on surrender of the contract during the accumulation period, the insurer will pay a lump sum to the contract owner in lieu of an annuity benefit.

Provisions Included in Fixed-Premium Annuity Contracts

- **Grace period provision:** gives the contract owner the right to pay any premium within a specified period—such as 31 days—following the premium due date.

- **Reinstatement provision:** gives the contract owner the right to reinstate a lapsed contract to fully paid-up status by paying all unpaid and outstanding premiums and satisfying other requirements specified in the provision.

Provisions Included in Contracts That Provide Lifetime Benefits

- **Misstatement of age or sex provision:** states that if the insurer discovers that the annuitant's age or sex was misstated on the annuity application, then the annuity benefits payable will be those that the premiums paid would have purchased for the correct age or sex.

---

provision is designed to protect both the contract owner and the insurer. The entire contract provision protects contract owners by ensuring that they will have a written copy of all the rules governing the annuity contract and that no part of the contract can be modified after issue without their consent. The entire contract provision protects the insurer by stipulating that changes to the contract can only be made in writing by an authorized officer of the insurance company. In addition, the provision typically stipulates that any oral statements made by any party to the contract are not part of the contract. In other words, if something is not in writing, it is not part of the contract.

Incontestability Provision

An *incontestability provision* states that after the contract becomes effective, the insurer generally cannot contest it. This provision is much more restrictive to the insurer than its counterpart in life insurance policies. Most life insurance applications ask for information regarding the insured's insurability—information that the insurer uses to make its underwriting decision. Because the application may include misstated insurability information, the insurer is allowed to contest a life insurance policy on the grounds of misstatements in the application for as long as two years after policy issue. Annuity applications typically do not request insurability or underwriting information. The incontestability provision in an annuity contract, therefore, generally stipulates that the insurer cannot contest the contract once it has become effective.

An exception to the incontestability of annuity contracts may arise if a contract includes a **waiver of premium for disability rider**, which allows contract owners to stop making premium payments in the event that they become disabled. To obtain a waiver of premium for disability rider, the applicant is required to provide proof of insurability. An incontestability provision like the one found in life insurance policies then becomes a part of the contract and the insurer can use misstatements made in the application to contest the waiver of premium rider for a specified period—usually two years—after the effective date. The annuity contract itself remains in force.

Free Look Provision

A *free look provision* states that the contract owner has a period of time—usually 10 to 20 days after receiving the contract—to examine the annuity contract, with the option of returning it to the insurer during this time for a full refund of the premium paid. In some states, if the contract owner returns a variable annuity contract under the free look provision, the insurer refunds the current market value of the contract.

Assignment Provision

An *assignment provision* grants the contract owner of a nonqualified annuity the right to temporarily or permanently transfer ownership of the contract. For example, a contract owner might wish to use the cash value of a nonqualified annuity as collateral for a loan by temporarily assigning the ownership rights in the annuity to a bank during the loan repayment period. We will discuss the possible tax consequences of assignments in Chapter 7.

Federal tax laws prohibit the assignment of certain types of qualified retirement plan contracts. If an annuity contract is part of one of these specified types of qualified retirement plans, the assignment provision typically states that the contract may not be sold, assigned, transferred,

---

incontestability provision.
A provision in an annuity contract which states that, after the contract becomes effective, the insurer generally cannot contest it.

waiver of premium for disability rider.
A rider included in annuity contracts which allows contract owners to stop making premium payments in the event that they become disabled.

free look provision.
A provision in an annuity contract which states that the contract owner has a period of time—usually 10 to 20 days after receiving the contract—to examine the contract with the option of returning it to the insurer during this time for a full refund of the premium paid or the current market value of the contract.

assignment provision.
A provision in a nonqualified annuity contract that grants the contract owner the right to temporarily or permanently transfer ownership of the contract.

or pledged to another person or entity as collateral for a loan or for any other purpose.

Payout Options Provision

A **payout options provision**, or *settlement options provision*, identifies and describes each of the options the contract owner may elect for the distribution of annuity benefits during the payout period. These options are described in detail later in this chapter.

Because different insurers use different terminology, some of the provisions in actual annuity contracts are not described in the same way as they are in the text discussion. Also, not all of the provisions discussed in the text are included in actual contracts.

Administration of Annuities During the Accumulation Period

Certain activities performed during the accumulation period of a deferred annuity directly affect the value and operation of the annuity contract. These activities include crediting earnings, assessing fees and charges, and paying death benefits. Because payments for immediate annuities begin within one annuity period of the purchase of the annuity contract, immediate annuities have no accumulation period and are therefore not affected by these activities.

Crediting Earnings

As you recall from Chapter 1, a deferred annuity can be purchased either with a single lump-sum premium payment or with a series of premium payments. These premiums are left on deposit with the insurer and generate earnings. The amount that premiums earn during the accumulation period and the way in which earnings are credited depend on whether the annuity is a fixed annuity or a variable annuity.

Earnings on Fixed Annuity Premiums

Under the terms of a fixed annuity, contract earnings typically take the form of interest. All fixed annuity contracts specify a **guaranteed interest rate** that is the minimum rate the insurer will pay on the annuity's accumulated value. In some cases, the insurer also specifies a **current interest rate**, which is the rate it will pay on the annuity during the time period specified as the contract duration. Most insurers offer different current interest rates for different contract duration periods, as shown in Figure 2.2.

---

payout options provision. A provision in an annuity contract which identifies and describes each of the options the contract owner may elect for the distribution of annuity benefits during the payout period. Also known as a settlement options provision.

guaranteed interest rate. The minimum rate an insurer will pay on a fixed annuity's accumulated value.

current interest rate. The interest rate prevailing in the economy, generally offered for the contract duration of a fixed annuity.

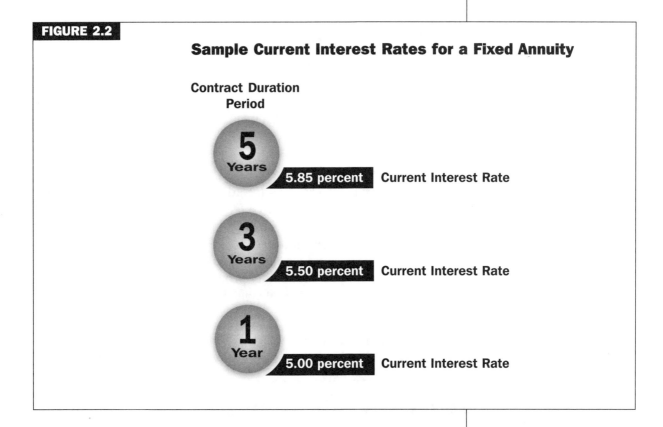

FIGURE 2.2 Sample Current Interest Rates for a Fixed Annuity

At the end of the contract duration period, the insurer will determine a new interest rate—the **renewal rate**—that will be paid for the next period. The renewal rate may be higher or lower than the current interest rate, depending on conditions in the general economy and how the insurer has invested the annuity funds. Neither the current rate nor the renewal rate can drop below the guaranteed interest rate specified in the contract.

Earnings on Variable Annuity Premiums

Premiums for a variable annuity are used to purchase **accumulation units**, which represent ownership shares in selected subaccounts of the insurer's separate account. The contract owner specifies in the application how the premiums and the accumulated balance of the annuity are to be distributed among these accounts. The values of accumulation units increase or decrease with increases or decreases in the values of the investments included in the subaccounts.

Rates of return for subaccounts are not guaranteed, but depend on the market performance of the included investments. If subaccount investments increase in value, contract owners earn a return on their investments. If subaccount investments decrease in value, contract owners will experience a loss. If markets decline sufficiently, contract owners may even lose part of their investment principal.

renewal rate.
The interest rate an insurer will pay for the next period of a fixed annuity; may be higher or lower than the current interest rate, depending on conditions in the general economy and how the insurer has invested the annuity funds.

accumulation units.
Ownership shares in selected subaccounts of an insurer's separate account that are purchased with premiums for a variable annuity.

Fees and Charges

Most annuity contracts are subject to a variety of administrative fees and transaction charges during the accumulation period. The types and amounts of these fees and charges depend on the type of annuity. Figure 2.3 shows how some of the more common fees and charges are applied.

Administrative Fees

Insurers generally charge fees for administering both fixed and variable annuities. An ***administrative fee*** is a charge the insurer levies to cover the costs of issuing the annuity, making administrative changes to the annuity contract and records, preparing the contract owner's statements, and performing other "maintenance" activities. Generally, the more maintenance an annuity product requires on the part of the insurer, the more likely it is that some type of administrative fee will be charged.

For fixed annuities, administrative fees often are included in the premiums charged for the contract. For variable annuities, administrative

administrative fee.
A charge an insurer levies on an annuity contract to cover the costs of issuing the contract, making administrative changes to the contract, preparing the contract owner's statements, and performing other "maintenance" activities.

FIGURE 2.3

Annuity Contract Fees and Charges

Fee or Charge	Fixed Annuities	Variable Annuities
Administrative fee	Usually included in premiums charged for the contract	Separate from premiums; ranges from $15 to $50 annually
Mortality and expense risk charge	Not applicable	Amount typically ranges from 1.00 percent to 1.75 percent of contract value
Surrender charge	Amount calculated as a percentage of the amount withdrawn; conditions and timing of withdrawals specified by contract	Amount calculated as a percentage of the amount withdrawn; conditions and timing of withdrawals specified by contract
Loan fee	Applied to each loan taken by the contract owner; usually deducted from the amount of the loan	Applied to each loan taken by the contract owner; usually deducted from the amount of the loan

fees are separate from premiums and range from $15 to $50 annually. Some insurers charge administrative fees for variable annuity contracts only if the contract value is below a certain amount—$50,000, for example—on the contract anniversary date.

Variable annuity contracts typically include two additional fees: a mortality and expense risks charge and an asset management fee. A ***mortality and expense risks (M&E) charge*** is a fee designed to compensate the insurer for risks under the contract. The mortality risk portion of the charge covers the insurer's obligation to provide annuity payments for an annuitant's lifetime, no matter how long it might be. The expense risk portion of the charge covers the insurer's obligation to issue and administer the contract, no matter what the cost. The M&E charge also includes amounts designed to reimburse the insurer for administrative and distribution costs associated with providing variable subaccount options. A typical M&E charge ranges from 1.00 percent to 1.75 percent of the contract value. The addition of guaranteed benefits—such as minimum death benefits, minimum accumulation benefits, and minimum withdrawal benefits—may increase the amount of the charge.

An ***asset management fee*** is a fee assessed by an investment fund manager to cover the fund management costs and operating expenses associated with a variable annuity's underlying investment funds.

Transaction Fees and Charges

Although most people purchase annuities to provide income during retirement, insurers generally allow the contract owner to withdraw funds from the contract's accumulated value during the accumulation period in the form of surrenders, withdrawals, or contract loans. These transactions typically are subject to fees or charges levied by the insurer.

Surrenders and Withdrawals. A ***surrender*** is a transaction in which the contract owner receives the annuity contract's entire ***cash surrender value***—the accumulated value of the contract less any charges. If a contract owner surrenders an annuity, the annuity contract ends before the annuity matures and no annuity benefit payments are made. A ***withdrawal*** is a transaction in which the owner of an annuity removes a portion of the annuity's accumulated value from the contract account. A withdrawal reduces the value of the contract and the amount of future benefit payments, but it does not cancel the contract. Some insurers refer to a withdrawal as a partial surrender.

To recoup the costs of issuing and administering the contract, insurers frequently impose a penalty known as a ***surrender charge*** on surrenders and withdrawals. For share-based variable annuities, the surrender

---

mortality and expense risks (M&E) charge.
A fee designed to compensate the insurer for risks under the contract and to reimburse the insurer for administrative and distribution costs associated with providing variable subaccount options.

asset management fee.
A fee assessed by an investment fund manager to cover the fund management costs and operating expenses associated with a variable annuity's underlying investment funds.

surrender.
A transaction in which the contract owner receives the annuity contract's entire cash surrender value and thereby cancels the contract.

cash surrender value.
The amount available to a contract owner who surrenders the contract; equal to the accumulated value of the contract, less any charges.

withdrawal.
A transaction in which the owner of an annuity removes a portion of the annuity's accumulated value from the contract account, but does not cancel the contract.

surrender charge.
A penalty imposed by an insurer when a contract owner withdraws funds from or surrenders an annuity contract.

FIGURE 2.4

Sample Surrender Provision

At or before the commencement of an annuity payment, part or all of the contract's value may be withdrawn on request of the contract owner. The amount of cash paid on a surrender will be the accumulated value withdrawn, less any surrender charge on such value.

Partial surrenders may be subject to one or more of the following conditions:

1. Only one partial surrender may be made in a policy year.
2. A partial surrender may not be for less than $1,000.
3. A partial surrender may not be made if the remaining accumulated value would be less than $5,000.

The surrender charge may be deducted from any partial surrender made during the first policy year. During any subsequent policy year, no surrender charge will be deducted from the first partial surrender made during the year for any amount withdrawn that is less than or equal to 10% of the accumulated value on the date of the withdrawal.

However, if the entire accumulated value is withdrawn, appropriate surrender charges will be deducted from the full amount withdrawn.

---

contingent deferred sales charge (CDSC).
A charge imposed by an insurer when the owner of a share-based variable annuity withdraws funds from or surrenders the annuity.

charge is often referred to as a **contingent deferred sales charge (CDSC)** and is similar to the back-end loads, described in Chapter 1, that are assessed on certain mutual funds. Imposition of a surrender charge also may discourage early withdrawal of funds intended for retirement.

The amount of the surrender charge or CDSC—which is calculated as a percentage of the amount withdrawn—and the conditions under which surrenders and withdrawals are allowed are specified in the contract. Some insurers use separate provisions to cover surrenders and withdrawals. Others cover surrenders and withdrawals under a single surrender provision such as the one shown in Figure 2.4.

Surrender charges and CDSCs are generally higher during the early years of an annuity contract and then decrease over time. In most cases, after the contract owner has owned the annuity for a certain number of years, surrender charges and CDSCs do not apply. Figure 2.5 shows a sample surrender charge schedule for a fixed annuity.

CDSCs on share-based variable annuities follow similar schedules. For example, traditional variable annuities, or B-share annuities, assess CDSCs, on a decreasing scale, for a period of six to eight years. L-share annuities include scaled CDSCs over a period of three to four years. A-share annuities do not include CDSCs, but do include premium-based

FIGURE 2.5

Sample Surrender Charge Schedule

Contract Year	Surrender Charge (Percentage of Withdrawal)
1	7.0%
2	6.0%
3	5.0%
4	4.0%
5	3.0%
6	2.0%
7	1.0%
8 and thereafter	no surrender charge

front-end charges. C-share annuities do not include front-end or back-end charges.

In addition to surrender charges assessed by the insurer, contract owners must pay taxes on contract surrenders and withdrawals. For example, contract owners typically are required to pay federal income taxes on any portion of a withdrawal that previously has not been taxed. Contract owners also must pay tax penalties—usually 10 percent of the taxable amount—on surrenders or withdrawals made before the contract owner reaches age 59½. We will discuss the tax implications of withdrawals and surrenders in more detail in Chapter 7.

Because insurers know that many potential annuity purchasers are reluctant to tie up funds they might need in case of an emergency, annuity contracts typically include provisions that afford annuity contract owners a certain degree of protection from surrender charges. These provisions include the

- ***Free withdrawal provision***, which grants the contract owner the right to withdraw a portion of the annuity's accumulated value during the accumulation period without a surrender charge. Free withdrawal provisions typically allow for withdrawals of between 10 and 15 percent of the annuity's value per year.

free withdrawal provision. A provision in an annuity contract that grants the contract owner the right to withdraw a portion (typically between 10 and 15 percent) of the contract's accumulated value during the accumulation period without a surrender charge.

waiver of surrender charge provision. A provision in an annuity contract which states that no surrender charge will be assessed on surrenders or withdrawals in excess of specified levels under certain conditions, such as disability, poor medical condition, terminal illness, unemployment, and confinement in a nursing home or hospital.

bailout provision. A provision in an annuity contract that enables the contract owner to surrender the annuity, usually without a surrender charge, if renewal interest rates on a fixed annuity fall below a pre-established level. Also known as an escape clause *or* cash-out provision.

- ■ *Waiver of surrender charge provision*, which states that, under certain circumstances, no surrender charge will be assessed to surrenders or withdrawals in excess of specified levels. The most common circumstances under which the insurer will waive surrender charges include disability or poor medical condition, terminal illness, unemployment, and confinement of the contract owner in a nursing home or hospital. Surrender charges also are waived if a contract owner elects to begin receiving annuity payments.

- ■ *Bailout provision*, sometimes known as an *escape clause* or *cash-out provision*, which enables the contract owner to surrender the annuity contract, usually without a surrender charge, if renewal interest rates on a fixed annuity fall below a pre-established level, typically 1 percent below the initial interest rate.

Contract owners who exercise their rights under the provisions described above generally are exempt from surrender charges imposed by the insurer. However, they still are subject to taxes and penalties imposed by the federal government.

Loans on Qualified Annuities. Although loans generally are not available under nonqualified annuities, many qualified annuity contracts include a contract provision that allows the contract owner to obtain a loan against the annuity's accumulated value. Loans against annuity balances are not considered to be assignments because they do not involve the transfer of ownership rights under the contract.

Loans also are distinguishable from surrenders or withdrawals. For example, a loan requires the contract owner to repay the amount received, plus interest. Surrenders and withdrawals do not require any repayment. In addition, because the cash value securing the loan will be available to the contract owner again as soon as the loan is repaid, a loan represents a temporary reduction in the accumulated value of the contract. A surrender or withdrawal is a permanent reduction of the contract value. A loan also is not subject to the same tax penalties or surrender charges that apply to surrenders and withdrawals.

Some insurers charge a fee for processing loans on qualified annuities. This fee generally is deducted from the amount of the loan at the time payment is made. Separate loan fees are charged for each loan made against the contract's accumulated value.

Payment of Death Benefits

Most fixed annuity contracts pay death benefits if the contract owner dies during the accumulation period of the contract. In most cases, the insurer pays the beneficiary the value of the annuity account as of the date the insurer receives the proof of death. If the contract owner dies during the payout period, the insurer may continue to make annuity benefit payments to a contingent payee, depending on the way the contract owner elects to have benefits distributed.

Although variable annuities typically do not provide guarantees with regard to interest rates or safety of principal, they usually include a minimum death benefit guarantee which ensures that the beneficiary will receive at least the amount that was deposited into the variable annuity contract, less any withdrawals. The death benefit guarantee will be described in more detail in Chapter 4.

Distributions

As you recall, the period during which annuity benefit payments are made is known as the payout period. When the payout period begins, an annuity is said to mature. The date on which the insurer begins to make annuity benefit payments, or distributions, is often called the annuity's **maturity date**, or *annuity date*. When an annuity matures, the insurer uses the money that has accumulated in the annuity to make periodic benefit payments according to the terms of the payout option selected by the contract owner. In the case of an immediate annuity, the contract owner chooses the payout option during the application process. In the case of a deferred annuity, the contract owner chooses the payout option just prior to the beginning of the payout period.

maturity date.
The date on which an insurer begins to make annuity payments, or distributions, under an annuity contract. Also known as the annuity date.

The particular payout option a contract owner selects affects the amount of each annuity benefit payment, the length of the payout period, and the total amount distributed. Payout options also have different tax implications. As a result, choosing the correct option for a person's unique circumstances is an important decision.

Distributions made during the payout period of either fixed or variable annuities can be categorized as nonannuitized payouts or annuitized payouts, depending on whether payments are linked to a life expectancy.

Nonannuitized Payout Options

Although annuities are designed to provide lifetime benefits, distributions can be structured to provide benefits of a designated amount or for a designated period. These nonannuitized distributions, which are not linked to any life expectancy, include (1) lump-sum distributions, (2) designated period distributions, and (3) designated amount distributions.

Lump-Sum Distributions

Some contract owners choose to have the accumulated value of their annuity distributed in a single payment, known as a **lump-sum distribution.** Such a distribution is not tied to any life expectancy. The major

lump-sum distribution.
A form of nonannuitized payout in which the accumulated value of an annuity contract is distributed in a single payment.

advantage of a lump-sum distribution is that it provides a large amount of money immediately that can be used for purposes such as buying a retirement home, paying for an extended trip, or covering planned expenses. The major drawback of this option is that the taxes incurred on a lump-sum distribution generally are due when payment is made and can reduce the amount of the distribution significantly.

Designated Period Distributions

As an alternative to a lump-sum distribution, a contract owner can elect to receive annuity payments for a designated period of time. This option usually is referred to as a ***fixed period option***. Under the fixed period option, the amount of each payment is determined by the accumulated value of the annuity on the maturity date and the number of payments specified by the option. For example, suppose Elena Varga elected to receive annual annuity benefit payments over a period of ten years. If the accumulated value of Ms. Varga's annuity on the maturity date is $150,000, then she will receive ten annual payments of $15,000 each. Additional interest earned during the payout period can increase the amount of individual annuity payments, but it typically will not increase the number of payments.

Under the fixed period option, the length of the payout period does not depend on any life expectancy. In addition, the fixed period option guarantees that all of the accumulated value of the annuity contract will be distributed, either to the payee or to a contingent payee. An annuity that is payable for a stated period of time, regardless of whether the annuitant is living at the end of the period, is called an ***annuity certain***. The specified period of time over which the insurer guarantees payments is called the ***period certain***.

Designated Amount Distributions

Contract owners also can elect to have annuity benefits distributed in payments of a designated minimum amount for as long a period as the contract's accumulated value will provide. This nonannuitized payout option generally is called a ***fixed amount option***. For example, suppose Demetrius Carter elected to receive monthly annuity payments of $1,000 during the payout period of his annuity. If the accumulated value of his annuity on the maturity date is $150,000, then Mr. Carter will receive $1,000 each month for a period of 12.5 years, or 150 months. Interest earned during the payout period can increase the number of payments, but it typically will not increase the amount of each payment.

The fixed amount option is similar to the fixed period option in that the length of the payout period under the fixed amount option does not

---

fixed period option.
A form of nonannuitized payout in which a contract owner elects to receive annuity payments for a designated period of time.

annuity certain.
An annuity that provides benefit payments for a stated period of time, regardless of whether the annuitant is living at the end of the period.

period certain.
The specified period of time over which an insurer guarantees payments under an annuity certain.

fixed amount option.
A form of nonannuitized payout in which the contract owner elects to receive payments of a designated minimum amount for as long a period as the contract's accumulated value will provide.

depend on any life expectancy. The fixed amount option also guarantees that the entire accumulated value of the annuity will be distributed, either to the payee or a contingent payee.

The features of the nonannuitized payout options described in this section are summarized in Figure 2.6.

Annuitized Payout Options

Annuitized payout options tie annuity benefit payments to a life expectancy. An annuity that provides periodic payments for at least the lifetime of the annuitant is referred to as a **life annuity**. Life annuities can be structured as (1) life only, or straight life annuities, (2) joint and survivor annuities, (3) life income with period certain annuities, and (4) life income with refund annuities. To simplify our discussion of these payout options, we will assume that the annuitant, whose life expectancy determines the amount and duration of annuity benefit payments, and the payee, who receives the annuity payments, are the same person and refer to them both as the annuitant.

Life Only Annuity

A **life only annuity**, or *straight life annuity*, provides periodic payments only for as long as the annuitant lives. Upon the death of the

life annuity.
An annuity that provides periodic payments for at least the lifetime of the annuitant.

life only annuity.
An annuity that provides periodic payments only for as long as the annuitant lives; upon the death of the annuitant, the insurer makes no further payments. Also known as a straight life annuity.

FIGURE 2.6

Nonannuitized Payout Options

Payout Option	Payment Amount	Length of Payout Period	Effect of Earnings During Payout Period
Lump-Sum Distribution	Equal to contract's accumulated value less taxes, if any	Payout period ends with payment of lump sum	No additional earnings; entire value distributed at maturity
Fixed Period Option	Determined by length of fixed period	Specified by contract owner; not linked to any life expectancy	Increases payment amount but not number of payments
Fixed Amount Option	Specified by contract owner	Determined by fixed payment amount; not linked to any life expectancy	Increases number of payments but not payment amount

annuitant, the insurer makes no further payments. Because of the uncertainty of when an annuitant will die, contract owners who choose a life only annuity run the risk that they may pay a great deal more in premiums than the annuitant will receive in annuity payments. Of course, it is also possible that the annuitant will live well beyond the projected life expectancy. In this case, the annuity payout will exceed the amount that the contract owner paid into the contract.

Joint and Survivor Annuity

A **joint and survivor annuity** is a form of life only annuity that provides a series of periodic payments based upon the life expectancies of two or more annuitants, and those payments continue until the last annuitant dies. The terms of a joint and survivor annuity contract determine whether the amount of each periodic benefit payment will remain the same after the first annuitant dies or decrease by a stated amount, such as 50 percent, following the death of the first annuitant. The premium amount required to fund the annuity will vary depending on the age and gender of the annuitants and the amounts that are to be paid out. The larger the expected amount of payments, the larger the premium required to pay for the annuity.

Life Income with Period Certain Annuity

An alternative available to contract owners who are unwilling to accept the risks associated with a life only annuity is a **life income with period certain annuity**. This type of annuity guarantees that annuity payments will be made throughout the annuitant's lifetime and that payments will continue for at least a specified period, even if the annuitant dies before the end of that period. The contract owner selects the period certain, which can be 5, 10, 15, or 20 years. Typically, for annuities that are similar in all other particulars, the longer the period certain, the smaller the amount of each benefit payment. The contract owner also selects a contingent payee who will receive annuity benefit payments throughout the remainder of the period certain if the annuitant dies before the period certain expires.

For example, assume that Brenda Bishop purchased a life income annuity with a 10-year period certain. If Ms. Bishop dies after having received five annual benefit payments, then the insurer will continue making payments to Ms. Bishop's contingent payee for a total of five years after Ms. Bishop's death—in other words, until the end of the period certain. If Ms. Bishop is living when the period certain expires, she will continue to receive payments for the rest of her life and payments will cease at the time of her death.

---

joint and survivor annuity. *A form of life only annuity that provides a series of periodic payments based upon the life expectancies of two or more annuitants, and those payments continue until the last annuitant dies.*

life income with period certain annuity. *An annuity that guarantees that payments will be made throughout the annuitant's lifetime* and *that payments will continue for at least a specified period, even if the annuitant dies before the end of that period.*

Life Income With Refund Annuity

Another alternative to a life only annuity is a life income with refund annuity. A *life income with refund annuity*, also known as a *refund annuity*, provides annuity benefit payments throughout the lifetime of the annuitant and guarantees that at least the purchase price of the annuity will be paid out. This guarantee means that if the annuitant dies before the total purchase price of the annuity has been paid in benefits, the insurer will issue a refund to the contingent payee equal to the difference between the purchase price and the amount that has been paid out. The refund can be paid in a lump sum or in installments. Note that the payout guarantee offered in a life income with refund annuity is similar to the death benefit that most annuities pay during the accumulation period.

The features of the annuitized payout options described in this section are summarized in Figure 2.7.

Payout Options for Variable Annuities

In addition to choosing how benefits are to be distributed during the payout period, owners of variable annuity contracts are allowed to specify whether payments under the selected distribution option will be fixed, variable, or a combination of both fixed and variable.

Fixed Payouts

If a variable annuity contract owner chooses a **fixed payout** option, the insurer makes a series of payments to the payee that are of a fixed amount throughout the payout period. Under this option, the insurer transfers the accumulated value of the annuity from the separate account to its general account. The accumulation units the contract owner holds in the various variable subaccounts are, in effect, "cashed in" and the money is distributed to the annuitant in a series of equal payments. This is the same system used to make annuity benefit payments under a fixed annuity contract.

Variable Payouts

If a contract owner selects a **variable payout** option, the insurer makes a series of payments to the annuitant that vary throughout the payout period according to the performance of subaccount investments. Under this option, the accumulation units in the subaccounts are not "cashed in." Instead, they are converted to annuity units before the first annuity payment is made. An **annuity unit** is a share in an insurer's separate account during the payout period of a variable annuity.

---

life income with refund annuity.
An annuity that provides annuity payments throughout the lifetime of the annuitant and guarantees that at least the purchase price of the annuity will be paid out. Also known as a refund annuity.

fixed payout.
A variable annuity payout option in which the insurer makes a series of payments to the payee that are of a fixed amount throughout the payout period.

variable payout.
A variable annuity payout option in which the insurer makes a series of payments to the annuitant that vary throughout the payout period according to the performance of subaccount values.

annuity unit.
A share in an insurer's separate account that is obtained by converting accumulation units in various subaccounts before the first annuity payment is made.

FIGURE 2.7

Annuitized Payout Options

Payout Option	Payment Amount	Length of Payout Period	Amount Distributed
Life Only Annuity	Determined by contract value at maturity and the life expectancy of the annuitant	Lifetime of the annuitant; payments cease at death of annuitant	Determined by length of time annuitant lives
Joint and Survivor Annuity	Determined by contract value at maturity and the life expectancies of two or more annuitants	Lifetime of last remaining annuitant; payments cease at death of last surviving annuitant	Determined by length of time all covered annuitants live
Life Income with Period Certain Annuity	Determined by contract value at maturity and the life expectancy of the annuitant	Lifetime of the annuitant **or** the period certain specified in the contract, whichever is longer	Minimum amount determined by length of period certain; maximum amount determined by length of time annuitant lives
Life Income with Refund Option	Determined by contract value at maturity and the life expectancy of the annuitant	Lifetime of the annuitant; any funds remaining at the death of the annuitant are paid out as a refund	Guaranteed to equal at least the purchase price of the annuity

The number of annuity units the insurer credits to the contract owner's account depends on the accumulated value of the contract and the current value of an annuity unit. Because annuity unit values vary from one subaccount to another, the number of annuity units credited to a contract owner also depends on the subaccounts in which assets are placed.

During the payout period, contract owners can allocate annuity units among variable subaccounts in much the same way they allocated premiums during the accumulation period. Exchanging annuity units between subaccounts can result in either an increase or a decrease in the number of annuity units, depending on the unit value of each subaccount.

Fixed and Variable Payouts

The owner of a variable annuity contract also can choose to combine a fixed payout with a variable payout. Under this option, the insurer transfers a portion of the contract's accumulated value to the general account. This portion will provide regular and fixed annuity benefit payments. The insurer converts the remainder of the contract's accumulated value to annuity units, and the contract owner invests this portion in one or more variable subaccounts within the separate account. This portion of the annuity's accumulated value will provide an annuity benefit payment that varies according to the performance of investments in the specified subaccounts. Contract owners can choose any proportions they desire for the split. After contract owners establish the proportions, however, they cannot transfer assets between the fixed and variable portions of the annuity.

Calculating Annuity Benefit Payments

Although actual annuity benefit payment calculations are beyond the scope of this text, it is possible to describe the effects of various factors on fixed and variable payouts.

Fixed Payout Amounts

The amount of an annuity benefit under a fixed payout option depends on the following variables:

- The amount of the contract's accumulated value that is transferred into the insurer's general account

- The number of periodic annuity payments

- The stated interest rate for the general account

In simple terms, the amount of fixed payouts is calculated by dividing the accumulated value of the contract in the insurer's general account by the number of periodic payments. For example, suppose that when Jonas Ruskin's deferred variable annuity matured, he transferred $60,000 of his contract's accumulated value to the insurer's general account to provide fixed monthly annuity payments over a period of ten years. Without accounting for interest earnings, Mr. Ruskin would receive 120 payments (12 months × 10 years) and the amount of each payment would be $500 ($60,000 ÷ 120 payments). As Figure 2.8 illustrates, changes to any of the variables used in the calculation would change the amount of each payment.

FIGURE 2.8

Effect of Changing Variables on the Size of Periodic Payments Under a Fixed Payout Option

Variable	If you …	Then the size of the periodic payments will …
Accumulated Value in General Account	**Increase** the amount allocated to the general account ↑	**Increase**, because the account value will be larger ↑
	Decrease the amount allocated to the general account ↓	**Decrease**, because the account value will be smaller ↓
Number of Periodic Payments	**Increase** the number of periodic payments in the series of payments ↑	**Decrease**, because the same amount of money will be spread over a larger number of payments ↓
	Decrease the number of periodic payments in the series of payments ↓	**Increase**, because the same amount of money will be spread over a smaller number of payments ↑
Stated Interest Rate	**Increase** the stated interest rate ↑	**Increase,** because the account will earn more interest ↑
	Decrease the stated interest rate ↓	**Decrease,** because the account will earn less interest ↓

Variable Payout Amounts

Variable payout calculations are more complex than fixed payout calculations. Simply stated, the amount of variable payouts depends on the number and value of annuity units held by the contract owner at the time annuity payments are made. Figure 2.9 illustrates how the amount of variable annuity payments changes with changes in the value of annuity units.

Keep in mind that this illustration of variable payout calculations is overly simplified. In reality, a number of other factors also affect the calculation of variable payout amounts. One of these factors is the assumed investment rate specified in some variable annuity contracts. An **assumed investment rate (AIR)** is the minimum rate of return that the subaccount investments are expected to earn. If the actual rate of return on the underlying subaccount investments is less than the AIR, the annuity payments will decrease. If the actual rate of return is greater than the AIR, the annuity payments will increase. Actual AIR calculations used to arrive at payment amounts are highly complex and

assumed investment rate (AIR). The minimum rate of return that variable annuity subaccount investments are expected to earn.

> **FIGURE 2.9**
>
> ## Calculating Variable Annuity Payouts
>
> Tamika Broadbent held 100 annuity units in Subaccount Z on the maturity date of her deferred variable annuity contract. The following table shows the value of these units on the date of three scheduled annuity payments and the amount of each of these payments.
>
> | Payment Number | Value of Annuity Units | Amount of Annuity Payment |
> |---|---|---|
> | Payment 1 | $5.00 | $500 ($5.00 × 100 units) |
> | Payment 2 | $4.75 | $475 ($4.75 × 100 units) |
> | Payment 3 | $5.25 | $525 ($5.25 × 100 units) |

are beyond the scope of this text. Most states have limitations on AIRs, but the most commonly used AIRs are 3 percent and 5 percent. Under some variable annuity contracts, the contract owner can select the AIR from within a certain range.

Because the value of annuity units varies with market changes, variable payout options entail a degree of risk for the contract owner that does not exist under fixed payout options. However, variable payout options also offer the potential that payments will increase over time, allowing payments to keep pace with inflation.

Key Terms

contract duration

entire contract provision

incontestability provision

waiver of premium for disability rider

free look provision

assignment provision

payout options provision

guaranteed interest rate

current interest rate

renewal rate

accumulation units

administrative fee

mortality and expense risks (M&E) charge

asset management fee

surrender

cash surrender value

withdrawal

surrender charge

contingent deferred sales charge (CDSC)

free withdrawal provision

waiver of surrender charge provision

bailout provision

maturity date

lump-sum distribution

fixed period option

annuity certain

period certain

fixed amount option

life annuity

life only annuity

joint and survivor annuity

life income with period certain annuity

life income with refund annuity

fixed payout

variable payout

annuity unit

assumed investment rate (AIR)

Endnote

1. Linda Koco, "'To Age 100' Features Proliferate in Life Insurance and Annuities," *National Underwriter*, Life & Health/Financial Services ed. (26 August 2002): 17.

Annuity Principles and Products

CHAPTER 3

Fixed Annuities

After studying this chapter, you should be able to

- Describe the principal, interest rate, and payout guarantees included in traditional fixed annuity contracts

- Describe three basic methods insurers use to calculate and credit excess interest under equity-indexed annuity contracts

- Describe the fund-management options available to owners of market value adjusted annuity contracts and the effects these options have on contract values

OUTLINE

Traditional Fixed Annuities
Principal Guarantees
Interest Rate Guarantees
Payout Guarantees
Inflation Erosion

Equity-Indexed Annuities
Principal Guarantees
Interest Rate Guarantees
Vesting Rights

Market Value Adjusted Annuities
Investment Options
Market Value Adjustments

Future of the Fixed Annuity Market

In the first two chapters of this text, we introduced fixed annuities and described some of the characteristics that distinguish fixed annuities from variable annuities. In particular, we described how premium payments are invested and the way interest is paid on those premiums.

In this chapter, we provide a more detailed discussion of the features and guarantees included in traditional fixed annuities, equity-indexed annuities, and market value adjusted (MVA) annuities.

Traditional Fixed Annuities

One of the primary characteristics that distinguishes traditional fixed annuities from variable annuities is the presence of guarantees made by the insurer to the contract owner. These guarantees can be classified as (1) principal guarantees, (2) interest rate guarantees, and (3) payout guarantees.

Principal Guarantees

As you recall from Chapter 1, premiums for fixed annuities are deposited into the insurer's general account, which consists of the assets and investments the insurer uses to support its traditional insurance products. In choosing investments for its general account, the insurer must comply with numerous state insurance laws designed to protect the assets in the account. Whatever financial risk arises from investments made from the general account is borne entirely by the insurer. As a result, the ***principal*** of a fixed annuity—the total amount of premiums paid into the annuity, exclusive of any investment returns—is secure no matter how poorly the insurer's investments perform. This guarantee against loss of principal is a key benefit of fixed annuities.

principal.
The total amount of premiums paid into an annuity, exclusive of any investment returns.

Interest Rate Guarantees

The guaranteed interest rate that insurers typically apply to fixed annuity contracts ensures that contract owners will earn a specified minimum return on their principal, regardless of how the investments in the insurer's general account perform. To illustrate how this minimum return is generated, suppose that Roberta Harker purchases a fixed annuity that offers a guaranteed interest rate of 5 percent. At the end of the contract year, Ms. Harker's contract will be credited with a 5 percent gain, even if the insurer's investments earned less than that amount. If the insurer's investments earn more than 5 percent, Ms. Harker's contract will still be credited with a 5 percent gain—the guaranteed interest rate for her contract. Ms. Harker will receive no additional earnings from the insurer's general account investments.

As you recall from Chapter 2, insurers can offer additional interest rate guarantees in the form of current and renewal rates. For example, assume that instead of a fixed interest rate, Ms. Harker's annuity contract specifies a contract minimum guaranteed interest rate of 5 percent and a 3-year current interest rate of 5.5 percent. During the first three years of the contract, Ms. Harker's annuity will earn 5.5 percent, regardless of how the investments in the insurer's general account perform. If, at the end of the 3-year contract duration period, conditions improve and the insurer sets a renewal rate of 6.0 percent, then Ms. Harker's annuity will earn 6.0 percent for the next year. If the interest rate at renewal is 5.2 percent, then Ms. Harker's annuity will earn 5.2 percent for the next year. However, even if economic conditions during any contract duration period worsen enough to drop interest rates to less than 5.0 percent, Ms. Harker's annuity is guaranteed to earn 5.0 percent.

Payout Guarantees

The investment and interest rate guarantees associated with fixed annuity contracts allow the insurer to guarantee that a fixed annuity will have at least a minimum accumulated value at maturity. As a result, the insurer can guarantee a minimum annuity benefit payment for each dollar of premium used to purchase the contract. Most fixed annuities specify that when the insurer begins making benefit payments, the amount of each payment will not change.

In very basic terms, the insurer determines the amount of each annuity benefit payment by dividing the accumulated value of the contract, which includes anticipated future earnings, by the number of payments due. For immediate fixed annuities, this calculation is fairly simple. As you recall from Chapter 1, an immediate annuity has no accumulation period; therefore, the accumulated value of the annuity is equal to the premium used to purchase the contract. The length of the payout period—and the expected number of annuity payments—are specified in the payout option. For example, under a lump-sum distribution, fixed period, or fixed amount option, the number of payments is determined by the contract owner. Under life annuity options, the number of payments is based on the annuitant's life expectancy.

Calculation of payment amounts for deferred fixed annuities is more complex. Because the accumulated value of a deferred fixed annuity depends on the length of the contract's accumulation period and the earnings on premiums deposited in the insurer's general account, the value of the contract is not known until the annuity matures. Because the contract owner typically does not select a payout option until shortly before the contract's maturity date, the number of payments also is uncertain. Using the guaranteed interest rate, however, the insurer can provide information about the minimum amounts guaranteed by a deferred fixed annuity for various ages and payout options. This information typically is presented in the form of a chart such as the one in Figure 3.1, which shows sample minimum monthly payments guaranteed for each $1,000 of accumulated value for a deferred fixed annuity.

According to this chart, an annuitant who begins receiving annuity benefit payments at age 40 under a life only payout option will receive $4.13 each month for each $1,000 of accumulated value. If the accumulated value of the contract on the maturity date is $20,000, then the annuitant will receive monthly payments of $82.60 each (20 × $4.13 = $82.60) for the remainder of his life. Note that in Figure 3.1, the calculated amounts are based on monthly payments; calculations for annual payments would result in different amounts. Note, too, that the amounts included in the chart are the minimum amounts the insurer guarantees when it issues the contract. If the insurer's investment experience is more favorable than expected or if current and renewal interest rates are higher than the guaranteed interest rate, then the insurer may pay more than the guaranteed amount.

FIGURE 3.1

Chart of Annuity Values for a Deferred Fixed Annuity

Minimum Monthly Payments for Each $1,000 Applied

Annuitant's Age	Payments for Life Only	Payments Guaranteed for 10 Years	Payments Guaranteed for 15 Years	Payments Guaranteed for 20 Years
40	$4.13	$4.12	$4.11	$4.09
45	4.36	4.34	4.32	4.28
50	4.65	4.62	4.58	4.52
55	5.05	4.99	4.91	4.82
60	5.56	5.45	5.32	5.14
65	6.27	6.07	5.82	5.48
70	7.33	6.89	6.38	5.76
75 & over	8.95	7.89	6.87	5.92

Inflation Erosion

Although the guarantees included in a fixed annuity contract protect the contract owner's investment during economic downturns, they can result in a loss of purchasing power during periods of inflation. Most fixed annuity contracts specify that annuity benefit payment amounts will not change over the course of the payout period. This means that the annuitant will receive the same amount each period even if expenses increase because of inflation. Many contract owners or annuitants, however, are willing to risk a loss of purchasing power to obtain the guarantees offered by a fixed annuity.

Equity-Indexed Annuities

Equity-indexed annuities, which were introduced in the early 1990s, combine the guarantees associated with traditional fixed annuities with additional earnings potential, making them an appealing alternative for some investors.

Principal Guarantees

The majority of premiums for equity-indexed annuities are deposited in the insurer's general account and used to purchase low-risk investments. Like premiums for traditional fixed annuities, premiums for equity-indexed annuities that are deposited into the insurer's general account are protected against loss. Insurers use the remaining premiums to purchase investments whose performance is closely tied to the performance of groups of investments tracked by indexes such as the Standard & Poor's (S&P) 500™ Composite Stock Price Index, the S&P Midcap 400™ Index, the NASDAQ 100™ Index, or the Russell 2000™ Index. As you recall from Chapter 1, an index is a measurement system that tracks the performance of a group of similar investments. Premiums used to purchase index-based investments are not guaranteed.

Because only that portion of the contract owner's investment deposited in the general account is guaranteed, equity-indexed annuities offer less investment security than traditional fixed annuities. Instead of guaranteeing the entire amount of principal paid into the contract, equity-indexed annuities typically offer a partial guarantee, usually expressed as a percentage of the total principal paid into the contract. To qualify as a fixed annuity under the terms of the Standard Non-Forfeiture Law for Individual Annuities, an equity-indexed annuity contract must guarantee a minimum account value of at least 90 percent of the premium amount.

Interest Rate Guarantees

Like traditional fixed annuities, equity-indexed annuities also specify a guaranteed minimum interest rate for premiums paid into the insurer's general account. This rate sets the lower limit of the potential earnings for the fixed portion of the contract and protects this portion of the contract value from market downturns. To qualify as fixed annuities, contracts issued prior to 2003 were required to guarantee a minimum interest rate of at least 3 percent. For contracts issued in 2003 or later, the guaranteed rate can vary from a low of 1 percent to a high of 3 percent. Earnings on premiums used to purchase index-based investments are credited to the contract in the form of excess interest that is tied to increases in the value of the specified index. The earnings generated by gains in the index can be substantial.

Calculating Excess Interest

The first step in determining excess interest earnings for an equity-indexed annuity is to establish the contract *term*, which is the length of time over which the interest will be calculated. The term is similar to the contract duration period of a traditional fixed annuity. Most equity-indexed annuities have terms that range from one year to ten years.

term.
The length of time over which excess interest on an equity-indexed annuity is calculated.

Insurers can calculate the excess interest applied to an equity-indexed annuity contract in a variety of ways depending on contract provisions. These methods can be classified as (1) annual interest methods, which calculate an interest rate for each year of the contract term, (2) total interest methods, which calculate one interest rate for the entire contract term, or (3) combination methods, which credit interest less frequently than annually but more often than once. A number of variations are available under each of these methods.

Rather than attempting to describe all of these variations, we will focus our discussion on the following three basic methods: the annual reset method, the point-to-point method, and the high water mark method.

Annual Reset Method. The most basic annual interest calculation method is the **annual reset method**, also known as the *ratchet method*, which involves comparing the value of the index at the end of each contract year with the value at the start of that year. For the next year, the starting value is reset to the ending value from the previous year. Figure 3.2 illustrates this resetting process. Contract values are reset at the beginning of each contract year during the term of the contract.

annual reset method.
A method of calculating excess interest on an equity-indexed annuity that involves comparing the value of the index at the end of each contract year with the value at the start of that year. The ending value of each year is then used as the starting value for the next year. Also known as the ratchet *method.*

The annual reset method allows the contract owner to lock in gains each year and avoid losses. When the market goes up, the contract owner earns excess interest. When the market remains stable or goes down, the contract neither gains nor loses value.

FIGURE 3.2

Annual Reset Method of Calculating Excess Interest

Contract Year	Beginning Value	Ending Value	Excess Interest
1	$300	$350	$50
2	350	250	0
3	250	250	0

point-to-point method.
A method of calculating excess interest on an equity-indexed annuity that involves comparing the value of the index at the start of the annuity contract term to the value at the end of the term to determine what, if any, excess interest has accrued because of a change in the index.

Point-to-Point Method. The *point-to-point method* is a total interest calculation method that compares the value of the index at the start of the annuity contract term to the value at the end of the term to determine what, if any, excess interest has accrued because of a change in the index. If the value of the index at the end of the term is higher than the value of the index at the beginning of the term, the contract will earn excess interest. If the index shows no growth or negative growth, the contract will not earn excess interest.

Because earnings depend only on the value of the index at the end of the term, they are insulated from the effects of short-term fluctuations during the term. As long as index values rise overall, the insulating effect can be an advantage. If values stagnate or decline, it can be a disadvantage because contract owners cannot lock in periodic gains.

high water mark method.
A method of calculating excess interest on an equity-indexed annuity that involves comparing the value of the index at the beginning of the contract term with the highest value that the index reaches on any contract anniversary date during the term.

High Water Mark Method. The *high water mark method* involves comparing the value of the index at the beginning of the contract term with the highest value—or high water mark—that the index reaches on any contract anniversary date during the term. If the index has gained in value on the high water mark compared to the value at the beginning of the term, the contract will earn excess interest for the contract term. However, if the index value at the high water mark is the same or less than the index value at the start of the contract term, the contract will not earn excess interest. As a result, the high water mark method—like the annual reset method and point-to-point method—allows the contract owner to take advantage of index gains without being subject to index losses.

The advantage of using high water marks rather than year-end or term-end values to calculate excess interest is that earnings are not dependent on index growth at the end of each contract year or at the end of the term. Using this method, the index need only show growth on any contract anniversary date. The disadvantage of using the high water mark method is that earnings are determined by looking at only one day.

Crediting Excess Interest

To compensate insurers for the investment and interest rate guarantees offered to the contract owner, equity-indexed annuity contracts typically do not credit contracts with the full amount of index gains. Instead, insurers use participation rates, spreads, and caps to determine the actual amount of excess interest that will be credited to the contract. The **participation rate** is the percentage of the specified index's gain in value that the equity-indexed annuity contract will earn. For example, if an index increases by 10 percent and the contract specifies an 80 percent participation rate, then the excess interest earned on the annuity will be 8 percent (0.8 × 0.10). Insurers offer different participation rates depending on their investment strategies and crediting methods. The participation rate can be specified for the term of the contract or for a contract year. If the rate is specified for a contract year, then the insurer will declare the participation rate each year of the contract term.

As an alternative to participation rates, some insurers apply spreads to excess interest. A **spread**, or *margin*, is a specified percentage that is deducted from the index gain. Thus, if an index increases by ten percent for a given period and the contract specifies a two percent spread, then the excess interest earned on the annuity will be eight percent (10 percent – 2 percent).

The **cap** is a specified interest rate that is the maximum amount of excess interest earned that will be credited to an equity-indexed annuity contract. If excess interest earnings are below the specified cap, the annuity will be credited with the entire amount of excess interest. If excess interest earnings are higher than the cap, the amount credited will be limited to the specified cap.

To illustrate how the participation rate and the cap work in combination, consider a contract that specifies a 90 percent participation rate and a 12 percent cap on earnings. If the value of the index increases by 20 percent over the evaluation period, then the amount of excess interest earned during the period would be 90 percent (the participation rate) of 20 percent (the index gain), or 18 percent (0.90 × 0.20 = 0.18). Because of the cap on earnings, the amount of excess interest actually credited to the annuity contract would be 12 percent.

Figure 3.3 shows how excess interest is calculated and credited under the annual reset, point-to-point, and high water mark methods over a five-year contract term. Each method assumes a 90 percent participation rate and a 12 percent cap.

The amount of excess interest earned is determined by multiplying the index gain/loss by the participation rate specified in the contract—in this case, 90 percent. The 12 percent cap then is applied to earned

participation rate.
The percentage of the specified index's gain in value that an equity-indexed annuity contract will earn.

spread.
A specified percentage that is deducted from the index gain to determine the amount of gain that an equity-indexed annuity contract will earn. Also known as a margin.

cap.
The upper limit on the amount of excess interest that will be credited to an equity-indexed annuity contract.

FIGURE 3.3

Calculating and Crediting Excess Interest

Value of Index	Annual Reset Method			Point-to-Point Method			High Water Mark Method		
Beginning value=400	Gain/ Loss	Interest earned[a]	Interest credited[b]	Gain/ Loss	Interest earned[a]	Interest credited[b]	Gain/ Loss	Interest earned[a]	Interest credited[b]
End of year 1 =420	5.0%	4.5%	4.5%	------	0%	0%	5.0%	4.5%	0%
End of year 2 =454	8.0%	7.2%	7.2%	------	0%	0%	13.5%	12.2%	12.0%
End of year 3 =445	-2.0%	0%	0%	------	0%	0%	11.3%	10.2%	0%
End of year 4 =445	0%	0%	0%	------	0%	0%	11.3%	10.2%	0%
End of year 5 =449	1.0%	0.9%	0.9%	12.3%	11.1%	11.1%	12.3%	11.1%	0%
Total:		12.6%			11.1%			12.0%	

[a] 90 percent participation rate applied to index gain
[b] 12 percent cap applied to earned interest

excess interest to determine the amount actually credited to the contract. Under the annual reset method, excess interest is calculated and credited annually during the contract term. Under the point-to-point and high water mark methods, excess interest is credited only at the end of the term, using either end-of-term or high-water-mark values.

Vesting Rights

Most equity-indexed annuity contracts require the contract owner to hold the contract until the end of the term to receive the full value of the annuity, including excess interest credits. In some cases, however, the contract owner is allowed to make withdrawals in accordance with a vesting schedule included in the contract. A **vesting schedule** is a timetable that specifies how much the contract owner can withdraw—before the end of the contract term—of the excess interest that has been credited to the contract. Generally, the percentage available increases over the term of the contract. By the end of the term, the contract owner can withdraw 100 percent of the gains.

vesting schedule.
A timetable that specifies how much a contract owner can withdraw—before the end of the contract term—of the excess interest that has been credited to an equity-indexed annuity.

Market Value Adjusted Annuities

Although market value adjusted (MVA) annuities are similar to traditional fixed annuities, they offer contract owners greater earnings potential by providing multiple interest rate options and increased access to funds. The increased earnings potential, however, carries increased risk.

Investment Options

As you recall, premiums for traditional fixed annuity contracts are deposited into the insurer's general account and earn a guaranteed interest rate for a specified contract duration period. MVA annuities allow contract owners to divide premium deposits among as many as ten different guarantee periods, ranging in length from one to ten years. Each guarantee period offers its own interest rate that remains fixed for the length of the period. At the end of each guarantee period, the contract owner has the option to leave funds under that same guarantee period for another term, switch funds to a different guarantee period, or withdraw the money from the account.

Market Value Adjustments

As long as the contract owner leaves all funds in the account until the end of the guarantee period, the value of the invested assets will increase at the fixed rate. If the contract owner withdraws funds before the end of the guarantee period, the insurer will make a market value adjustment. This adjustment can result in an increase, a decrease, or no change in the total value of the contract.

Most insurers allow contract owners to make partial withdrawals—up to a specified percent of total contract value—without an adjustment. Insurers typically also waive adjustments for withdrawals made within a specified period of time—usually 30 days—before the end of the guarantee period.

Calculating Market Value Adjustments

Although the actual calculation of market value adjustments is beyond the scope of this text, it is possible to describe the adjustment process. In general terms, market value adjustments are determined by comparing the fixed rate assigned to the guarantee period to prevailing rates in the market at the time of withdrawal.

The fixed rate is set at the time the contract is purchased and is based on the type of investments made with account funds. In some cases, insurers back MVA annuity accounts with investments that are linked to a specified market index. More often, insurers back MVA annuity contracts with investments in bonds and money market instruments. When a contract owner withdraws funds from an MVA annuity account, the insurer sells account investments to cover the amount of the withdrawal. The prices at which the insurer can sell account investments depend on the prevailing market rates.

Bonds and money market instruments generally decrease in value as interest rates rise. Therefore, sales made when prevailing interest rates are higher than fixed rates generally result in losses because the value of the investments has decreased. On the other hand, bonds and money market instruments generally increase in value as interest rates fall. Consequently, sales made when prevailing rates are lower than fixed rates result in gains because the value of the investments has increased.

The gains or losses that occur as a result of investment sales determine the direction of market value adjustments. If investments are sold at a loss, withdrawals create a negative market value adjustment. Under these conditions, contract owners will lose a portion of their investment earnings and—depending on the terms of the contract—also may lose a portion of their principal. If sales of investments result in a gain, a positive market value adjustment is made and contract owners will realize a gain above the fixed rate specified for the guarantee period.

Although negative market value adjustments are often difficult for customers to accept, the potential for increased earnings makes MVA annuities an attractive alternative to traditional fixed annuities.

Future of the Fixed Annuity Market

During the 1980s and early 1990s, fixed annuities became a popular vehicle for accumulating and protecting assets. The overwhelmingly positive performance of the U.S. stock market between 1993 and 2000 shifted the focus from fixed products to variable products and sales of fixed annuities during this period rose only 2 percent each year.[1] Subsequent downturns in the market caused investors to look again at fixed annuities as safe investment alternatives.

In times of economic uncertainty, fixed annuities will probably maintain a significant share of the annuities market. However, the focus is likely to shift from traditional forms to more innovative forms. Equity-indexed annuities and MVA annuities, which offer contract owners some level of protection against market losses and a share of market gains, are likely to increase in popularity. Annuity developers already are enhancing the appeal of these annuities by offering additional features, such as CD-indexing, treasury indexing, and guarantees for more than one year.

Key Terms

principal

term

annual reset method

point-to-point method

high water mark method

participation rate

spread

cap

vesting schedule

Endnote

1. Jennifer C. Rankin, "Back to Basics," *Resource* (August 2002): 8.

Annuity Principles and Products

CHAPTER 4

Variable Annuities

After studying this chapter, you should be able to

- Describe the risk and return features that distinguish variable annuities from fixed annuities
- Describe the various investment options available in variable annuity subaccounts
- Describe the purpose of asset allocation
- Discuss the special services, payout options, and benefits that are unique to variable annuities

OUTLINE

Investment Risk and Return

Subaccount Investments
Asset Classes
Asset Allocation
Subaccount Values
Contract Values

Special Services
Automatic Dollar Cost Averaging
Transfers Between Subaccounts
Automatic Rebalancing

Guaranteed Living Benefits

Guaranteed Death Benefits

In this chapter, we turn our attention to variable annuities, which as you recall from Chapter 1, are annuities under which the accumulated value of the contract and the amount of periodic annuity benefit payments fluctuate according to the performance of a specified pool of investments.

Because investment risk and return are critical features of variable annuities, we begin the chapter with a description of these concepts. We then describe the characteristics and functions of separate accounts, including asset classes, asset allocation methods, and investment value calculations. We end the chapter with a discussion of three features available under variable annuity contracts: special services, guaranteed living benefits, and guaranteed death benefits.

Investment Risk and Return

In our discussion of fixed annuities, we noted that the two most important features of these annuities are that premiums are deposited in the insurer's general account and that contract owners are given certain principal, interest rate, and payout guarantees. These features offer contract owners protection against investment **risk**—which is the possibility that an investment will lose value—and a guaranteed rate of **return**—which is the profit investors earn on their investments. The interplay between the risks and returns offered by various investment options—in which higher risks usually generate higher returns and lower risks usually generate lower returns—is known as the **risk-return trade-off**.

Under the terms of a variable annuity contract, premiums are deposited into a separate account and used to purchase investments in various subaccounts. Within certain limits, contract owners determine where and in what amounts their premiums will be invested. The insurer, however, offers no minimum investment value or interest rate guarantees. As a result, contract owners bear all of the risk for their investment choices. During periods of market decline, losses can be substantial and can even result in a loss of the contract owner's investment principal. However, because earnings are not "locked in" at a fixed rate, the contract owner also keeps all positive investment returns, excluding any applicable expense charges. When market conditions are favorable, investment returns—and the value of the annuity contract—increase. Insight 4.1 describes the effects of risk and return on the values of fixed and variable annuity contracts.

Subaccount Investments

The subaccount investments included in the separate account represent a wide variety of risk and return options. Some subaccount investments are designed to preserve principal while generating a steady stream of income. Bonds and money market investments generate

risk.
The possibility that an investment will lose value.

return.
The profit an investor earns on his investment.

risk-return trade-off.
The interplay between risks and returns offered by various investment options, in which higher risks usually generate higher returns and lower risks usually generate lower returns.

INSIGHT 4.1

Effects of Risk and Return on Fixed and Variable Annuity Values

On January 1, Pamela Chase and David Croft each purchased a $10,000 deferred annuity from the Tradewind Insurance Company. Ms. Chase purchased a fixed annuity with a one-year fixed interest rate of 5 percent. Mr. Croft purchased a variable annuity and directed that his premiums be used to purchase investments in specified subaccounts. The following examples illustrate the effects of risk and return on these two annuity contracts.

Example One: Market Gains

During the period between January 1 and December 31, interest rates rose, and Tradewind was able to earn a 10 percent return on investments from its general account. On December 31, Tradewind credited Ms. Chase's fixed annuity with 5 percent interest, as specified in her contract. This credit increased the value of her annuity from $10,000 to $10,500. Because the earnings on Ms. Chase's contract are fixed, she received no additional earnings from the investments in Tradewind's general account.

Market performance during the same period also was exceptional, and, like Tradewind's general account investments, Mr. Croft's subaccount investments earned a 10 percent return, increasing the value of his variable annuity from $10,000 to $11,000. Because earnings on variable annuity contracts are not fixed, Mr. Croft was able to earn a higher return on his annuity than Ms. Chase earned on her fixed annuity contract.

Example Two: Market Losses

During the period between January 1 and December 31, interest rates fell, and Tradewind lost 2 percent on investments from its general account. All other factors remained the same. On December 31, Tradewind credited Ms. Chase's account with 5 percent interest as specified in her contract, even though the insurer's actual earnings were negative. The value of Ms. Chase's annuity thus increased from $10,000 to $10,500. No matter how far interest rates drop, Ms. Chase's fixed annuity contract is guaranteed 5 percent earnings.

Market values also dropped, and Mr. Croft lost 2 percent on his subaccount investments. Because Mr. Croft's contract does not offer any interest rate guarantees, the value of his contract decreased from $10,000 to $8,000. In this case, Mr. Croft's variable annuity earned a lower return than Ms. Chase's fixed annuity earned.

---

interest.
A fee that banks and other financial institutions pay for the use of borrowed money.

dividend.
A share of a company's profits from its stock.

income in the form of **interest,** which is a fee that banks and other financial institutions pay for the use of borrowed money. Stocks generate income in the form of dividends. A **dividend** is a share of a company's profits. Other subaccount investments focus on long-term growth through capital appreciation. **Capital appreciation** is an increase in the market value of invested assets. These different types of investment options are designed to meet individual investors' goals, risk tolerances, and personal needs.

Variable annuity contracts typically allow contract owners to use their premium deposits to purchase investments in multiple variable subaccounts. Contract owners also can use a portion of their premiums to purchase investments in a fixed account. A *fixed account*, sometimes called a *variable guaranteed account*, guarantees payment of a fixed rate of interest for a specified period of time. Premiums invested in the fixed account are held in the insurer's general account.

Asset Classes

Regardless of the number of subaccounts offered and the variety of investment objectives represented, all of the underlying investments of a variable annuity's subaccounts can be divided into groups based on their risk and return features. A group of similar investment instruments linked by related risk and return features is known as an **asset class**.

Variable annuity subaccounts can be divided into the following three types based on the asset classes in which funds are invested:

- A **money market subaccount** is a subaccount in an insurance company's separate account that consists of short-term money instruments or cash equivalents, such as United States Treasury bills. Money market instruments generally carry less risk for investors, but also tend to generate lower returns than either bond or stock investments.

- A **bond subaccount** is a subaccount in an insurance company's separate account that consists of a variety of both short-term and long-term government and corporate bonds. A **bond** is a type of debt that reflects money an organization has borrowed and must repay to the bond-holder. Because bond values tend to fluctuate more than money market values in response to market conditions, bonds generally involve a greater amount of risk for the investor. However, they also offer greater returns than do money market investments.

- A **stock subaccount** is a subaccount in an insurance company's separate account that consists of an array of domestic and foreign stocks. A **stock** is an ownership share in a company. Because dividend amounts and stock prices depend on corporate and market performance, stocks involve higher potential risks—and offer the potential for higher returns—than either bonds or money market instruments.

Figure 4.1 presents a list of the types of subaccounts commonly found in variable annuity contracts sold by U.S. insurers. Although the names and subaccount classifications used within variable annuity contracts differ from insurer to insurer, the general categories and types of subaccounts are fairly similar.

capital appreciation.
An increase in the market value of invested assets.

fixed account.
A variable annuity account that guarantees payment of a fixed rate of interest for a specified period of time. Also known as a variable guaranteed account.

asset class.
A group of similar investment instruments linked by related risk and return features.

money market subaccount.
A subaccount in an insurance company's separate account that consists of short-term money instruments or cash equivalents, such as U.S. Treasury bills.

bond subaccount.
A subaccount in an insurance company's separate account that consists of a variety of both short-term and long-term government and corporate bonds.

bond.
A type of debt that reflects money an organization has borrowed and must repay to the bond-holder.

stock subaccount.
A subaccount in an insurance company's separate account that consists of an array of domestic and foreign stocks.

stock.
An ownership share in a company.

FIGURE 4.1

Variable Annuity Subaccounts

Asset Class	Subaccount Name	Typical Investments
Money Market	Money Market	U.S. Treasury bills
Bond	Government	Bonds issued by the U.S. government and its agencies
	Corporate	Bonds issued by U.S. corporations
	International	Bonds issued by foreign governments and corporations
Stock	Large Cap	Stocks of large U.S. corporations
	Mid Cap	Stocks of medium-sized U.S. corporations
	Small Cap	Stocks of small U.S. corporations
	Value	Stocks of U.S. corporations that currently appear to be priced below market value
	Growth	Stocks of U.S. corporations that demonstrate strong potential for capital appreciation
	Income	Stocks of U.S. corporations with a stable dividend payment history
	Growth & Income	A mixture of stocks of U.S. corporations with strong potential for capital appreciation and stocks of U.S. corporations with a stable dividend payment history
	International	Stocks of foreign corporations
	Global	Stocks of both foreign and U.S. corporations
Money Market, Bond, Stock	Sector	Stocks or bonds from a particular industry or market segment (such as telecommunications, utilities, health care)
	Index	Stocks or bonds that make up one of the financial market indices
	Balanced or Asset Allocation	A mix of money market instruments, bonds, and stocks
Fixed rate	Fixed/Variable Guaranteed	Investments included in the insurer's general account

Asset Allocation

At the time contract owners purchase variable annuity contracts, they must select at least one subaccount in which to invest annuity premiums. When contract owners choose more than one subaccount, they must specify what percentage of premiums they wish to invest in each subaccount. The insurer then invests the initial premium payment and any additional premiums in the specified subaccounts in the percentages indicated. The process of investing in fixed accounts, money markets, bonds, and stocks in predetermined proportions is known as *asset allocation*. Figure 4.2 illustrates how assets are allocated to subaccounts.

asset allocation. The process of investing premiums for variable annuities in fixed accounts, money markets, bonds, and stocks in predetermined proportions.

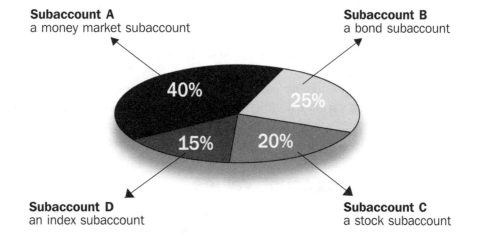

FIGURE 4.2

Allocating Premiums to Variable Subaccounts

Janine Mason purchased a variable annuity from the Lakeside Insurance Company with an initial premium payment of $10,000 and chose to allocate her premium payment as indicated below:

Subaccount A — a money market subaccount — 40%
Subaccount B — a bond subaccount — 25%
Subaccount C — a stock subaccount — 20%
Subaccount D — an index subaccount — 15%

In investing Ms. Mason's premium deposit, Lakeside purchased $4,000 (.40 × $10,000) in money market instruments from Subaccount A, $2,500 (.25 × $10,000) in bonds from Subaccount B, $2,000 (.20 × $10,000) in stocks from Subaccount C, and $1,500 (.15 × $10,000) in indexed stocks and bonds from Subaccount D.

After a variable annuity has been issued, contract owners can (1) transfer money among subaccounts, (2) change the percentage of premiums allocated to specific subaccounts, or (3) change the subaccounts in which future premiums are invested.

Contract owners can establish asset mixes that match their tolerance for risk, desired return on investment, and investment time frame by diversifying investments among several subaccounts and including each asset class in the total distribution. **Diversification,** which is the process of investing in a number of financial instruments to minimize the risk associated with any one investment or type of investment, allows contract owners to use positive returns earned from some of the investments held in a subaccount to offset the negative impact of poorly performing investments.

diversification.
The process of investing in a number of financial instruments to minimize the risk associated with any one investment or type of investment.

Asset Allocation Models

Many insurers use asset allocation models to help variable annuity contract owners diversify their investment holdings and choose the best possible asset mixes. In this context, an **asset allocation model** is a tool that uses an investor's personal and financial data to generate options for strategically distributing assets among different types and classes of investments.

asset allocation model.
A tool that uses an investor's personal and financial data to generate options for strategically distributing assets among different types and classes of investments.

A typical asset allocation model gathers personal and financial information about a contract owner, including age, current income, tax bracket, investment objectives, time constraints, risk tolerance, and the amount of other investments or financial obligations. The model then generates one or more asset mixes that take these factors into consideration. The contract owner can apply the resulting asset allocation by proportionally allocating premiums to corresponding subaccounts within the variable annuity contract. Figure 4.3 presents three representative asset allocation options generated by an asset allocation model and their corresponding risk and return characteristics.

Subaccount Values

When a contract owner pays premiums, the insurer uses those premiums to purchase accumulation units—or ownership shares—in the subaccounts specified in the contract. The value of the contract owner's investment in these subaccounts is determined by the current value and number of accumulation units the contract owner holds in each subaccount.

Current Value of an Accumulation Unit

The current value, or price, of an accumulation unit on a given day is equal to the value of a subaccount's invested assets at the close of business divided by the number of subaccount accumulation units

Chapter 4 — Variable Annuities | 65

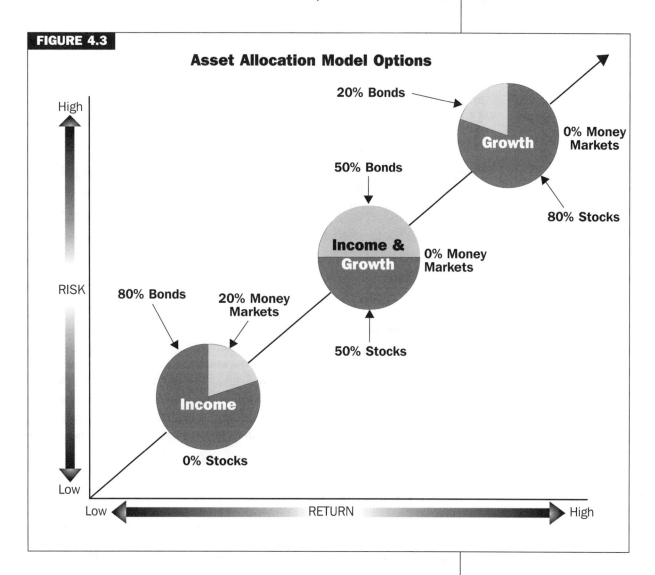

outstanding. Unit values fluctuate according to market conditions and can vary from day to day. Figure 4.4 demonstrates how accumulation unit values are calculated.

Number of Accumulation Units

The number of accumulation units that can be purchased with a premium deposit is determined by dividing the amount of the deposit by the value of an accumulation unit on the day of the deposit. Because accumulation unit values are determined at the close of business, premiums are not actually applied to purchase accumulation units until the following day, when values are known. For example, suppose a contract owner makes a $100 premium payment into Subaccount A on June 1. If the current value of an accumulation unit in Subaccount A is $20 at the close of business on June 1, as shown in Figure 4.4, then the contract

FIGURE 4.4

Calculating Accumulation Unit Value

At the close of business on June 1, Variable Subaccount A has a value of $500,000 and 25,000 outstanding accumulation units. Therefore, the current value/price of an accumulation unit in Variable Subaccount A at the close of business on June 1 is equal to:

$500,000 ÷ 25,000 = $20.00
(Value of invested assets) (Accumulation units outstanding) (Value/price of each accumulation unit)

owner's premium will purchase 5 accumulation units in the subaccount ($100 premium ÷ $20.00 unit value = 5 units purchased). Because the unit value is not determined until the close of business on the day of the premium payment, the actual purchase will not be made until the following day, June 2. If the contract owner increases or decreases the amount of the premium, or the value of an accumulation unit increases or decreases, the number of accumulation units the premium purchases also will increase or decrease.

Contract Values

The total value of a variable annuity contract is determined by adding the values of all subaccount investments. Because changes in the value of accumulation units caused by changes in market conditions affect the value of variable subaccount investments, changes in unit values also result in changes in the value of the contract. Figure 4.5 demonstrates how subaccount and contract values are affected by market performance.

Special Services

Insurance companies issuing variable annuity contracts often offer contract owners special services or investment program options that are not available under fixed annuity contracts. Typically, these services are included in contract provisions designed to help contract owners more efficiently manage their variable subaccount investments. The most common services included in variable annuity contracts include (1) automatic dollar cost averaging, (2) transfers between subaccounts, and (3) automatic rebalancing.

FIGURE 4.5

Calculating Subaccount and Contract Values for Variable Annuities

On April 30, Michael Huang purchased a deferred variable annuity and selected Subaccount A and Subaccount B as the investment vehicles for his annuity. He paid a premium of $1,200 on April 30, May 30, and June 30. The premium was to be divided equally between Subaccount A and Subaccount B. The value of the subaccounts and the value of Mr. Huang's annuity on each of these dates are shown below.

April 30	May 30	June 30
Subaccount A	**Subaccount A**	**Subaccount A**
Premium deposited ....$600 Current unit value .... $2.00 Units purchased.................300 Total premium invested ....$600 Total units purchased 300	Premium deposited ....$600 Current unit value .... $3.00 Units purchased.................200 Total premium invested .... $1,200 ($600 + $600) Total units purchased ....500 (300 + 200)	Premium deposited ....$600 Current unit value .... $2.50 Units purchased.................240 Total premium invested .... $1,800 ($600 + $600 + $600) Total units purchased ....740 (300 + 200 + 240)
Subaccount value .... $600 (300 × $2.00)	**Subaccount value ..... $1,500** (500 × $3.00)	**Subaccount value ..... $1,850** (740 × $2.50)
Subaccount B	**Subaccount B**	**Subaccount B**
Premium deposited ....$600 Current unit value .... $2.50 Units purchased.................240 Total premium invested ....$600 Total units purchased 240	Premium deposited ....$600 Current unit value .... $2.00 Units purchased.................300 Total premium invested .... $1,200 ($600 + $600) Total units purchased ....540 (240 + 300)	Premium deposited ....$600 Current unit value .... $2.50 Units purchased.................240 Total premium invested .... $1,800 ($600 + $600 + $600) Total units purchased ....780 (240 + 300 + 240)
Subaccount value .... $600 (240 × $2.50)	**Subaccount value ..... $1,080** (540 × $2.00)	**Subaccount value ..... $1,950** (780 × $2.50)
Contract (Subaccount A + Subaccount B)	**Contract** (Subaccount A + Subaccount B)	**Contract** (Subaccount A + Subaccount B)
Total premium invested .... $1,200 ($600 + $600) Total units purchased ....540 (300 + 240)	Total premium invested .... $2,400 ($1,200 + $1,200) Total units purchased .... 1,040 (500 + 540)	Total premium invested .... $3,600 ($1,800 + $1,800) Total units purchased .... 1,520 (740 + 780)
Total Contract Value .... $1,200 (600 + $600)	**Total Contract Value .... $2,580** ($1,500 + $1,080)	**Total Contract Value .... $3,800** ($1,850 + $1,950)

Automatic Dollar Cost Averaging

To maximize market earnings and minimize losses, investors typically must buy when prices are low and sell when prices are high. Unfortunately, timing market transactions can be difficult and errors can be costly. Investors can avoid the stress of market timing through **dollar cost averaging**, which involves investing a fixed dollar amount in one or more financial instruments on a regular, periodic basis—regardless of the current values of the selected instruments. In the context of variable annuity contracts, dollar cost averaging involves using premium payments to make periodic purchases of accumulation units in one or more variable subaccounts.

Contract owners can implement dollar cost averaging by making regular periodic premium payments, or by taking advantage of the dollar cost averaging service included in most variable annuity contracts. Under the terms of an **automatic dollar cost averaging provision,** the contract owner makes a single premium payment into the insurer's separate account and the insurer uses that premium to make regular, periodic purchases in selected subaccounts over a specified period of time.

Because accumulation unit values vary, the number of units fixed premium payments will purchase also varies. As you recall from our discussion of subaccount and contract values, when accumulation unit values are higher, the fixed dollar amount will purchase relatively fewer subaccount units. When accumulation unit values are lower, the fixed dollar amount will purchase more subaccount units.

Over time, dollar cost averaging typically produces gains because the average value of accumulation units tends to be higher than the average cost of the units. Figure 4.6 shows how dollar cost averaging works. In this example, a contract owner pays a $500 premium into the insurer's separate account on February 1, and the insurer uses that premium to purchase accumulation units in a specified subaccount on the first day of the month for five consecutive months. Contract charges, if any, are not included.

In our example, the average value of an accumulation unit was $2.60 [($2.00 + $2.50 + $4.00 + $2.50 + $2.00) ÷ 5], and the average cost of each unit was $2.44 ($500 ÷ 205 units). Thus, the contract owner earned a gain of $0.16 per unit. In general, the more volatile a subaccount is, the greater the long-term gains will be.

---

dollar cost averaging.
The process of investing a fixed dollar amount in one or more financial instruments on a regular, periodic basis, regardless of the current values of the selected instruments.

automatic dollar cost averaging provision.
A provision in a variable annuity contract that allows the contract owner to use a single premium payment to make periodic purchases of accumulation units in one or more variable subaccounts over a specified period of time.

FIGURE 4.6

Dollar Cost Averaging

Purchase Date	Premium Amount	Unit Value	Units Purchased
February 1	$100.00	$2.00	50
March 1	$100.00	$2.50	40
April 1	$100.00	$4.00	25
May 1	$100.00	$2.50	40
June 1	$100.00	$2.00	50

Transfers Between Subaccounts

A *transfer* is a special service that allows a contract owner to move assets among variable annuity subaccounts during the accumulation period or the payout period. The ability to shift assets from one subaccount to another enables the contract owner to respond to changing market conditions and to adjust asset allocations to meet changing financial needs and investment objectives. Most variable annuity contracts include provisions that specify the maximum number and minimum dollar amount of subaccount transfers a contract owner may authorize during the accumulation period. Some provisions require the contract owner to pay a fee if requested transfers exceed designated limits. Transfer provisions also may limit transfers among subaccounts to certain designated dates. In addition, when the payout period has begun, most variable annuity contracts do not allow contract owners to make transfers into and out of the fixed account.

transfer.
A special service that allows a contract owner to move assets among variable annuity subaccounts during the accumulation period or the payout period.

Automatic Rebalancing

As we mentioned earlier in this chapter, contract owners typically specify—at the time of purchase—the proportion of each premium they wish to allocate to specified variable subaccounts. Over time, fluctuations in subaccount values may cause the actual proportion of assets allocated to each subaccount to change. In other words, the proportional distribution of assets in the subaccounts may not always equal the proportional distribution of assets the contract owner specified at the time the annuity was purchased.

For example, assume that Ernesto Alvarez purchased a deferred variable annuity from the Jupiter Insurance Company with a single premium payment of $50,000. At the time he purchased the annuity, Mr. Alvarez elected to invest 50 percent of the premium in Stock Subaccount C and 50 percent of the premium in Bond Subaccount D. Later that year, stock values increased and bond values dropped. As a result, the return on investments in Stock Subaccount C began to rise and the return on investments in Bond Subaccount D began to decline. At the end of the year, the proportion of assets Mr. Alvarez had invested in Stock Subaccount C had increased to 60 percent of the total, and the proportion of assets invested in Bond Subaccount D had decreased to 40 percent of the total. Thus, the proportional distribution of invested assets no longer reflected Mr. Alvarez's original asset allocation. If Mr. Alvarez wishes to maintain the original asset allocation on his own, he will have to continually monitor the performance and value of his subaccount investments and transfer assets back and forth as needed.

To eliminate the need for constant monitoring and ensure the consistent distribution of assets among the subaccounts specified by the contract owner, many insurers include automatic rebalancing provisions in variable annuity contracts. An **automatic rebalancing provision** states that values automatically will be transferred among specified subaccounts to maintain the allocation percentages designated by the contract owner. In our example, an automatic rebalancing provision would ensure that funds from Stock Subaccount C would be transferred periodically to Bond Subaccount B to maintain Mr. Alvarez's original 50/50 allocation split.

automatic rebalancing provision.
A provision in a variable annuity contract which states that values automatically will be transferred among specified subaccounts to maintain the allocation percentages designated by the contract owner.

Guaranteed Living Benefits

To compete more effectively during market downturns, many insurers have added enhanced benefits to their variable annuity products. The most common of these enhancements include

- **Guaranteed Minimum Income Benefit (GMIB).** This feature guarantees that variable payouts will not fall below a certain amount—usually a specified percentage of the first payment—even if investments drop in value as a result of poor market performance. For example, if an annuity contract includes an 80 percent guaranteed income benefit and the first monthly payment is $600, then the minimum amount the contract owner will receive on any future monthly payment will be $480 (0.80 × $600).

- **Guaranteed Minimum Withdrawal Benefit (GMWB).** This feature guarantees that a minimum amount of investment earnings will be available for withdrawals, even if subaccount investments perform poorly. In some cases, insurers also increase the maximum allowable withdrawal level. Increases can range from 7 percent to as high as 12 percent above the usual withdrawal levels.

- **Guaranteed Minimum Accumulation Benefit (GMAB).** This feature guarantees a return of principal if the contract remains in force for a specified period of time. Some contracts offer even more liberal guarantees, such as a guarantee of a multiple of principal.

- **Long Term Care Benefit.** This feature, usually offered as a rider, provides long term care insurance benefits if the annuitant requires home health care or nursing home care as a result of accident or illness. The benefit covers the cost of care without decreasing monthly annuity payments.

- **Nursing Home Care Benefit.** This feature allows contract owners to terminate the contract, without surrender charges, to cover nursing home care. To qualify for the benefit, (1) care must be prescribed by a physician and delivered in an eligible facility, (2) the contract owner must satisfy an 18-month waiting period, and (3) the contract must have been in force for more than one year.

Because these guarantees increase risk for the insurer, insurers usually charge contract owners extra for these benefits.

Guaranteed Death Benefits

Although, excluding any money held in fixed accounts, variable annuity contracts do not provide investment guarantees, they often do include a minimum death benefit guarantee. The **death benefit guarantee** states that if the contract owner dies before annuity payments begin, the beneficiary named by the contract owner will receive a benefit equal to the greater of (1) the total amount of premium payments made for the annuity, less any withdrawals, or (2) the accumulated value of the annuity at the time of the contract owner's death. The death benefit guarantee thus provides protection against the loss of principal invested in a variable annuity during the contract's accumulation period and, in some cases, also protects against the loss of investment earnings.

For example, assume that Robert Harding purchased a single-premium deferred variable annuity with a $50,000 payment on January 2 and named his wife, Emily, as the beneficiary. Three years later, during the contract's accumulation period, Robert died. On the date of Robert's death, the accumulated value of his subaccount investments had fallen to $40,000 because of poor investment performance. Under the terms of the contract's death benefit guarantee, the amount of the death benefit paid to Emily, would be equal to the amount of premiums paid—in this

death benefit guarantee. A provision in a variable annuity contract which states that if the contract owner dies before annuity payments begin, the beneficiary named by the contract owner will receive a benefit equal to the greater of (1) the total amount of premium payments made for the annuity, less any withdrawals made, or (2) the accumulated value at the time of the contract owner's death.

case $50,000. If the value of Robert's annuity at the time of his death had increased to $60,000, Emily would receive the contract's accumulated value, or $60,000.

Some insurers also offer variations on these guarantees. For example, the contract owner may choose to have the account value determined using a date other than the date of death, such as the last contract anniversary date. Contracts also may offer a guaranteed growth option. Under this option, the insurer agrees to credit a minimum interest rate (usually 3 to 5 percent) on premiums if the total accumulated value of the contract at the time of death is equal to or less than the sum of premiums paid.

Key Terms

risk

return

risk-return trade-off

interest

dividend

capital appreciation

fixed account

asset class

money market subaccount

bond subaccount

bond

stock subaccount

stock

asset allocation

diversification

asset allocation model

dollar cost averaging

automatic dollar cost averaging provision

transfer

automatic rebalancing provision

death benefit guarantee

Annuity Principles and Products

CHAPTER 5

Investment Basics

After studying this chapter, you should be able to

- Identify the major factors that affect a person's ability and willingness to accept risk
- Describe the major types of investment risk and their impact on various investments
- Discuss the importance of the time value of money on investments
- Describe the advantages and disadvantages of various investment products

OUTLINE

Investment Principles
Risk and Return
Time Value of Money
Dollar Cost Averaging
Diversification and Asset Allocation

Investment Features of Variable Annuities and Other Financial Products
Investment Security
Access to Funds
Tax Advantages
Payout Options

In our discussion so far, we have made numerous references to financial planning. In this chapter, we provide an overview of some of the basic principles of investing that underlie financial planning and explain how different types of investments function.

We begin the chapter with a discussion of the principles of risk and return, the time value of money, dollar cost averaging, and diversification and asset allocation. We then describe some of the investment advantages and disadvantages of variable annuities and other financial products.

Investment Principles

Because a comprehensive discussion of the financial planning process is beyond the scope of this text, we will focus our attention in this section on some of the basic concepts involved in developing an investment strategy. These concepts include risk and return, time value of money, dollar cost averaging, and diversification and asset allocation.

Risk and Return

As you recall from Chapter 4, risk is the possibility that investors will experience a loss on their investments as a result of market conditions and return is the profit investors earn for taking a risk. Although all investments in financial products involve risk and return, some investments carry higher risks and offer higher returns than others.

For example, a person who purchases shares of stock faces considerable risk. Small decreases in market values can result in the loss of part of the initial investment. Large decreases, such as those experienced in the U.S. stock market during the fourth quarter of 2001, can be devastating. The trade-off for accepting high risk from stock investments—and the feature that makes these investments appealing to many people—is the possibility of earning high returns.

Other investments carry very little risk. For example, if a person opens a savings account or purchases a **certificate of deposit (CD)**— a contractual agreement issued by a bank that returns the investor's principal, with interest, on a specified date—the investment is protected even if the bank fails. This protection is provided through the **Federal Deposit Insurance Corporation (FDIC)**, a U.S. federal agency that guarantees up to $100,000 per individual account on deposit in member institutions. Investments in CDs are not entirely without risk. If the entire economy of the United States were to fail and the government were to go bankrupt, then the bank might not be able to cover the investment. However, the chance of such a situation occurring is so remote that investors typically ignore the risk. The risk-return trade-off for greater investment security is lower returns.

certificate of deposit (CD).
A contractual agreement issued by a bank that returns the investor's principal, with interest, on a specified date.

Federal Deposit Insurance Corporation (FDIC).
A U.S. federal agency that guarantees funds on deposit— up to a $100,000 limit— in member institutions.

For most investors, the amount of risk they are willing to accept in exchange for investment returns depends on their risk tolerance and the type of risk involved.

Risk Tolerance

A person's risk tolerance, or comfort level with risk, is affected by a variety of personal factors, including the person's age, circumstances, and personality. For example, younger people typically have more time to achieve financial goals than do older people. As a result, younger people are better able and more willing to accept a greater amount of risk. Similarly, people with more resources—or those with the potential for building resources—generally can accept higher levels of risk than can people with limited resources. People who are "aggressive" investors also tend to be more comfortable with risk than those who are more "conservative." Characteristics such as marital status, family size, and education level also contribute to risk tolerance.

Risk tolerance is affected by external factors as well. For example, in a bull market, when the economy is strong and stock prices rise, people tend to be willing to accept more risk than they are willing to accept in a bear market, when economic conditions and stock prices are weak.

Understanding risk tolerance is an important part of retirement planning because people's willingness or unwillingness to accept risk can affect the amount that they can earn on various retirement savings products and the type of investment strategy that can best meet their needs. Figure 5.1 contains a quiz designed by a financial services company to help group retirement plan participants determine their risk tolerance and select the most appropriate investment strategy.

FIGURE 5.1

Investment Risk Strategy Quiz

Do you want to put money away and take as little risk as possible or do you want to put your money to work and assume a bit more risk? Maybe you want to be somewhere in the middle. Before you choose your investment selections you should determine a strategy.

Here's a quick quiz to help you identify how much risk you may be comfortable taking with your investments. Remember, this is only a general guideline to help you determine a possible investment strategy and feel comfortable with whatever investment decisions you make.

Read through each question and enter your answer in the box to the right of the question. For example, if you are 20–29 years old, you would enter "5" in the box to the right of question A. When you've finished, add up the numbers in the boxes to get your "risk tolerance" score. Then you will be ready to figure out a strategy and choose the investment options that are right for you.

(continued on next page)

Chapter 5 — Investment Basics

FIGURE 5.1 *continued*

Investment Risk Strategy Quiz

A. How old are you?

20–29	30–39	40–49	50–59	60+
5	4	3	2	1

B. How many years until you retire?

5	10	15	20	25+
1	2	3	4	5

C. Many types of investments involve significant ups and downs in the total value of your account, especially in the short term. How willing are you to ride out the following losses in your account?

Down 5% or Less	Down 10%	Down 15%	Down 20% or More
1	2	3	4

D. Do you consider yourself knowledgeable about investments and do you believe that there are many advantages to investing in the stock market?

Strongly Agree	Agree	Neutral	Disagree	Strongly Disagree
5	4	3	2	1

E. Do you understand the trade-off between risk and potential reward and are you willing to accept more risk to possibly achieve higher returns?

Strongly Agree	Agree	Neutral	Disagree	Strongly Disagree
5	4	3	2	1

F. Do you feel that given your current income level and assets (e.g., home equity, IRAs, savings accounts), you will achieve your retirement goals?

Strongly Agree	Agree	Neutral	Disagree	Strongly Disagree
5	4	3	2	1

Total Score ☐

What type of strategy are you comfortable with? From the quiz, see where your score falls and place a check mark next to the strategy that best matches your tolerance for risk:

( ) 26–29 points **Aggressive Strategy (High Risk):** You want to maximize the long-term growth of your retirement savings. You understand the ups and downs of stocks and are comfortable with taking a lot of risk to maximize returns. You have plenty of time to wait out the stock market cycles.

( ) 21–25 points **Growth Strategy:** You are looking to grow your money by investing and may have more time on your side. You are somewhat comfortable riding out the ups and downs of the stock market in exchange for the possibility of higher long-term results.

( ) 16–20 points **Balanced Strategy:** You want a balance between growth and security. You will accept some risk in order to have the potential for higher returns over time.

( ) 11–15 points **Moderate Strategy:** You feel a strong need to protect and grow your assets with emphasis on security. You are cautious but may be willing to diversify to spread out some of your risk.

( ) 6–10 points **Conservative Strategy:** Security is your most important concern. You may be approaching retirement or simply prefer to preserve more of your initial investment.

Source: Excerpted from Manulife Financial's *Your Guide to Building Financial Security*. Reprinted with permission.

The closer people get to the time when they need income from their investments—for example, as they near retirement—the more conservative their investment choices tend to become. However, as Insight 5.1 points out, even seniors need to retain some aggressive investments as a hedge against inflation and to provide for additional income to cover longer life spans and unexpected expenses.

Type of Risk

A person's willingness to accept risk also depends on the type of risk involved. Investment risks can be divided into three broad categories: (1) interest rate risk, (2) inflation risk, and (3) market risk.

Insight 5.1

Insurers Say Seniors Should Keep Some Risk in Their Investments

As longevity increases and retirement ages drop, insurers are adapting their investment products to include more aggressive and flexible vehicles.

Experts say older people are showing a newfound acceptance of risk. The experts cite various reasons for this, but they give most of the credit to public realization that people must hedge against inflation.

Ted Benna, president of the 401(k) Association, a Langhome, Pennsylvania, defined-contribution consulting firm, explained that people must now consider that they may live over 30 years in retirement. "In the past you retired at 65 and lived 10 years," he said.

A man aged 65 can expect to live to be 80 or 81, and a 65-year-old woman can reasonably hope to reach 85, noted Scott Dunn, assistant scientist at LIMRA International, Windsor, Connecticut.

Retirees should avoid being unduly conservative in their asset allocation, said Bob Howley, a pension actuary at Buck Consultants in New York. Even a low inflation rate of 3 percent annually would more than halve the value of money over 25 years, he said.

Older Americans do need to keep at least part of their assets liquid, in order to cover sudden expenses, like emergency medical care, said Ron Goldman, an independent financial planner and sales desk director at First Penn Pacific, Oakbrook Terrace, Illinois. However, he said he advises his senior financial planning clients to keep at least part of their assets in aggressive holdings.

Where should they put this type of money? Mr. Benna said variable annuities (VAs) are optimal insurance products for retirees looking to invest more aggressively.

Source: Adapted from Joseph D'Allegro, "Insurers Say Seniors Should Keep Some Risk in Their Investments," *National Underwriter*, Life & Health/Financial Services ed.(10 August 1998): 7, 26. Used with permission.

Interest rate risk is the chance that unpredictable fluctuations in interest rates will jeopardize the opportunity to maximize the return on an investment. Investments that guarantee a specified interest rate—such as CDs, savings accounts, and bonds—are especially susceptible to interest rate risk. For example, suppose that at the time a person purchased a CD, the guaranteed interest rate was 4 percent. Three months later, interest rates rose and new CDs offered guaranteed interest rates of 6 percent. Because fixed-rate investments do not allow owners to take advantage of increases in interest rates that occur during the contract period, they are subject to interest rate risk. Equity-based investments, such as stocks, mutual funds, and variable annuities, generally carry no interest rate risk because they allow investors to realize increased earnings during market upswings.

Inflation risk is the risk that the average level of prices for goods and services during an investment period will increase at a higher rate than investment earnings. During a period of inflation, if the value of an investment does not increase at a rate equal to or greater than the inflation rate, the purchasing power of the investor's dollars will decrease and the investment will not purchase as many goods and services as the investor had anticipated.

Fixed-rate investment products are sensitive to inflation risk. For example, suppose a couple saving for their child's college education purchases a ten-year bond that guarantees 4 percent interest. The expected return on the couple's investment may be high enough to cover college tuition and other expenses at current prices. However, if education costs increase significantly during the next ten years, the couple's investment return may not be adequate to cover their expenses. In such a scenario, inflation will adversely affect the value of the investment. Equity-based investments such as variable annuities, which can increase in value when market prices increase, offer a buffer against rising prices and decreased purchasing power.

A third type of investment risk is ***market risk***, which is the risk associated with fluctuations in stock prices. Because fixed-rate investments offer a guaranteed return, regardless of how the market performs, they are shielded from market risk. Fixed-rate investments also are protected against ***stagnant market risk***, which is the risk that the stock market will experience neither a significant gain nor a significant loss. These investments will still increase in value during periods of stagnation because of their interest rate guarantees.

Market-based investments are subject to both market risk and stagnant market risk. For example, market risk affects variable annuity contracts in two ways. Market rates that are lower than expected can prevent subaccount investments from providing desired returns. A significant drop can erode the principal invested in the account. Stagnant

interest rate risk.
The chance that unpredictable fluctuations in interest rates will jeopardize the opportunity to maximize the return on an investment.

inflation risk.
The risk that the average level of prices for goods and services during an investment period will increase at a higher rate than investment earnings.

market risk.
The risk associated with fluctuations in stock prices.

stagnant market risk.
The risk that the stock market will experience neither a significant gain nor a significant loss.

market risk does not cause variable annuity products to lose value, but it does prevent them from increasing in value. Over time, a lack of earnings can cause the value of the investment, and annuity payments, to be lower than expected.

Time Value of Money

The *time value of money* is an investment principle which states that the value of a sum of money will change over time as a result of the effects of interest. According to the time value of money principle, money invested in an interest-bearing financial product—such as a variable annuity or a savings account—has both a present value and a future value. At its most basic level, the present value of an investment is the original sum, or principal, used to make the investment. The future value of the investment is equal to the sum invested plus the interest earned over the investment period.

Financial planning often views the investment process in reverse, looking first at how much a person will need to cover expenses at some future point in time and then determining how much the person will need to invest, starting now, in order to have the necessary amount later. In this context, the *future value (FV)* of the investment is the amount that the original sum is expected to be worth at the end of a specified period of time, if it is invested at a specified interest rate. The *present value (PV)* is the amount that must be invested now, at a given rate of interest, to accumulate a specified amount by a certain future date.

The interest earned on investments can take one of two forms. Occasionally, investments earn *simple interest*, which is interest earned only on the principal. For example, assume that a person deposits $100 into an account earning 5 percent simple interest. At the end of the first year, the amount in the account will be $105 [$100 + (0.05 × $100)]. If the account earns interest only on the principal, then at the end of the second year, the amount in the account will be $110 [$105 + (0.05 × $100)]. More often, investments earn *compound interest*, which is interest earned on both the principal and the accumulated interest. If the account in our example above earns compound interest, the amount in the account at the end of the first year will still be $105. However, because interest is earned on the entire account balance—including the accumulated interest—the amount in the account at the end of the second year will be $110.25 [$105 + (0.05 × $105)].

Over time, compounding can have a tremendous impact on the value of an investment. Insight 5.2 provides a comparison of the effects of beginning a retirement savings program at age 25 versus age 35.

---

time value of money.
An investment principle which states that the value of a sum of money will change over time as a result of the effects of interest.

future value (FV).
The amount that an original sum is expected to be worth at the end of a specified period of time, if it is invested at a specified interest rate.

present value (PV).
The amount that must be invested now, at a given rate of interest, to accumulate a specified amount by a certain future date.

simple interest.
Interest that is earned only on the principal.

compound interest.
Interest that is earned on both the principal and the accumulated interest.

Chapter 5 — Investment Basics | 81

> **Insight 5.2**
>
> ### Saving for Retirement: The Cost of Procrastination
>
> The sooner you start saving for retirement, the better, because the younger you are, the longer your money has a chance to compound. The best way to explain compounding is with an example. It's a story about two siblings—Anne and Jenny. Anne began contributing $100 a month to her 401(k) company retirement plan at the age of 25 and continued contributing until age 65.
>
> Jenny, on the other hand, procrastinated. She never got around to investing for retirement until she was 35 years old (10 years after Anne). She began putting $100 a month away in her company 401(k) plan, and did so until she reached age 65. Both Anne and Jenny earned an average annual return of 8 percent on their accounts.
>
> As you can see from the accompanying charts, both Anne and Jenny retired at age 65, but because Anne started saving 10 years earlier than Jenny, she earned $169,253 more in interest alone—and saved $181,253 more for her retirement. That's the benefit of compounding.
>
> | | Anne | Jenny |
> |---|---|---|
> | Starts contributing at age ... | 25 | 35 |
> | Years of contribution .... | 40 | 30 |
> | Monthly deposit .... | $100 | $100 |
> | Total contributions ..... | $48,000 | $36,000 |
> | Total interest .... | $274,108 | $104,855 |
> | Total Savings .... | $322,108 | $140,855 |
>
>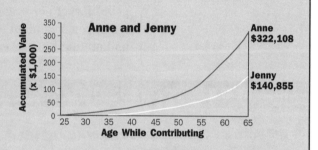
>
> **Source:** "How Early Should You Start?" *Manulife Financial,* http://www.manulife.com/usa/wwusdpen/early.htm (10 October 1998). Reprinted with permission.

Dollar Cost Averaging

As you recall from Chapter 4, dollar cost averaging allows investors to invest a fixed amount in one or more financial instruments at regular intervals, regardless of the current price of the selected instruments. In Figure 4.6, we illustrated the effects of dollar cost averaging on the average cost of accumulation units. In our example, the insurer used a variable annuity contract owner's $500 premium payment to purchase accumulation units in a specified subaccount over a five-month period. At the end of the five months, the average cost of the units was $2.44, and the contract owner owned 205 units. If our contract owner had invested the entire $500 at the beginning of the period, the average cost of the units would have been $2.50 instead of $2.44. The contract owner would have realized no gain. In addition, the premium would have purchased 200 units ($500 ÷ $2.50) rather than 205. Over time, the effects of dollar cost averaging tend to increase, as shown in Insight 5.3.

Diversification and Asset Allocation

As you recall from Chapter 4, diversification involves investing in a number of different financial instruments. Overall, diversification reduces risk and increases the likelihood of higher returns by allowing investors to use gains generated by investments that perform well to offset losses generated by investments that perform poorly.

Investors can achieve broad-based diversification by including financial products with different levels and types of risk and return in their investment portfolios. For example, suppose that an investor established a portfolio that included CDs, municipal bonds, a variable annuity contract, and mutual fund shares. During periods when the market performs well and interest rates rise, the CDs and bond investments will suffer from interest rate risk, but this risk will likely be offset by gains from the variable annuity and mutual fund investments. During periods of poor market performance, gains on the CDs and bond investments will offset some or all of the effects of market risk on the variable annuity and mutual fund investments.

Insight 5.3

Effects of Dollar Cost Averaging on a Deferred Variable Annuity

Valerie Taylor paid a $1,200 premium on a deferred variable annuity on January 1 of each year from 1970 until 1996. The insurer deposited the premium payments into its separate account and then, on the first day of each month, purchased accumulation units in Stock Subaccount H, which consisted of stocks included in Standard & Poor's Composite 500 Stock Index. The table below shows the average unit values, average unit costs, and unit gains generated by these stocks between January 1, 1970, and December 31, 1996.[1]

Period	Average Unit Value	Average Unit Cost	Unit Gain
Jan. 1, 1970 – Dec. 31, 1979	$12.75	$12.35	$0.40
Jan. 1, 1980 – Dec. 31, 1989	$28.15	$18.23	$9.92
Jan. 1, 1990 – Dec. 31, 1996	$55.35	$23.40	$31.95

At the end of 10 years, the $0.40 unit gain for the investments in Subaccount H would have produced a moderate gain on Ms. Taylor's investment. At the end of 26 years, with unit values more than twice as high as unit costs, the gain on Ms. Taylor's investment would have been significant.

Owners of variable annuity contracts can achieve similar results by allocating assets among a variety of different subaccounts. The overall effect of asset allocation, like that of diversification, will be to reduce risk and improve the likelihood of high investment returns.

Investment Features of Variable Annuities and Other Financial Products

Investors typically base their investment decisions on how well various products meet their investment needs. For investors saving for retirement, those needs often include security, access to funds, tax advantages, and a steady stream of retirement income. Figure 5.2 compares various investment products on each of these features.

Investment Security

The ability of an investment product to provide investment security is a primary consideration for many investors saving for retirement. Traditionally, such investors have relied on savings accounts, CDs, and bonds—which offer guaranteed rates of return—to provide this security. They have avoided market-based investments such as stocks and mutual funds because these products generally do not offer guaranteed returns. The trade-off for this security is lower returns.

The limited guarantees that are now being included in variable annuities offer investors a way to improve their returns without entirely sacrificing security. As we indicated in Chapter 4, most variable annuities offer death benefit guarantees that ensure the return of principal if the contract owner dies during the accumulation period. In some cases, insurers are increasing death benefits by linking them to contract values and allowing contract owners to lock in increases through ratchet or step-up features. Some variable annuities also offer minimum guaranteed accumulation benefits and minimum guaranteed income benefits.

Access to Funds

Access to principal and earnings is another important consideration when choosing investments. Although all investment options allow some access, the ease with which an investor can move money from one vehicle to another or liquidate assets to cover unexpected expenses varies. Some investments, such as stocks and mutual funds, offer fairly liberal access. Investors can buy and sell shares or transfer money from one fund to another at their discretion. Other investments restrict the amount and/or timing of withdrawals or transfers. For example, variable

FIGURE 5.2

Investment Features of Various Financial Products

Investment Product	Investment Security	Access to Funds	Tax Advantages	Payout Options
Savings Accounts	Guaranteed rate of return FDIC protection	Unlimited access	Earnings taxed annually No tax penalty for early withdrawals	Lump-sum distribution
CDs	Guaranteed rate of return FDIC protection	Owners charged for early withdrawals	Earnings taxed annually No tax penalty for early withdrawals	Lump-sum distribution
Bonds	Guaranteed rate of return	Owners charged for early payout	Earnings taxed annually Gains from transfer or sale subject to capital gains tax No tax penalty for early withdrawals	Lump-sum distribution
Stocks	No guarantees	Unlimited access Owners charged fees for purchases and sales	Earnings taxed annually Gains from transfer or sale subject to capital gains tax No tax penalty for early withdrawals	Lump-sum distribution
Mutual Funds	No guarantees	Unlimited access Owners charged fees for purchases and sales	Earnings taxed annually Gains from transfer or sale subject to capital gains tax No tax penalty for early withdrawals	Lump-sum distribution
Variable Annuities	Death benefit guarantee Limited guarantees on income, accumulated value	Limited access Contract owners may be subject to surrender charges for withdrawals	Earnings and gains from transfer or sale tax deferred Earnings taxed as ordinary income at distribution Early withdrawals subject to federal tax penalty	Lump-sum distribution Periodic payments over lifetime of owner

annuity contracts generally restrict the amount a contract owner can withdraw without charge to a certain percentage of the contract value each year.

Access usually comes at a cost. For example, investors typically pay a fee for buying and selling stocks and mutual fund shares. Owners of variable annuities, which are structured to provide payment on a specified date, typically must pay surrender charges on withdrawals made before the contract matures. In most cases, withdrawals from variable annuities also are subject to income taxes. Investors who surrender CDs, bonds, or variable annuities before they mature and contract owners who terminate variable annuity contracts before reaching a specified age also may be subject to additional charges and tax penalties.

Tax Advantages

In the United States and Canada, different types of investments are treated differently for tax purposes. These differences often are an important consideration when developing an investment strategy and selecting investment products.

One of the most important differences in the tax treatment of investment products is the way in which investment earnings are taxed. Earnings on savings accounts, CDs, bonds, stocks, and mutual fund shares are considered to be income to the investor and are taxed in the calendar year in which they are earned. Because the amount of tax payable reduces the value in these investments, the after-tax rate of return typically is less than the advertised rate, as shown in Figure 5.3.

Earnings on variable annuity subaccount investments, on the other hand, are excluded from the contract owner's yearly income and taxes are deferred until the contract matures or the contract owner withdraws money from the account. Thus, the after-tax interest rate on variable annuity earnings is the same as the posted rate.

To illustrate the effects of differences in tax treatment on investment values, suppose that on January 2, Edward Monroe deposits $2,000 in a savings account earning 8 percent interest. At the end of the first year, Mr. Monroe will have earned $160 in interest ($2,000 × 0.08). This $160 is subject to income taxes. If Mr. Monroe is in a 28 percent tax bracket, he will owe $44.80 ($160 × 0.28) in taxes. The effects of this tax on Mr. Monroe's investment are shown below:

Actual earnings	**$115.20**	($160.00 - $44.80)
Actual rate of return	**5.76%**	($115.20 ÷ $2,000)
Total investment value	**$2,115.20**	($2,000 + $115.20)

FIGURE 5.3

Advertised Interest Rates vs After-Tax Interest Rates

	If your current advertised interest rate is:					
	3.00%	4.00%	5.00%	6.00%	7.00%	8.00%
And your tax bracket is:	Your after-tax equivalent interest rate will be:					
10.0%	2.70%	3.60%	4.50%	5.40%	6.30%	7.20%
15.0%	2.55%	3.40%	4.25%	5.10%	5.95%	6.80%
27.0%	2.19%	2.92%	3.65%	4.38%	5.11%	5.84%
30.0%	2.10%	2.80%	3.50%	4.20%	4.90%	5.60%
35.0%	1.95%	2.60%	3.25%	3.90%	4.55%	5.20%
38.6%	1.84%	2.46%	3.07%	3.68%	4.30%	4.91%

Source: Excerpted from Jefferson Pilot Financial Insurance Company, "Things Are Not Always What They Seem," *Financial Chapter: Annuities* (November 2002). Used with permission.

Now suppose that on the same day, Marie Yost used $2,000 to purchase a deferred variable annuity. If Ms. Yost's subaccount investments earn an 8 percent return, then she will have earned $160 in interest at the end of the first year—the same amount Mr. Monroe earned. However, because earnings on a variable annuity accumulate on a tax-deferred basis, no taxes are due. The effects of tax deferral on Ms. Yost's investment values are shown below:

Actual earnings	**$160.00**	($2,000 × 0.08)
Actual rate of return	**8.0%**	($160.00 ÷ $2,000)
Total investment value	**$2,160.00**	($2,000 + $160)

Over time, the combined effects of tax-deferred earnings and compounded interest can be substantial, as shown in Insight 5.4. For comparison purposes, we will assume that market rates in our example remain at 8 percent over the entire investment period. Remember, though, that actual market values can vary widely over time and variable annuities generally do not offer guaranteed rates of return.

Insight 5.4

Long-Term Effects of Tax-Deferred Earnings on Investment Values

Mr. Monroe and Ms. Yost continued to make $2,000 payments into their respective investments each year for a period of 20 years. Neither made any withdrawals. At the end of the 20-year period, both investors elected to receive the proceeds in their accounts in a lump sum.

The value of Mr. Monroe's savings account and Ms. Yost's variable annuity contract at the end of the 20-year investment period are shown below:

	Savings Account	Variable Annuity
Amount deposited	$40,000	$40,000
Earnings	$35,938	$58,846
Total value of investment	$75,938	$98,846

Because the interest earned on his savings account is taxed annually, Mr. Monroe will not owe any taxes when he receives payment. He will receive the entire amount in his account—$75,938—at distribution. Ms. Yost's earnings are taxable at distribution. If Ms. Yost is in a 28 percent tax bracket, she will owe $16,477 in taxes ($58,846 × 0.28). This amount will be deducted from her account value, and she will receive $82,369—$6,431 more than the amount Mr. Monroe received.

The tax-deferral feature of variable annuities also offers tax advantages during retirement. At distribution, that part of the payment that represents earnings becomes taxable. However, because tax rates generally decrease as income levels decrease, the amount of tax payable on those earnings may be less than it would have been during the contract owner's working years.

Gains generated when an investor transfers money from one vehicle to another also are taxed differently. For example, if owners of stocks and mutual fund shares held outside of a qualified plan wish to transfer money from one stock or mutual fund account to another, they must first sell the original shares and then buy shares in the new account. If owners sell shares for more than they paid for the shares, they must pay taxes on the **capital gain**—the difference between the purchase price and the selling price. If a mutual fund itself sells shares of stock for a profit or receives dividends, share owners also must pay taxes on their portion of the profit or dividends. Short-term gains (gains on investments held for less than 12 months) typically are taxed as ordinary income. Long-term gains (gains on investments held for 12 months or more) are taxed as capital gains at a maximum rate of 20 percent.

capital gain.
The difference between the purchase price of a stock or mutual fund share and its selling price.

Earnings generated when the owner of a variable annuity contract transfers money from one variable subaccount to another are not subject to current taxation. Like other annuity earnings, gains resulting from account transfers are tax-deferred. However, when annuity earnings are taxed, they are classified as ordinary income, which is subject to higher tax rates than earnings classified by the Internal Revenue Code as capital gains.

A final tax difference is the treatment of withdrawals from investment accounts. In general, investors can withdraw money from savings accounts or sell stocks or mutual fund shares at any time, without tax penalties. Owners of investments that have a specified maturity date, such as bonds or CDs, may be charged a fee for withdrawing funds early, but they are not subject to tax penalties. Contract owners who withdraw money from variable annuities before they reach age 59½ typically are subject to a 10 percent federal tax penalty on the taxable portion of the withdrawal. This penalty tax is in addition to income taxes on earnings and any surrender charges assessed by the insurer.

Payout Options

A final consideration when selecting a retirement investment is the availability of payout options. When bonds or CDs mature or stocks or mutual fund shares are sold, proceeds typically are paid as lump-sum distributions. The amount distributed—equal to the amount invested plus accumulated interest, less any applicable charges—is not affected by the investor's extended life or early death. The advantage of a lump-sum distribution is that it provides investors with a fairly large sum of money all at once. The disadvantage of a lump-sum distribution is that investors must either manage the amount or reinvest it to provide an income stream during retirement.

Although variable annuity contracts can distribute contract proceeds in a lump sum, they also offer additional payout options that are not available with other products. The most important of these options in terms of retirement savings is the ability to receive periodic payments that provide a steady stream of income throughout the annuitant's lifetime. A retiree who lives a very long life potentially can receive an amount that is much greater than the amount invested and accumulated in the annuity contract.

On the other hand, the early death of an annuitant receiving lifetime benefits might mean that total payments are less than the principal invested in the contract. As we mentioned in Chapter 2, contract owners can eliminate this risk by choosing payout options that allow a contingent payee or beneficiary to recover the owner's investment.

Key Terms

certificate of deposit (CD)

Federal Deposit Insurance Corporation (FDIC)

interest rate risk

inflation risk

market risk

stagnant market risk

time value of money

future value (FV)

present value (PV)

simple interest

compound interest

capital gain

Endnote

1. Ibbotson Associates, *Stocks, Bonds, Bills, and Inflation: 1996 Yearbook* (Chicago: Ibbotson Associates, 1996).

Annuity Principles and Products

CHAPTER 6

Individual and Group Annuities

After studying this chapter, you should be able to

- Explain the difference between a qualified retirement plan and a nonqualified retirement plan

- Describe how people use individual annuities to save for retirement, manage lump-sum distributions, and pay for the cost of education

- Explain the important differences among traditional IRAs, Roth IRAs, and non-IRA individual annuities

- Explain how government regulations affect employer-sponsored retirement plans in the United States and Canada

- Describe the types of retirement plans most commonly offered by employers in the United States and Canada

Outline

Individual Annuities
Saving for Retirement
Managing Lump-Sum Distributions
Funding Education

Group Annuities
Qualified Retirement Plans in the United States
Registered Retirement Plans in Canada
Nonqualified Retirement Plans

In Chapter 1, we described how annuities can be classified according to when benefit payments begin and how premiums are paid and invested. In this chapter, we focus on two categories of annuities determined by contract ownership and coverage: individual annuities and group annuities.

We begin the chapter with a discussion of individual annuities and the types of financial objectives they are designed to meet. We then describe the role of group annuities in employer-sponsored retirement plans.

Individual Annuities

Individual annuities can be structured in any of the basic forms we have described in this text, including immediate or deferred annuities, single-premium or periodic-premium annuities, and fixed or variable annuities. In this section, we will describe how individual annuities are used to (1) provide income for retirement, (2) manage lump-sum distributions, and (3) fund education.

Saving for Retirement

People in the United States and Canada can use a variety of financial products to help them accumulate and manage the resources they will need to meet financial obligations during retirement. These products can function as part of an informal savings program or as part of a designated individual retirement arrangement. An **individual retirement arrangement (IRA)**, or *individual retirement account*, is a retirement savings plan that allows people with taxable compensation—that is, wages, salaries, professional fees, or other amounts received for services rendered—to deposit a portion of that income in a tax-deferred savings plan. Although all individual annuities—whether they are separate from or part of IRAs—are nonqualified annuities, those that are IRA-based receive different tax treatment than non-IRA annuities. In our discussion we will distinguish these annuities by referring to annuities that are purchased separate from IRAs as individual nonqualified annuities and referring to annuities that are purchased in conjunction with IRAs as IRA-based annuities.

individual retirement arrangement (IRA). A retirement savings plan that allows people with taxable compensation to deposit a portion of that income in a tax-deferred savings plan. Also known as an individual retirement account.

Individual Nonqualified Annuities

One of the primary benefits of individual nonqualified annuities is their virtually unlimited availability. All people, whether or not they have any taxable compensation, can purchase individual nonqualified annuities. Legal entities such as trusts or corporations also can purchase individual nonqualified annuities. In addition, premiums paid on individual nonqualified annuities are not subject to legally defined maximum limits. Unless premium payments are limited by contract terms, contract owners can pay as much as they wish in premiums. Finally, although most contracts specify the age at which annuity payments must begin, this required distribution age is typically higher than the required distribution age of 70½ years that is standard for most IRAs and qualified retirement plans.

The primary disadvantage of individual nonqualified annuities is that they offer only limited tax advantages. Like all annuity contracts, individual nonqualified annuities allow earnings to accrue on a tax-deferred basis. However, premiums used to purchase an individual nonqualified annuity are not tax-deductible. This means that no portion of the premiums can be deducted from the contract owner's current taxable income. Because income tax rates during employment typically are higher than rates during retirement, the amount of taxes that are payable when premiums are paid is often greater than the amount that would be payable if premiums were taxed at the time money is withdrawn from the account.

IRA-Based Annuities

In the United States, IRAs typically are established by a sponsoring financial institution such as an insurance company, a bank, or an investment company. The sponsoring institution manages the account and invests the IRA contributions at the owner's direction. Contributions can be invested in a variety of funding vehicles, including bank savings accounts, mutual funds, money market instruments, and individual annuities. How contributions are made and how they are treated for tax purposes depends on whether the IRA is a traditional IRA or a Roth IRA.

Traditional IRAs. Annuities that are part of traditional IRAs offer certain advantages over individual nonqualified annuities. Perhaps the most important of these advantages is the tax treatment of annuity premiums. Unlike premiums for individual nonqualified annuities, premiums paid for traditional IRA-based annuities—like all other contributions to traditional IRAs—may be deductible in part or in whole from the contract owner's current taxable income. The portion of traditional IRA contributions that is tax-deductible depends on the person's (1) gross income, (2) tax filing status, and (3) coverage under an employer-sponsored retirement plan. Taxes on deductible contributions, along with taxes on all earnings, are deferred until money is withdrawn from the account.

The ability to make contributions with pretax dollars—that is, tax-deductible earnings—offers contract owners two important tax advantages. Because contributions are deducted from the person's taxable compensation when deposits are made, the amount of income taxed each year is reduced. Contributions made with pretax dollars are taxed as income when money is withdrawn from the IRA, but because income during retirement generally is taxed at a lower rate than income during a person's employment years, the amount of taxes paid on contributions also is reduced. Premiums for individual nonqualified annuities, which are not tax-deductible, do not receive these same tax advantages.

Traditional IRA-based annuities also have certain drawbacks. Unlike premium payments for individual nonqualified annuities, premium payments for traditional IRA-based annuities and other contributions that qualify for tax deduction currently are limited by law to 100 percent of an individual's taxable compensation or $3,000, whichever is less. For individuals age 50 or older, annual contributions are limited to the lesser of taxable compensation or $3,000 plus a "catch-up" contribution of $500. Contribution limits are scheduled to rise to $4,000 in 2005 and to $5,000 in 2008. After that, limits will adjust in $500 increments, based on the government's inflation index. "Catch-up" contributions for individuals age 50 or older will increase to $1,000 in 2006. If a person has more than one IRA (including Roth IRAs), the contribution limits apply to the total amount paid into all accounts for the year. Individual nonqualified annuities are not subject to these legally mandated maximum contribution limits.

In addition, laws in the United States and Canada impose financial penalties if contract owners withdraw funds from traditional IRAs early or fail to begin making withdrawals within a specified timeframe. For example, withdrawals from a traditional IRA made before the owner reaches age 59½ may be subject to a 10 percent federal tax penalty. This penalty is in addition to any income tax due on the withdrawal. Tax penalties also apply if contract owners fail to begin receiving payments from traditional IRAs by April 1 of the year after they reach age 70½. Penalties may be as high as 50 percent of the amount not distributed as required. Owners of individual nonqualified annuities also are subject to tax penalties for making early withdrawals and failing to begin receiving payments by a specified age.

Roth IRAs. Contributions to Roth IRAs, including premiums paid for Roth IRA-based annuities, are made entirely with after-tax dollars. As a result, no portion of the amount contributed to a Roth IRA is deductible from a contract owner's current taxable income. The amount a contract owner can contribute to a Roth IRA also is subject to limits and requirements similar to those imposed on contributions to traditional IRAs.

These disadvantages are offset by the fact that, if certain criteria are met, all investment earnings generated from premiums for Roth IRA-based annuities and other Roth IRA contributions can be withdrawn on a tax-free basis. In other words, earnings from a Roth IRA are not taxed as income, even at the time of withdrawal. Earnings typically are awarded tax-free status if the contract owner maintains the contract for a minimum of five years and is age 59½ or older. Earnings also are tax free if the contract owner dies, becomes disabled, or uses $10,000 or more to purchase a first home.

Withdrawals from a Roth IRA made before the contract owner reaches age 59½, like those from individual nonqualified annuities and traditional IRAs, may be subject to a 10 percent federal tax penalty. However, no tax penalty is imposed if contract owners fail to make withdrawals from a Roth IRA by the time they reach age 70½. Contract owners can leave funds in Roth IRAs for their heirs, who then will be able to withdraw money, untaxed, over their lifetimes.

Figure 6.1 compares the features of individual nonqualified annuities, traditional IRAs, and Roth IRAs. Note that the regulations governing IRAs apply whether the IRA contributions are used to purchase an annuity or some other investment vehicle, such as a savings account or mutual fund.

Managing Lump-Sum Distributions

As you recall from Chapter 1, many employer-sponsored retirement plans distribute benefits—either upon separation from the sponsoring company or at retirement—in a lump sum. Life insurance proceeds, court-ordered awards, large cash prizes, gifts, bonuses, and money due from settlement of an estate or sale of property generally are payable as lump-sum distributions as well. Benefits from IRAs also can be paid in a lump sum.

One way a person can manage a lump-sum distribution is to invest the proceeds in an individual annuity. Benefit payments then can be structured to provide a regular income during retirement. Applicable income taxes on lump-sum distributions are payable when the distribution is received. In the case of lump-sum distributions paid to plan participants from employer-sponsored retirement plans, the payer is required to withhold 20 percent of the taxable portion of distributions for federal income taxes. Earnings on the amount in the annuity contract then accrue on a tax-deferred basis.

A person also can "roll over" lump-sum distributions from certain retirement plans. A **rollover** is a tax-free movement of cash or other assets disbursed from one retirement plan into another retirement plan. As long as funds are transferred directly from the original plan to the new plan and not paid to the plan participant, income taxes on the amount of the rollover amount are deferred until money is disbursed by the new plan.

rollover.
A tax-free contribution of cash or other assets disbursed from one retirement plan into another retirement plan.

FIGURE 6.1

A Comparison of Individual Nonqualified Annuities, Traditional IRAs, and Roth IRAs

Feature	Individual Nonqualified Annuity	Traditional IRA	Roth IRA
Taxable Compensation Requirements	No	Yes	Yes
Contributions Deductible from Current Taxable Income	No	Yes	No
Investment Earnings Tax-Deferred	Yes	Yes	Yes (tax free after five years)
Contributions Taxable at Withdrawal	No	Yes	No
Investment Earnings Taxable at Withdrawal	Yes	Yes	No (after five years)
Tax Penalties for Early Withdrawal*	Yes	Yes	Yes
Maximum Age for Payouts	Yes (as specified in contract)	Yes (70½)	No
Contribution Limits	No (Unless specified in contract)	Yes (100 percent of taxable compensation or $3,000** annually, whichever is less)	Yes (100 percent of taxable compensation or $3,000** annually, whichever is less)

* Penalties may be waived under certain circumstances

** Scheduled to rise to $4,000 in 2005, $5,000 in 2008, and in $500 increments indexed to inflation starting in 2009. Individuals age 50 or older allowed to make "catch-up" contributions in addition to specified maximums.

Current tax laws in the United States allow the following types of rollovers:

- **From a traditional IRA to another traditional IRA.** In general, both the taxable and nontaxable portions of disbursements from traditional IRAs—which consist of (1) earnings and (2) contributions—can be rolled over to a new traditional IRA.

- **From a traditional IRA to an employer-sponsored qualified plan.** Only the taxable portion of disbursements from traditional IRAs can be rolled over into qualified plans, including 401(k), 403(b), and 457 plans. Qualified plans may, but are not required to accept rollover contributions.

- **From a traditional IRA to a Roth IRA.** Contributions must satisfy certain tax requirements. In addition, no deductible contributions can be made to a Roth IRA.

- **From an employer-sponsored qualified plan to a traditional IRA.** Both the taxable and nontaxable portions of distributions from employer-sponsored qualified plans, including 401(k), 403(b), and 457 plans, can be rolled over.

- **From a SEP plan, SIMPLE IRA, or Roth IRA to a Roth IRA.** Transfers to Roth IRAs, which are called conversions, can be accomplished through rollovers, trustee-to-trustee transfers, or same trustee transfers. Conversions are treated as rollovers and typically are subject to income and tax filing requirements. Deductible amounts cannot be rolled over. In addition, conversions from SIMPLE IRAs are not allowed during the first two years of an employee's participation in the plan.

- **From an employer-sponsored qualified plan to another employer-sponsored qualified plan.** The taxable portion of distributions from employer-sponsored qualified plans may be rolled over to other employer-sponsored qualified plans if the receiving plan accepts such rollovers. The nontaxable portions of distributions may be rolled over to qualified plans of the same type as the original plan by direct trustee-to-trustee transfer if the receiving plan agrees to separately account for such after-tax amounts.

Rollover contributions from Roth IRAs to traditional IRAs or to employer-sponsored qualified plans are not allowed. Figure 6.2 illustrates the tax benefits of direct rollovers over lump-sum distributions.

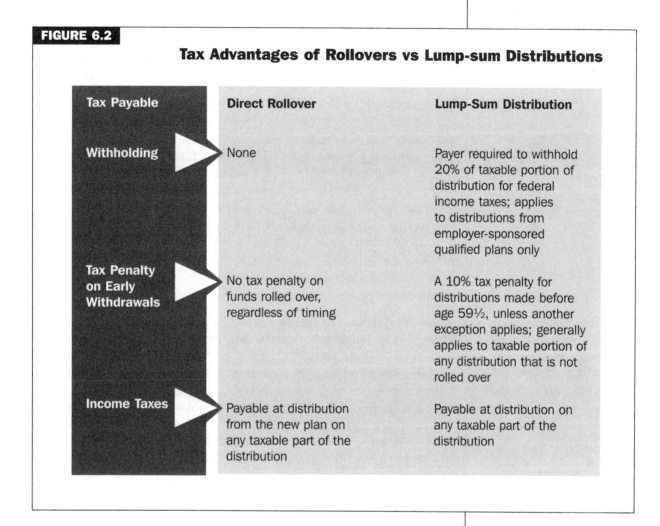

FIGURE 6.2 Tax Advantages of Rollovers vs Lump-sum Distributions

Tax Payable	Direct Rollover	Lump-Sum Distribution
Withholding	None	Payer required to withhold 20% of taxable portion of distribution for federal income taxes; applies to distributions from employer-sponsored qualified plans only
Tax Penalty on Early Withdrawals	No tax penalty on funds rolled over, regardless of timing	A 10% tax penalty for distributions made before age 59½, unless another exception applies; generally applies to taxable portion of any distribution that is not rolled over
Income Taxes	Payable at distribution from the new plan on any taxable part of the distribution	Payable at distribution on any taxable part of the distribution

Funding Education

Another use for individual nonqualified annuities and IRA-based annuities is to provide funds to cover the costs of a college education for a child or grandchild. However, as we mentioned earlier, withdrawals generally are subject to taxation. In addition, the Internal Revenue Service imposes tax penalties if funds are withdrawn before the contract owner reaches age 59½, unless another exception applies.

Education IRAs (which were renamed Coverdell Education Savings Accounts in 2001) and qualified tuition programs offer exceptions to the standard tax treatment of withdrawals. A **Coverdell Education Savings Account,** or *education IRA*, is a special form of IRA that allows the owner to make withdrawals at any time—without penalty—as long as the money is used to cover qualified education costs. Qualified costs typically include expenses for tuition, fees, books, supplies, and—

Coverdell Education Savings Account. A special form of IRA that allows the owner to make withdrawals at any time—without penalty—as long as the money is used to cover qualified education costs. Also known as an education IRA.

for individuals who are at least half-time students—room and board. In addition, both contributions and all accumulated earnings can be withdrawn on a tax-free basis if they are used for education purposes.

Like contributions to individual nonqualified annuities and Roth IRAs, contributions to education IRAs are not tax deductible. Like other IRAs, education IRAs also impose limits on the amount an investor can contribute annually to the account. Prior to 2002, annual contributions were limited to $500 and could be made only by individuals. After the beneficiary reached age 18, no further contributions were allowed. The Economic Growth and Tax Relief Reconciliation Act of 2001 (EGTRRA) relaxed the restrictions on contributions, contributors, and use of funds. The annual contribution limit for education IRAs is currently $2,000, and contributions can be made by corporations and other legal entities as well as by individuals. In addition, funds can be used to cover elementary and secondary school costs as well as college expenses.

qualified tuition program.
A form of prepaid tuition plan designed to help parents save for their children's college tuition. Also known as a 529 program.

A **qualified tuition program**, also known as a *529 program*, is a form of prepaid tuition plan designed to help parents save for their children's college education. Initially, qualified tuition programs were restricted to state-sponsored plans and covered only the cost of tuition. Contributions were made with nondeductible, after-tax dollars and taxes on earnings were deferred until funds were distributed. As a result of EGTRRA, privately sponsored plans also are allowed and, beginning in 2004, distributions made for all qualified education costs will be tax free. A 10 percent tax penalty will be imposed on any distributions not made for education purposes.

Group Annuities

The annuity features and tax advantages we described in the previous sections of this chapter provide substantial incentives for people to use individual annuities as part of retirement savings plans. Tax laws in the United States and Canada offer similar incentives for employers to establish retirement plans for their employees. In most cases, these incentives come in the form of economic benefits to the **plan sponsor**—an employer that establishes a private retirement plan on behalf of employees—and the **plan participant**—an employee who is covered by a private employer-sponsored retirement plan.

plan sponsor.
An employer that establishes a private retirement plan on behalf of its employees.

plan participant.
An employee who is covered by a private employer-sponsored retirement plan.

As you recall from Chapter 1, group retirement plans that meet specific legal requirements receive certain federal tax benefits. In the United States, a plan that meets these requirements is known as a qualified plan. In Canada, such a plan is known as a registered retirement plan. Group retirement plans that do not meet specific requirements, and therefore do not receive the same favorable tax treatment, are classified as nonqualified plans.

Qualified Retirement Plans in the United States

To qualify for favorable tax treatment in the United States, nongovernmental employer-employee group retirement plans must comply with the federal Employee Retirement Income Security Act (ERISA). Qualified plans also must meet specific requirements included in the U.S. Internal Revenue Code (IRC). These IRC requirements are described in Figure 6.3.

When an employer establishes a qualified retirement plan, the employer typically appoints a **plan trustee**, who holds legal title to the retirement plan assets on behalf of the plan participants. The trustee is responsible for administering and maintaining plan assets. If an employer funds a retirement plan with an annuity, a trust is not required. The employer purchases an annuity and then invests plan assets according to the terms of the contract.

The employer can purchase a group annuity covering all participants or an individual annuity for each participant. If the employer purchases a group annuity, the employer is the owner of the group master contract. Participating employees receive a certificate when they enroll in the plan. For ease of administration, group annuities most commonly are used in plans covering large numbers of employees. If individual annuities are used, a separate contract covers each participant. The employer, however, usually owns the individual contracts.

The three most common types of employer-sponsored qualified retirement plans in the United States are (1) pension plans, (2) profit sharing plans, and (3) retirement savings plans. Small businesses that cannot bear the administrative expense of establishing a qualified plan, can gain tax advantages by establishing specialized plans such as simplified employee pension plans and savings incentive match plans. Self-employed persons generally participate in Keogh plans. Figure 6.4 briefly describes these types of retirement plans.

Pension Plans

For the purposes of our classification system, a **pension plan** is a type of employer-sponsored qualified retirement plan under which an employer makes contributions on behalf of employees to provide those employees with a lifetime monthly income benefit that begins at retirement. These mandatory contributions are used to fund at least a portion of the pension plan's promised benefits. Employer contributions generally are deductible from the employer's taxable income and are not included in employees' wages. Employees typically do not contribute to pension plans.

plan trustee.
A person, appointed by the sponsor of a qualified retirement plan, who holds legal title to the retirement plan assets on behalf of plan participants.

pension plan.
A type of qualified employer-sponsored retirement plan under which an employer makes contributions on behalf of employees to provide those employees with a lifetime monthly income benefit that begins at retirement.

FIGURE 6.3

IRC Requirements for Qualified Group Retirement Plans

To receive favorable tax treatment, employer-sponsored group retirement plans in the United States must meet Internal Revenue Code requirements in the following areas:

- **Participation.** Participation in the plan must be open to all employees who meet certain age and employment requirements. In most cases, any employee who is age 21 or older *and* who has completed at least one year of employment must be eligible to participate. However, if an employee will be fully vested in the plan after two years of service, the plan can impose a minimum employment requirement of two years.

- **Vesting.** Participants' interest in a plan is vested when they are entitled to receive partial or full benefits under the plan even if they no longer work for the sponsoring employer at the time of their retirement. Benefits funded by employer contributions must vest within a specified period after the participant becomes eligible to join the plan. Benefits funded by personal contributions must vest immediately.

- **Nondiscrimination.** The plan cannot discriminate in favor of highly compensated employees.

- **Distribution.** The plan must contain specific provisions regarding when benefit payments will begin and what, if any, benefits will be payable upon the death of the plan participant.

- **Investments.** A variety of regulations govern the ways insurers and other financial services providers must invest retirement plan assets. These regulations are designed to ensure the safety of retirement benefits.

- **Reporting.** The plan sponsor is required to provide periodic reports about the plan's provisions and performance to governmental agencies and to plan participants.

Although employers can select from various types of pension plans, each qualified pension plan can be categorized as either a defined benefit plan or a defined contribution plan.

A ***defined benefit plan*** is a type of pension plan that specifies the amount of benefit—based on the employee's income, years of service, or both income and years of service—a participant will receive at retirement. The retirement benefit usually is described in terms of a monthly annuity, and the plan sponsor is obligated to deposit enough

defined benefit plan.
A type of pension plan that specifies the amount of benefit—based on the employee's income, years of service, or both income and years of service—a participant will receive at retirement.

Chapter 6 — Individual and Group Annuities   103

FIGURE 6.4

U.S. Retirement Savings Plans

Qualified retirement savings plans. In the United States, employers can establish tax-deferred retirement savings plans on behalf of their employees. These plans generally take one of the following three forms:

- **Pension plans.** Employers make mandatory contributions on behalf of employees to provide those employees with lifetime retirement income. Employees typically do not make contributions.

- **Profit sharing plans.** Employers make voluntary contributions payable from, and usually based on, the employers' profits. Because contributions are linked to company profits, the amount can change from year to year. Employees typically do not make contributions.

- **Retirement savings plans.** Plans are funded by voluntary employer and employee contributions. Plans include: (1) 401(k) plans, covering employees of for-profit organizations; (2) 403(b) plans, covering employees of not-for-profit organizations; and (3) 457 plans, covering employees of state and local governments.

Simplified employee pension (SEP) plans. Small business owners establish and make contributions into an IRA for each participating employee. Employees typically do not make contributions. Employers were prohibited from establishing new plans after December 31, 2002.

Savings incentive match plans for employees (SIMPLE plans). Small business owners establish one of two types of tax-deferred retirement savings plans on behalf of their employees: (1) SIMPLE IRAs and (2) SIMPLE 401(k) plans. Both employers and employees can contribute to the plans.

Keogh plans. Self-employed persons who are not eligible to participate in employer-sponsored plans can gain tax advantages by depositing a portion of their earned income—up to a specified maximum—in a tax-deferred retirement plan.

assets into the plan to provide the promised benefit. An actuary determines the amount of the employer's contributions by estimating employee mortality, turnover, future salaries, administrative expenses, and plan investment earnings. For investment purposes, the plan trustee typically pools all of the contributions the employer makes on behalf of all plan participants into one account. As plan participants retire, the plan trustee distributes the retirement plan benefits in accordance with the plan's provisions.

defined contribution plan.
A type of pension plan that specifies the annual contribution an employer will deposit into a pension plan on behalf of each plan participant.

A ***defined contribution plan*** is a type of pension plan that specifies the annual contribution the employer will deposit into the plan on behalf of each plan participant. Defined contribution plans include money-purchase plans, target benefit plans, profit-sharing plans, 401(k) plans, stock bonus plans, and employee stock option plans. Usually, the employer's contribution is a specified percentage of the participant's salary or wages. The plan trustee can allocate employer contributions to individual accounts for each participant or pool contributions into one account with relative percentages assigned to each participant. The plan trustee or plan administrator provides record keeping services so that individual accounts can be maintained. Plan contributions are invested and accumulate earnings on behalf of each plan participant.

When a plan participant retires, the total amount allocated to that person is available either in a lump sum or in the form of monthly annuity benefit payments, depending on the provisions of the plan. The amount of the annuity payment that a retiree receives depends on the amount that has accumulated in the account during the retiree's working years. Thus, although the amount of money going into the plan is clearly specified, the exact amount of the payment is not known until the retiree begins to receive payments.

In recent years, plan sponsors have tended to establish defined contribution plans rather than defined benefit plans. When an employer establishes a defined contribution plan, the employer knows in advance what the cost will be to fund the plan each year and will not have to rely on actuarial estimates. In addition, the ERISA requirements for defined contribution plans are less complex than the requirements for defined benefit plans.

Profit Sharing Plans

profit sharing plan.
A type of qualified employer-sponsored retirement plan that is funded by employer contributions payable from, and usually based on, the employer's profits.

A ***profit sharing plan*** is a type of qualified employer-sponsored retirement plan that is funded by employer contributions payable from, and usually based on, the employer's profits. Employer contributions are deductible from the employer's taxable income as a business expense and are not included in employees' wages. Employees generally do not make contributions.

A qualified profit sharing plan functions in most respects like a defined contribution pension plan. However, unlike defined contribution pension plans in which employer contributions are mandatory and are determined in accordance with a formula included in the plan, employer contributions to profit sharing plans are voluntary and are determined annually. Because contributions are linked to company profits, the contribution amount can change from year to year. In some years, the employer may not make any contributions.

Retirement Savings Plans

Retirement savings plans are another form of qualified plan that employers in the United States can use to provide retirement benefits to their employees. One of the most common plans offered by for-profit organizations is the ***401(k) plan***, an arrangement that allows both employers and employees to make contributions to a tax-deferred retirement savings plan established for the benefit of employees. The name *401(k)* refers to the section of the U.S. Internal Revenue Code that permits the creation of these plans.

Under a 401(k) plan, the employer establishes an individual account for each participant. Employers can, but are not obligated to, make contributions to employees' 401(k) accounts. If an employer does make contributions, the amount usually is equal to the amount contributed by the employee or a percentage of that amount, subject to a specified maximum. The amount of an employer's contribution to a 401(k) plan is deductible from the employer's current taxable income.

To provide an incentive for employees to participate in 401(k) retirement savings plans, U.S. federal tax laws allow employees to contribute a percentage of their taxable compensation—up to a specified maximum amount—to the plan each year. Currently, the maximum contribution is $12,000 annually. This amount will increase annually until 2006, when the allowable contribution will reach $15,000. As is the case with IRAs, employees age 50 or older are allowed to make "catch-up" contributions of $500 annually through 2005 and $1,000 annually thereafter. Employee contributions are made with pretax dollars. In other words, when an employee contributes to a 401(k) plan, the amount of the contribution is excluded from the employee's current gross taxable income.

Taxes on both employee and employer contributions and taxes on all earnings from investments in the plan are deferred until money is withdrawn. Disbursements made prior to age 59½ usually are subject to a federal tax penalty. However, depending on plan guidelines, participants may be eligible to take penalty-free loans on 401(k) balances. We will discuss the tax treatment of 401(k) plans in Chapter 7. Disbursements made after a specified date also are subject to tax penalties. Participants in qualified retirement plans must begin to receive distributions by the later of April 1 of the year after they reach age 70½ or April 1 of the year after they retire.

Beginning in 2006, employers also will be able to offer Roth 401(k) plans. Unlike regular 401(k) plans, Roth 401(k) plans are funded with nondeductible, after-tax contributions and earnings are tax free after five years. In addition, no minimum annual distribution is required. As a result, contract owners can leave funds in the plan for use by their heirs. Roth 401(k) plans are particularly appealing to high-income employees who are not eligible to establish Roth IRAs.

401(k) plan.
An arrangement that allows both employers and employees to make contributions to a qualified tax-deferred retirement savings plan established for the benefit of employees.

403(b) plan.
An arrangement that allows not-for-profit employers and their employees to make contributions to a qualified tax-deferred retirement savings plan established for the benefit of employees.

457 plan.
An arrangement that allows state and local governments and their employees to make contributions to a qualified tax-deferred retirement plan established for the benefit of employees.

Tax Sheltered Annuity (TSA).
A retirement annuity sold only to public school teachers and employees of hospitals, colleges, and other organizations offering qualified retirement plans under section 403(b) of the U.S. Internal Revenue Code.

Although only 401(k) plans established for employees of for-profit organizations meet the original definition of "qualified" specified in the U.S. Internal Revenue Code, federal tax advantages also are provided for retirement savings plans established for employees of not-for-profit organizations and employees of state and local governments. A ***403(b) plan*** is an arrangement that allows not-for-profit employers and their employees to make contributions to a tax-deferred retirement savings plan established for the benefit of employees. A ***457 plan*** is an arrangement that allows state and local governments and their employees to make contributions to a tax-deferred retirement savings plan established for the benefit of employees. Like 401(k) plans, 403(b) and 457 plans are named for the sections of the U.S. Internal Revenue Code that permit the respective plan's creation. Like 401(k) plans, 403(b) and 457 plans allow participants to make pretax contributions to the plans, up to specified limits, and all investment earnings accumulate on a tax-deferred basis.

Participants in 403(b) plans and employees of certain tax-exempt organizations also are eligible to invest in a special type of annuity known as a Tax Sheltered Annuity. A ***Tax Sheltered Annuity (TSA)*** is a retirement annuity sold only to public school teachers and employees of hospitals, colleges, and other organizations offering qualified retirement plans under section 403(b) of the U.S. Internal Revenue Code. As with other retirement savings plans, TSAs are subject to regulations regarding maximum contribution limits, early withdrawals, and loans against account balances. A detailed discussion of the regulations governing 403(b) and 457 plans and TSAs is beyond the scope of this text.

Simplified Employee Pension Plans

Because of the complexity of the laws governing retirement plan administration and the costs associated with establishing a retirement plan, many employers—especially small employers—are unable to offer pension and other retirement savings benefits to their employees. To make retirement plans more available to the employees of these businesses, U.S. federal tax laws provide tax advantages for employer-sponsored plans known as simplified employee pension plans.

simplified employee pension (SEP) plan.
An arrangement under which an employer makes contributions to an IRA for each participating employee.

Under a ***simplified employee pension (SEP) plan***, an employer establishes and makes contributions into an IRA for each participating employee. Generally, participating employees do not make contributions to the plan. Although employers can no longer establish new SEP plans, they may still contribute to existing plans established prior to December 31, 2002. In doing so, employers must ensure that the plan meets legal requirements concerning the eligible employees the plan must cover and the contribution amounts that the employer can make on behalf of specific classes of employees.

The amount of an employer's contribution to a SEP plan, subject to designated maximums, is deductible as a business expense from the employer's taxable income. Also, the amount of this contribution is excluded from the employee's taxable income. The maximum amount that can be deducted as a contribution to a SEP IRA is considerably higher than the maximum amount permitted for a traditional IRA.

Many employers established SEP plans because these plans are easy to administer and they reduce the amount of paperwork normally associated with establishing a qualified pension plan or other type of qualified retirement savings plan. Because of the higher deductible amounts available through a SEP plan, many self-employed people also established SEP IRAs.

Savings Incentive Match Plans for Employees

Small business owners in the United States have two alternatives to the retirement savings plans we have discussed: the Savings Incentive Match Plan for Employees (SIMPLE) IRA and the Savings Incentive Match Plan for Employees (SIMPLE) 401(k). A **Savings Incentive Match Plan for Employees (SIMPLE) IRA** is an arrangement whereby an employer with fewer than 100 employees can establish a simplified IRA for employees. Under the plan, the employer and the employee can make contributions, up to specified maximums, to the IRA. Both employer and employee contributions are tax-deductible. However, the maximum annual contribution that can be deducted from an employee's taxable income under a SIMPLE IRA is considerably higher than that allowed for a traditional IRA. Currently, the maximum amount is $8,000. In 2005, the maximum will increase to $10,000. Like a traditional or Roth IRA, a SIMPLE IRA allows investment earnings to accumulate on a tax-deferred basis. Insight 6.1 offers a closer look at SIMPLE IRA plans.

Savings Incentive Match Plan for Employees (SIMPLE) IRA. An arrangement whereby an employer with 100 or fewer employees can establish a simplified IRA for employees.

A **Savings Incentive Match Plan for Employees (SIMPLE) 401(k)** is an arrangement whereby an employer with fewer than 100 employees can establish a simplified 401(k) retirement savings plan for employees. The SIMPLE 401(k) plan functions in much the same way as a regular 401(k) plan in that both the employer and the employee can make contributions to the plan up to a specified maximum. Employer contributions to the plan are deductible from the employer's current taxable income, employee contributions are made on a pretax basis, and all earnings on investments held in the account accumulate on a tax-deferred basis. However, a SIMPLE 401(k) does not require the same level of administrative support as a regular 401(k) plan. As with SEP plans and SIMPLE IRA plans, SIMPLE 401(k) plans allow employers to make contributions to an employee's retirement savings without incurring the higher administrative costs often associated with other types of qualified pension and retirement plans.

Savings Incentive Match Plan for Employees (SIMPLE) 401(k). An arrangement whereby an employer with 100 or fewer employees can establish a simplified 401(k) retirement savings plan for employees.

Insight 6.1

Whatever Happened to SIMPLE IRA Plans?

The Savings Incentive Match Plans for Employees (SIMPLE) became effective January 1, 1997, under the 1996 Small Business Jobs Protection Act.

When the SIMPLE IRA plan was first introduced, it seemed ideal for many small employers. After all, only 21 percent of companies with fewer than 100 employees had 401(k) plans, according to a 1997 study by Access Research (see *National Underwriter,* July 20, 1998). This low number is not surprising, considering the $1,500 to $2,000 annual administrative costs that even small 401(k) plans had to pay. Such costs posed too great a burden for small employers, in view of the small number of participants involved.

However, to date, the response to the SIMPLE concept from many insurance companies and other vendors has been less than enthusiastic.

In September 1998, The Advantage Group conducted an informal survey of 25 large insurance companies, asking if they were targeting the SIMPLE IRA market. Over three-quarters of the 25 companies which answered said they either didn't offer SIMPLE plans or didn't market them.

Why not? Some companies said they were allocating resources to Roth IRA marketing. Others said that they felt SIMPLE plans were a good idea, but they didn't feel there was a market for them yet.

While SIMPLE IRAs are on hold at a number of insurers, some carriers do believe in their potential.

One large insurer had over 1,000 SIMPLE IRA plans on the books with over 11,000 participants, as of mid-1998. The company's core market is closely held businesses typically with 10 or fewer employees. The insurer says small employers that can't afford the administrative costs of 401(k) plans are good candidates for SIMPLE IRA plans.

Another large insurer had opened over 600 SIMPLE IRA plans, as of mid-1998. It reports implementing plans ranging in size from sole proprietors to companies with as many as 65 employees. The plans are often used in businesses where owners are expecting little or no employee contributions or where owner contributions are restricted in an existing plan. Company officials say plans also are used by small tax-exempt employers, start-up firms, and companies with current top-heavy plans.

Source: Adapted from Jack Marrion, "Whatever Happened to the SIMPLE Plans?" *National Underwriter*, Life & Health/Financial Services ed. (28 September 1998): 8, 22. Used with permission.

Although the future of SIMPLE plans is unclear, they may become more popular now that SEP plans can no longer be established.

Keogh Plans

Self-employed persons can gain tax advantages by establishing Keogh plans. A **Keogh plan** is an arrangement that allows self-employed persons to deposit a portion of their income earned from self-employment, up to a specified maximum, in a tax-deferred retirement savings plan. A Keogh plan is set up by a sponsoring financial institution, such as an insurance company, a bank, or an investment company. The sponsoring financial institution manages the Keogh plan and invests plan contributions at the owner's direction. Plan contributions can be placed in any of several types of investments, including annuities.

The maximum annual contribution allowed under a Keogh plan currently is the lesser of 25 percent of net earnings or $40,000. Participants can deduct the amount of their contributions from their taxable income, and earnings accrue on a tax-deferred basis. Because contributions are tax-deductible and investment earnings are tax-deferred, all withdrawals from a Keogh plan are taxable as income. In addition, investors may have to pay federal tax penalties on withdrawals if they fail to meet certain requirements. These withdrawal penalties are designed to encourage people to use money held in Keogh plans for retirement.

Keogh plan.
An arrangement that allows self-employed persons to deposit a portion of their income earned from self-employment in a tax-deferred savings plan.

Registered Retirement Plans in Canada

In Canada, the federal government and all the provinces have each enacted a **Pension Benefits Act** that governs the terms and operation of private retirement plans. This legislation requires employers to register these plans with a specified government agency and to comply with a number of requirements. Although the requirements vary from province to province, they are similar in many respects to those imposed on qualified plans in the United States. However, unlike U.S. plans, Canadian legislation requires that all registered plan benefits be portable so that they can be moved from one registered plan to another.

Pension Benefits Act.
A Canadian federal law that governs the terms and operation of private retirement plans.

Canada currently recognizes the following three forms of registered retirement plans: (1) registered pension plans, (2) deferred profit sharing plans, and (3) registered retirement savings plans.

Registered Pension Plans

A *registered pension plan (RPP)* is a type of employer-sponsored retirement plan, available in Canada, under which an employer makes contributions on behalf of employees to provide those employees with a lifetime monthly income that begins at retirement. It is similar to the qualified pension plans available in the United States. Contributions to RPPs are tax-deductible, and are subject to specified annual maximum

registered pension plan (RPP).
A type of registered retirement plan in Canada; equivalent to a qualified pension plan in the United States.

amounts. Most of these plans require participants to contribute. Usually, the plan sponsor's contribution is a specified percentage of the participant's contribution.

Deferred Profit Sharing Plans

deferred profit sharing plan (DPSP).
A type of registered retirement plan in Canada that allows employers to make contributions on behalf of employees that are related to profits; similar to qualified profit sharing plans in the United States.

A *deferred profit sharing plan (DPSP)* is a Canadian registered retirement plan in which plan sponsor contributions are related to profits and are tax deductible by the plan sponsor, subject to specified annual maximum amounts. Prior to 1992, participants were allowed to contribute to DPSPs. These contributions, however, could not be required and were not tax-deductible. In 1992, participant contributions were no longer permitted. Deferred profit sharing plans are similar in most respects to the profit sharing plans available in the United States.

Registered Retirement Savings Plans

registered retirement savings plan (RRSP).
A type of registered retirement plan in Canada that allows people with earned income (not employers) to make tax-deductible contributions into a tax-deferred savings plan; equivalent to an individual retirement arrangement (IRA) in the United States.

A *registered retirement savings plan (RRSP)* is a Canadian registered retirement plan which allows people with earned income (not employers) to make tax-deductible contributions, subject to specified annual maximum amounts, into a tax-deferred savings plan. Some employers have established group RRSPs, which are basically a collection of individual RRSPs that offer employees the advantage of making contributions through payroll deductions. Employers may make contributions to group RRSPs on behalf of their employees. However, participants report employer contributions as wages and then take an offsetting deduction in the amount of the contribution. Thus, any employer contributions become employee contributions for tax purposes. In general, Canadian RRSPs are similar to U.S. individual retirement arrangements (IRAs).

Nonqualified Retirement Plans

Because qualified retirement plans receive favorable tax treatment, they often are popular among employers and employees. Some employers, however, elect to establish employee retirement plans that do not qualify for all the tax advantages available to qualified plans. An employer can establish a nonqualified plan as either (1) an alternative to establishing a qualified plan or (2) a supplement to an existing qualified plan.

The primary benefit to an employer of establishing a nonqualified retirement plan is that the employer is relieved from complying with the complex legislative and tax requirements that govern qualified plans. For example, an employer that establishes a nonqualified plan can provide additional benefits to certain classes of employees, such as highly paid executives, who cannot receive special treatment under a qualified plan. As with qualified plans, employer and employee contributions to a nonqualified plan can be placed in a variety of investments, including annuities.

Key Terms

individual retirement arrangement (IRA)

rollover

Coverdell Education Savings Account

plan sponsor

plan participant

plan trustee

pension plan

defined benefit plan

defined contribution plan

profit sharing plan

401(k) plan

403(b) plan

457 plan

Tax Sheltered Annuity (TSA)

simplified employee pension (SEP) plan

Savings Incentive Match Plan for Employees (SIMPLE) IRA

Savings Incentive Match Plan for Employees (SIMPLE) 401(k)

Keogh plan

Pension Benefits Act

registered pension plan (RPP)

deferred profit sharing plan (DPSP)

registered retirement savings plan (RRSP)

Annuity Principles and Products

Taxation of Annuities

After studying this chapter, you should be able to

- Describe how income taxes are levied in the United States on annuity contributions, earnings, benefit payments, withdrawals, and loans

- Describe the tax penalties imposed on premature withdrawals, late withdrawals, and distributions of less than the specified minimum amount

- Explain how annuities are treated with regard to estate taxes in the United States

- Describe the tax treatment of Section 1035 exchanges and rollovers

- Describe the Canadian tax treatment of individual annuity and registered retirement plan contributions, earnings, and benefit payments

OUTLINE

U.S. Income Taxes
Income Taxes on Annuity Premiums
Income Taxes on Annuity Earnings
Income Taxes on Annuity Benefit Payments
Income Taxes on Withdrawals
Income Taxes on Loans

U.S. Penalty Taxes

U.S. Estate Taxes

Other U.S. Taxes on Annuities
Exchanges
Rollovers

Canadian Taxation of Annuities

In the United States, ERISA and Internal Revenue Code provisions have generated hundreds of pages of detailed laws and rulings related to the establishment and taxation of pension plans, annuities, and other insurance and retirement products. We discussed some of these regulatory issues in Chapter 6.

Figure 7.1 describes some of the primary sources of information about U.S. tax requirements. In Canada, various Pension Benefits Acts outline standards and tax requirements for Canadian retirement plans.

In this chapter, we highlight the tax requirements that are most important for annuity products. We begin the chapter with a discussion of income taxes in the United States that apply to annuity premiums, earnings, benefits, and withdrawals. We then describe penalty taxes and specialized taxes that are imposed on annuities that are included in estates, exchanged for other annuities, or rolled over into qualified retirement plans. We end the chapter with a brief description of the Canadian taxation of individual annuities and registered retirement plans.

FIGURE 7.1

Sources of Information on the Establishment and Taxation of Annuities

The U.S. Internal Revenue Code describes tax laws and rulings that cover income, estate, gift, employment, and excise taxes. The following sections of the IRC contain specific information about the taxation of annuities and other retirement products:

- Section 72 — covers annuities
- Section 401 — covers retirement savings plans for employees of for-profit organizations
- Section 403 — covers retirement savings plans and tax sheltered annuities for employees of not-for-profit organizations
- Section 408 — covers individual retirement arrangements (IRAs)
- Section 457 — covers retirement savings plans for employees of state and local governments
- Section 1035 — covers nontaxable exchanges of insurance policies and annuity contracts

Individuals preparing annual tax returns can find additional information about the tax treatment of annuities and retirement plans in the following Internal Revenue Service publications:

- Publication 560: Retirement plans for Small Business—covers SEP, SIMPLE, and qualified plans
- Publication 571: Tax-Sheltered Annuity Plans—covers tax-sheltered annuities and 403(b) plans
- Publication 575: Pension and Annuity Income
- Publication 590: Individual Retirement Arrangements (IRAs)—covers traditional IRAs, Roth IRAs, SEP plans, and SIMPLE plans

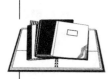

U.S. Income Taxes

Income tax is a tax levied on compensation that a person or business receives for services rendered. At some point in time, most annuity contract owners in the United States are required to pay income taxes on the money they invest in annuities and on the earnings those investments generate.

income tax.
A tax levied in the United States on compensation that a person or business receives for services rendered.

Income Taxes on Annuity Premiums

As you recall from Chapter 6, tax laws in the United States and Canada offer incentives for people to save money for retirement by granting tax advantages to (1) owners of certain individual annuities and (2) participants in and sponsors of qualified group retirement plans. One of these advantages is the tax treatment of annuity premiums and plan contributions.

Tax Advantages for Annuity Owners

As you recall from Chapter 6, contract owners typically can deduct part or all of the premiums paid on annuities used to fund traditional IRAs, up to specified maximums, from their federally taxable income. As a result, annuity contract owners get two tax advantages. First, if they are below a certain income level threshold, contract owners can deduct all or part of their annuity premium payments from their annual taxable income, thereby reducing the amount of taxes payable each year. Second, because income during retirement generally is taxed at a lower rate than income during working years, contract owners also may reduce the amount of tax that is eventually payable on premiums.

Owners of annuities used to fund Roth IRAs and individual nonqualified annuities do not receive the same tax benefits. For example, contributions to Roth IRAs and premiums paid on individual nonqualified annuities are not deductible from the contract owner's current income. As a result, contributions are taxed at current rates. However, because it has already been taxed, the amount of money contract owners pay into Roth IRAs and individual nonqualified annuities—often called the *tax cost basis*—is not subject to taxation when the contract is surrendered, money is withdrawn, or annuity payments begin.

tax cost basis.
The amount of money contract owners pay into Roth IRAs and non-IRA individual nonqualified annuities.

Tax Advantages for Participants in Qualified Retirement Plans

Participants in certain qualified group retirement plans (which we described in Chapter 6) receive tax advantages similar to those available to owners of traditional IRAs. For example, contributions to qualified 401(k) plans—up to specified maximums—are excluded from the plan participant's annual taxable income. Thus, plan participants can reduce their current taxes and will most likely pay less in taxes when plan funds are withdrawn during retirement.

Tax Advantages for Sponsors of Qualified Retirement Plans

Sponsors of qualified retirement plans also receive tax benefits. As we mentioned in Chapter 6, retirement plans in the United States must meet requirements specified in ERISA to be considered qualified plans. Qualified plans also must satisfy Internal Revenue Code requirements. The Internal Revenue Service does not require employers to obtain advance approval of their retirement plans in order to receive favorable tax treatment; however, most employers choose to do so to ensure that their plans meet the qualified plan requirements.

Under current tax laws, employer contributions to qualified retirement plans are considered a business expense. Thus, employers who make contributions to a qualified plan on behalf of employees can deduct those contributions, within stated limits, from their current taxable income.

Income Taxes on Annuity Earnings

Like other income, earnings from most annuities and other retirement savings vehicles are subject to income taxes. (Roth IRAs, in which earnings become tax-free after certain requirements are met, are an exception.) However, because earnings accrue on a tax-deferred basis, annuity owners and participants in retirement plans funded by annuities can postpone payment of income taxes on their investment earnings until funds are withdrawn from the account or annuity benefit payments are made. For example, suppose Miles Fortis purchased a deferred annuity at age 40, but waited 20 years before he began to receive annuity payments. Although the annuity contract earned investment income for 20 years, unless he made early withdrawals, Mr. Fortis did not have to pay taxes on this income until he began receiving annuity benefit payments at age 60.

The tax deferral of annuity earnings offers investors a definite incentive to save for retirement. However, only individuals are eligible for this special tax treatment. Corporations, trusts, and other legal entities that own annuities generally must pay income taxes on annuity earnings each year. Exceptions to this requirement include some types of trusts held for the benefit of a natural person. In these cases, income taxes on annuity earnings are deferred until benefit payments begin.

Income Taxes on Annuity Benefit Payments

For purposes of federal income taxes, annuity benefit payments consist of two parts:

- Principal—or tax cost basis—which is the amount the contract owner pays into the annuity

- Earnings, which are income generated by the investment

The way in which these parts are taxed depends on the type of annuity.

Taxation of Certain Nonqualified Annuity Benefit Payments

As we have mentioned, contributions to Roth IRAs, individual nonqualified annuities, and nonqualified group retirement plans are included in the contract owner's current taxable compensation. As a result, contract owners and plan participants can exclude the portion of annuity benefit payments that consists of a return of principal from their taxable income when benefit payments are received. Contract owners and plan participants must include the portion of annuity benefit payments that represents investment earnings in their taxable compensation and pay all applicable taxes.

If an annuity benefit is paid in a single lump-sum distribution, then the process of determining the taxable portion of the benefit is straightforward. The tax cost basis—the amount of principal on which the contract owner or plan participant already has paid taxes—is subtracted from the total contract value as of the date the annuity payment is made. The remaining amount—which consists of earnings—is taxed as income.

If an annuity benefit is paid in installments, determining the taxable portion of each benefit payment is more involved, especially if the total number of payments is not known in advance. In this case, contract owners can determine the amount of a fixed annuity benefit payment that is exempt from taxable income by using an Internal Revenue Code formula known as an ***exclusion ratio.*** The exclusion ratio is expressed by the following equation:

exclusion ratio.
An Internal Revenue Code formula used to calculate the amount of a fixed annuity benefit payment that is exempt from taxable income; equal to the investment in the contract as of the date annuity payments begin divided by the contract's expected return.

$$\text{Exclusion ratio} = \frac{\text{Investment in the contract as of date annuity payments begin}}{\text{Expected return}}$$

In this equation, the investment in the contract is equal to the contract owner's tax cost basis and the expected return is equal to the expected amount of each annuity payment multiplied by the expected number of payments.

If a contract owner elects to receive payments under a nonannuitized payout option (lump-sum distribution option, fixed period option, or fixed amount option), then the owner's expected return is equal to the total value of the amount distributed under the contract. If a contract owner elects to receive lifetime payments, the expected return depends on the annuitant's life expectancy and is contract specific. Insight 7.1 describes how the exclusion ratio is calculated for lifetime annuity payments in the case of a fixed monthly amount for the life of one annuitant.

For variable annuity payments, the Internal Revenue Code exclusion formula requires the insurer to divide the investment in the contract,

INSIGHT 7.1

Sample Exclusion Ratio Calculation

Ingrid Sorenson will begin receiving monthly payments of $500 from her fixed annuity on September 1, her 65th birthday. She is scheduled to receive these monthly payments for the remainder of her life. On the annuity's maturity date, Ms. Sorenson will have paid $50,000 into her annuity contract.

The insurer knows from the information above that Ms. Sorenson's investment is $50,000 and that she is scheduled to receive $500 each month for the rest of her life. What the insurer does not know is how long Ms. Sorenson will live, which will determine the total amount of the benefit Ms. Sorenson will receive.

To determine the total return Ms. Sorenson is expected to receive, the insurer uses the life expectancy information included in IRS Annuity Tables such as the one shown below:*

Ordinary Life Annuities—One Life—Expected Return Multiples

Age	Multiple	Age	Multiple
55	28.6	61	23.3
56	27.7	62	22.5
57	26.8	63	21.6
58	25.9	64	20.8
59	25.0	65	20.0
60	24.2	66	19.2

*Purchases made prior to July 1, 1986, may require different tables.

According to this table, Ms. Sorenson's life expectancy at the time the contract matures is 20.0 years, or 240 months. To calculate the total amount Ms. Sorenson is expected to receive from her annuity, the insurer multiplies Ms. Sorenson's monthly payment ($500) by the number of months she is expected to live (240) to arrive at an expected return of $120,000. The insurer can then calculate the amount of each payment excludable from Ms. Sorenson's income by inserting Ms. Sorenson's information into the exclusion ratio equation as shown below:

$$\frac{\text{Investment}}{\text{Expected return}} = \frac{\$50,000}{\$120,000} = 41.7\% \text{ excluded}$$

According to this calculation, Ms. Sorenson will receive $208.50 ($500 × 0.417) of each annuity payment tax free. The remainder of each payment, or $291.50, will be taxable as income.

adjusted for the value of any period certain or refund guarantee, by the number of periodic benefit payments that will be made. The periodic exclusion ratio that results from this calculation will remain the same each period even though the total payment amount will fluctuate each period because of the performance of the selected variable subaccounts. As is the case with fixed annuities, the contract owner can exclude only after-tax dollars paid into a variable annuity.

For both fixed and variable annuities purchased **on or after** January 1, 1987, as soon as contract owners recover their total tax cost basis, they must include any remaining amount in their gross income and pay income taxes on the full amount. However, if an annuity was purchased **before** January 1, 1987, the exclusion amount will continue to be applied, even after the annuitant recovers the tax cost basis.

For example, suppose Ms. Sorenson in Insight 7.1 purchased her annuity **on or after** January 1, 1987. In this case, after she recovers her tax cost basis, all remaining annuity payments will be included in her gross income and are fully taxable. If Ms. Sorenson purchased her annuity **before** January 1, 1987, the exclusion amount will continue to be applied for the remainder of her life.

Taxation of Traditional IRA and Qualified Annuity Benefit Payments

When an annuity is part of a traditional IRA or qualified retirement plan, premiums generally are not included in the contract owner's or plan participant's current taxable income. Both the principal and earnings of traditional IRAs and qualified annuities are then subject to income taxes when contract owners and plan participants begin to receive annuity benefit payments. However, if a person makes nondeductible contributions, the amount of those contributions that is included in annuity benefit payments would not be taxed.

Income Taxes on Withdrawals

In Chapter 2, we described the contract provision that allows the owner of an individual nonqualified annuity to withdraw a portion of the contract value at any time before annuity benefit payments begin. The way in which withdrawals are taxed depends on when premiums on the contract were paid.

Premiums Paid On or Before August 13, 1982

Premiums for individual nonqualified annuity contracts paid **on or before** August 13, 1982, are taxed using the ***cost recovery rule***, which states that withdrawals are considered first to be a return of the tax cost basis and are therefore not taxable income. After the contract owner withdraws an amount equal to the tax cost basis in the contract,

---

cost recovery rule.
A tax calculation method which states that withdrawals from nonqualified annuity contracts are considered to be a return of the tax cost basis first and are therefore not taxable income; applies to annuity contracts established on or before August 13, 1982.

withdrawals are considered interest and become taxable to the contract owner as income. The following example illustrates how the cost recovery rule works.

> Anthony Ricci purchased an individual deferred annuity on January 2, 1979, with a single $50,000 premium payment. On August 15, 1991, Mr. Ricci withdrew $10,000 from his annuity. Because the contribution was made before August 13, 1982, taxation of Mr. Ricci's withdrawal is subject to the cost recovery rule. According to the cost recovery rule, the entire $10,000 withdrawal—which is less than the $50,000 Mr. Ricci invested in the annuity—is treated as a recovery of the tax cost basis in the contract and is not taxable as income.

Premiums Paid After August 13, 1982

Contract owners who pay premiums for individual nonqualified annuity contracts **after** August 13, 1982, pay taxes on withdrawals according to the interest first rule. The *interest first rule* states that any amount that the contract owner takes out of the annuity will be considered a withdrawal of interest (which has not previously been taxed), until the contract owner has withdrawn all of the interest in the contract. Thereafter, withdrawals are considered to consist of the owner's investment in the contract and are not taxed. The interest first rule, which is essentially the opposite of the cost recovery rule, is illustrated below.

> In 1991, Margaret Malloy purchased an individual deferred annuity with a single $50,000 premium. In 1998, she withdrew $30,000 from the contract. The value of the contract at the time of the withdrawal was $75,000. Because Ms. Malloy purchased her annuity after August 13, 1982, her withdrawal is taxed under the interest first rule. According to this rule, the first $25,000 of Ms. Malloy's withdrawal is taxable because it is equal to the amount of interest earned on the contract ($75,000 value − $50,000 investment = $25,000 earnings). The remaining $5,000 is considered a return of her tax cost basis and is tax free.

interest first rule.
A tax calculation method which states that any amount a contract owner takes out of a nonqualified annuity will be considered a withdrawal of interest (which has not been taxed), until the contract owner has withdrawn all of the interest in the contract; applies to annuity contracts established after August 13, 1982.

Note that the cost recovery rule and the interest first rule apply only to those annuities that have a tax cost basis. Annuities used to fund traditional IRAs and qualified employer-sponsored retirement plans are paid for with deductible premiums and therefore do not have a tax cost basis.

Income Taxes on Loans

As we mentioned in Chapter 2, owners of certain types of annuities can obtain loans based on the value of their contracts. The type of loan a contract owner can obtain and how it is taxed depend on whether the annuity is a nonqualified annuity or a qualified annuity.

Loans on Individual Nonqualified Annuities

Most individual nonqualified annuities do not allow loans to be taken directly from the annuity contract balance because this would be considered a distribution. However, as you recall from Chapter 2, individual nonqualified annuities generally include an assignment provision that grants the contract owner the right to temporarily or permanently transfer ownership of the contract. As a result of this provision, contract owners of individual nonqualified annuities can use the value of their annuity contracts as security for loans from banks or other entities. Owners of annuities funding IRAs are prohibited from obtaining loans from the contract balance or from using their IRAs as security for loans.

In general, loans on individual nonqualified annuities are treated as distributions for tax purposes and taxes are based on when contract premiums were paid. For example, if a contract owner purchases an annuity contract **on or before** August 13, 1982 and later uses the contract value as security for a loan, the cost recovery rule applies to the amount of the loan. Under the terms of this rule, if the loan amount is less than or equal to the tax cost basis of the contract, the loan amount is not considered to be taxable income. If the loan amount exceeds the tax cost basis of the contract, the excess amount is considered to be a withdrawal of interest and is taxable as current income.

If the contract owner purchases an annuity contract **after** August 13, 1982, loans are subject to the interest first rule. In this case, any loan amount that is less than or equal to the contract's accumulated earnings at the time of the loan is considered to be a withdrawal of interest and is taxable as income. Loan amounts in excess of accrued earnings are considered to be a return of the tax cost basis and are not taxable. Insight 7.2 illustrates how loan amounts are treated for income tax purposes.

Loans on Qualified Annuities

The tax treatment of loans on qualified annuities differs significantly from the treatment of loans obtained through assignment of individual nonqualified annuities. Unlike individual nonqualified annuities, qualified annuities cannot be assigned and therefore cannot be used as security for a loan from a bank or other entity. However, qualified annuities generally include detailed loan provisions that allow participants of certain annuity-funded qualified plans, such as 401(k) and 403(b) plans, to obtain loans from the provider of the annuity contract based on the value of the account. The significance of these provisions is that loans may not be considered to be withdrawals and therefore may not be taxable as income.

> **INSIGHT 7.2**
>
> ### Taxes Payable on Loans from Individual Nonqualified Annuities
>
> Lewis Alverado purchased a $50,000 individual nonqualified deferred annuity contract in 1980. Andrea McCall purchased a similar $50,000 annuity contract in 1985. In 1998, Mr. Alverado and Ms. McCall, both of whom were age 60, used their annuity contracts as security for bank loans in the amount of $75,000.
>
> The value of Mr. Alverado's contract at the time of the loan was $105,000. Because Mr. Alverado purchased the contract before August 13, 1982, the cost recovery rule applies. As a result, the first $50,000 of his loan is considered a return of the tax cost basis of the contract and is nontaxable. The remaining $25,000 is considered earnings and is subject to income taxes.
>
> The value of Ms. McCall's contract at the time of the loan was $98,000. Because she purchased her annuity after August 13, 1982, the interest first rule applies. In this case, the first $48,000 of Ms. McCall's loan amount is considered earnings ($98,000 value minus $50,000 investment) and is taxable as income. The remaining $27,000 is considered a nontaxable return of the contract's tax cost basis.

For example, participants in 401(k) plans typically are allowed to obtain loans of up to $50,000 or 50 percent of their vested account value, whichever is less. Plan participants must pay the loan amount, with interest, back into their account, but they do not pay federal income taxes on the loan. Some participants who terminate employment with an unpaid loan balance may find that the unpaid portion of the loan is considered to be an early distribution subject to 20 percent withholding for federal income taxes and a premature distribution penalty. Whether or not a loan is considered a distribution after separation from employment depends on the terms of the plan or loan agreement and not on federal tax laws. To avoid any possible tax liability, the participant must repay the loan prior to termination.

U.S. Penalty Taxes

To discourage people from purchasing annuities as short-term tax-sheltered investments, the U.S. federal government imposes penalty taxes on annuity distributions that are received before a specified date.

FIGURE 7.2

Situations in Which Premature Distributions Are Exempt from Penalty Taxes

Generally

Premature distributions are exempt from the 10 percent penalty tax if payments are made:

- On or after the death of the contract owner (or, if the contract owner is not a natural person, on or after the death of the annuitant)
- While the contract owner (or annuitant) is disabled
- As part of a series of substantially equal periodic payments made for the life of the contract owner or the joint lives of the contract owner and beneficiary

For qualified plans

Premature distributions also are exempt from tax penalties if payments are made:

- Because of hardship
- After separation from employment when the plan participant is age 55 or older
- For certain medical expenses
- As a result of a qualified domestic relations order

For traditional IRAs

Premature distributions also are exempt from tax penalties if payments are made:

- For the purchase of a first home
- For qualified education expenses

The federal government also imposes penalty taxes on annuity distributions that (1) do not begin by a specified date or (2) are less than a specified minimum amount.

premature distribution.
A withdrawal of earnings from an annuity before the contract owner reaches age 59½.

In the case of a **premature distribution**, which is a withdrawal of earnings from an annuity before the contract owner reaches age 59½, the tax penalty is 10 percent, unless another exception applies. Figure 7.2 lists some of the situations in which premature distributions are exempt from federal tax penalties.

Tax penalties, which apply only to the taxable portion of the distribution, are in addition to the income taxes that are payable on the amount withdrawn and apply to both qualified and nonqualified annuities. Loans obtained by individual nonqualified annuity contract owners under age 59½ are subject to the same 10 percent federal tax penalty, in addition to the applicable income taxes payable on the loan.

Owners of traditional IRAs and participants in qualified retirement plans also pay tax penalties if they do not begin to receive distributions by a specified date. Owners of traditional IRAs must begin receiving distributions no later than April 1 of the year after they reach age 70½. Failure to comply with this requirement may result in a 50 percent excise tax on the amount not distributed as required. Participants in qualified retirement plans must begin to receive distributions by the later of April 1 of the year after they reach age 70½ or April 1 of the year after they retire. Owners of Roth IRAs are not required to receive a distribution at any time and may leave their accounts to their heirs tax free.

In addition, owners of traditional IRAs and participants in qualified retirement plans are subject to penalty taxes if the amount of the distribution they receive falls below a specified **minimum distribution** amount defined in the tax code. However, traditional IRA contract owners and 403(b) plan participants who have multiple accounts of the same type may choose to receive the total amount required for all of their accounts from one account of that type and not withdraw anything from other accounts of the same type.

minimum distribution. The minimum amount a contract owner is required to withdraw from an annuity contract at maturity.

U.S. Estate Taxes

When a U.S. citizen dies, the federal government imposes estate taxes on the value of that person's estate worth more than a specified amount. Currently, estate taxes apply to amounts greater than $1,000,000 and rates are set at up to 50 percent. Under the provisions of EGTRRA, the $1,000,000 estate tax exemption will rise periodically and tax rates will decrease until 2010, when estate taxes will be eliminated. This gradual repeal of estate taxes is scheduled to end on December 31, 2010. Unless Congress reinstates the repeal, the estate tax will go into effect again on January 1, 2011, with an exemption amount at the 2001 level of $675,000.

Estate taxes generally must be paid before a person's property can be distributed to the heirs of the estate. One exception to this rule is that a person can transfer all estate values to a spouse without incurring any estate taxes. A full explanation of estate taxes is beyond the scope of this text; however, we will discuss how estate taxes apply to annuity proceeds.

Whether an annuity is subject to estate taxes at the contract owner's death depends on whether the contract owner dies during the contract's accumulation period or payout period. If the contract owner dies during the accumulation period, the value of the annuity is included in the owner's **gross estate**, which is the total value of property subject to estate taxes. Estate taxes are levied on the deceased's property—

gross estate. The total value of property subject to estate taxes.

including annuity proceeds—if the value of the total estate exceeds the legally defined exemption.

If the contract owner dies during the contract's payout period, then the estate taxes payable on annuity proceeds depend on the type of annuity. If the annuity is a form of life only annuity, then the contract owner's death ends the annuity contract, no more payments are made, and no tax liability is incurred. On the other hand, if the annuity has some type of survivor benefit, then the present value of those future benefits is included in the contract owner's gross estate and is subject to applicable estate taxes.

Other U.S. Taxes on Annuities

Owners of annuity contracts in the United States may be subject to additional taxes if they (1) exchange the contract for another annuity contract or (2) roll over funds from a qualified plan or an IRA into another plan.

Exchanges

Occasionally, owners of individual annuity contracts or individual life insurance policies elect to exchange their existing contracts for new annuity contracts. Contract owners make these exchanges by surrendering their original contracts and then using the proceeds to purchase annuities. Contract owners can make exchanges by transferring the principal and interest from the surrendered contract to a new or existing contract issued by the same company or by a different company.

Because the contract owner technically is withdrawing the principal and earnings from the original annuity or insurance policy, taxation of the deferred income in the original contract becomes an issue. Section 1035 of the Internal Revenue Code allows owners of individual nonqualified annuity contracts to avoid this tax liability by making tax-free exchanges of individual nonqualified annuity contracts and life insurance policies. An exchange that meets the guidelines established by the Internal Revenue Code is referred to as a **Section 1035 exchange**. Other sections of the tax code include similar provisions for the tax-free exchange of one qualified annuity for another qualified annuity.

In order to qualify as a tax-free exchange, the original insurer must transfer contract values from the original contract to the new contract without any distribution passing through the hands of the contract owner. In addition, the contract owner and annuitant must be the same on the original contract and the new contract.

Section 1035 exchange. An arrangement under which an insurer transfers contract values, tax free, from an original life insurance or annuity contract to a new contract without any distribution passing through the hands of the contract owner.

Rollovers

As we discussed in Chapter 6, participants in qualified retirement plans who are no longer employed by the plan sponsor or who have met another distributable event have several options for managing the vested amounts in their accounts. If the balance in the account is large enough and the plan document allows, the person may simply leave the balance in the account until retirement. However, many people choose to roll over funds from one qualified plan to another qualified plan or to an IRA. To avoid an automatic withholding of 20 percent for federal income taxes, the entire account balance in the original qualified plan must be transferred directly to the new qualified plan, without any part of the distribution going to the plan participant. This type of rollover transfer is known as a *trustee-to-trustee transfer*. If the plan participant receives any part of the original distribution, 20 percent of the amount the individual receives will be withheld for income taxes. Owners of traditional IRAs also can roll over funds to other plans.

Individuals who receive cash distributions can recover the withholding amount if they roll over an amount equal to the original account balance within 60 days of the cash distribution. Individuals must add their own money to make up for the 20 percent withheld, but may receive a refund of the amount when they file federal income tax returns.

Canadian Taxation of Annuities

As you recall from Chapter 6, taxation of contributions to annuities and registered retirement plans in Canada is similar to the taxation of contributions in the United States. People who purchase individual annuities pay premiums with after-tax dollars and therefore cannot deduct contributions from their taxable income. These contributions, however, are not taxed when funds are withdrawn. Canadian employees can deduct the amount of their contributions to registered retirement savings plans (RRSPs), within specified limits, from their taxable income and defer payment of any applicable taxes on these contributions until funds are withdrawn. Employees must report any employer contributions as wages and then take an offsetting deduction in the amount of the contribution. Thus, any employer contributions become employee contributions for tax purposes.

In Canada, taxation of investment earnings and benefit payments from individual annuities and retirement plans varies in certain respects from taxation in the United States. For example, Canada taxes the investment income buildup on deferred annuities held by natural persons prior to withdrawal. For annuity contracts purchased in 1989 or later, taxes on earnings are assessed on an annual basis. For contracts purchased

trustee-to-trustee transfer. A type of rollover transfer in which the entire account balance in a qualified retirement savings plan is transferred directly to a new qualified plan, without any part of the distribution going to the plan participant.

before 1989, taxes on earnings are assessed every three years. Corporations and partnerships pay an annual tax on income accumulated in annuities during the year. In addition, owners of individual annuities in Canada and participants in RRSPs are required to include the full amount of each annuity payment in their taxable income. They then deduct the tax cost basis and any portion consisting of amounts previously taxed.

Key Terms

income tax

tax cost basis

exclusion ratio

cost recovery rule

interest first rule

premature distribution

minimum distribution

gross estate

Section 1035 exchange

trustee-to-trustee transfer

Annuity Principles and Products

CHAPTER 8

Regulation of the Annuity Industry

After studying this chapter, you should be able to

- Describe the role and function of the National Association of Insurance Commissioners (NAIC)
- Explain the purpose of solvency regulation
- Describe the U.S. market conduct requirements that apply to company and producer licensing, contract approval, advertising and disclosure, and product suitability
- Explain the focus of federal regulation of annuities in the United States
- Describe the regulatory functions of the Securities and Exchange Commission (SEC) and the National Association of Securities Dealers (NASD)
- Describe the provincial and federal laws and regulatory agencies that govern annuities in Canada

OUTLINE

U.S. State Regulation
Solvency Regulation
Market Conduct Regulation

U.S. Federal Regulation
Securities Regulation

Canadian Provincial Regulation
Solvency Regulation
Market Conduct Regulation

Canadian Federal Regulation

Because thousands of people own annuities and rely on them for future financial security, the development, sale, and administration of annuity products is subject to extensive regulation. In this chapter, we will look at the regulatory systems that have been established in the United States and Canada to govern annuity sales and operations.

We begin the chapter with a description of state and federal annuity regulations in the United States. We then examine comparable Canadian annuity regulation.

U.S. State Regulation

In 1945, the U.S. Congress passed the **McCarran-Ferguson Act**, which left the authority to regulate the insurance industry to the states as long as Congress considered state regulation to be adequate. As a result of this act, state governments—not the federal government—have primary authority to regulate insurance business, including the issue and sale of annuity products. Congress maintains the right to enact insurance legislation if it determines that state regulation is inadequate or not in the public interest.

To manage their regulatory authority over insurance business, each state has established an administrative agency, typically known as the **state insurance department**, or *state department of insurance*, which is charged with making sure that insurance companies operating within the state comply with all of that state's insurance laws and regulations. Usually, each state insurance department is under the direction of a state insurance commissioner or state superintendent of insurance.

The state insurance departments created the **National Association of Insurance Commissioners (NAIC)**, a private, nonprofit organization that consists of the insurance commissioners or state superintendents of insurance of each state, the District of Columbia, and the four U.S. territories. The purpose of the NAIC is to promote uniformity of state regulation. The NAIC provides a forum for discussions of common regulatory problems and develops solutions to these problems in the form of model laws and regulations that each state is encouraged to pass. A **model law** is sample legislation intended to serve as a guide for state lawmakers. State legislatures can adopt model laws exactly as written or use them as a basis for developing their own laws. State legislatures also develop laws without using NAIC model laws as a guide.

Because annuities are considered to be insurance products, many of the state regulations that apply to insurance also apply to annuities. However, many states have passed additional laws to regulate the issue and sale of annuity products. The NAIC model laws that form the basis for much of the regulation specific to annuities are summarized in Figure 8.1. We will discuss some of these model laws in more detail in the following sections.

McCarran-Ferguson Act.
A U.S. federal law that grants the authority to regulate the insurance industry to the states as long as Congress considers state regulation to be adequate.

state insurance department.
A state agency charged with making sure that insurance companies operating within a state comply with all of that state's insurance laws and regulations. Also known as the state department of insurance.

National Association of Insurance Commissioners (NAIC).
A private, nonprofit organization made up of the insurance commissioners or state superintendents of insurance of each state, the District of Columbia, and the four U.S. territories that works to promote uniformity of state regulation.

model law.
Sample legislation that is intended to serve as a guide for state lawmakers.

FIGURE 8.1

NAIC Model Laws Pertaining to the Issue and Sale of Annuities

New Annuity Mortality Table Model Rule
Recognizes certain new mortality tables as the minimum standard of valuation for annuity contracts.

Life and Health Insurance Policy Language Simplification Model Act
Specifies requirements—referred to as readability requirements—that policy forms for life and health insurance and annuity products must meet to be approved for use. These requirements cover (1) language level, (2) type size, (3) overall appearance, and (4) length.

Standard Nonforfeiture Law for Individual Deferred Annuities
Requires that individual deferred annuity contracts provide minimum nonforfeiture values in the event that premium payments stop or the contract is surrendered. The nonforfeiture value is equal to the contract's accumulated value, less any allowable charges, at the time the contract is terminated. Also requires disclosure of information on interest rates, death benefits, and mortality tables used in any calculations included in the annuity contract. (Note that these requirements apply only during the accumulation period of a deferred annuity. After the annuity's maturity date, the insurer must provide payments in accordance with the terms of the contract.)

Model Variable Annuity Regulation
Establishes qualifications an insurer must meet to issue and sell variable annuities. Specifies requirements for variable annuity products including the (1) use of separate accounts for annuity investments, (2) establishment of minimum reserve requirements, and (3) provision of minimum nonforfeiture values.

Producer Licensing Model Act
Specifies the requirements an individual must satisfy to sell insurance and annuity products.

Advertisements of Life Insurance and Annuities Model Regulation
Requires insurers to ensure full and truthful disclosure to the public of all material and relevant information in their advertisements for life insurance and annuity products.

Annuity Disclosure Model Regulation
Requires that prospective buyers of individual deferred annuities and certain group annuities be provided with basic information about annuities in general and about premiums, cash values, and surrender costs for the specific annuity contract the prospective buyer is considering.

Replacement of Life Insurance and Annuities Model Regulation
Specifies the procedures insurers and producers must follow when selling a new contract that will replace an existing contract issued by the same or a different insurer.

Whether they are based on NAIC model laws or developed independently, state regulations governing insurance companies and products generally fall into two broad categories:

- **Solvency regulation,** which addresses the need for insurance companies to be financially stable and capable of paying debts and disbursing life insurance benefits and annuity proceeds—including death benefits and annuity payments—when they are due

- **Market conduct regulation,** which is designed to ensure that insurance companies conduct business fairly and ethically

Solvency Regulation

The financial stability of an insurance company is an important concern for people who own insurance and annuity products. For this reason, each state has enacted laws that require any insurance company operating within the state to demonstrate its solvency. **Solvency** is the ability of an insurer to make specified payments to contract owners and to meet other financial obligations on time.

State regulators monitor the solvency of insurers by reviewing each company's **Annual Statement**, which is a financial report containing detailed accounting and statistical data about the company. Each insurer operating in the state must prepare an Annual Statement every year and file it with the state insurance department and the NAIC. In addition, regulators examine each insurer's operations and financial condition in detail at least every three to five years. Regulators can conduct examinations more often if necessary.

In the event that an insurer becomes insolvent and cannot meet its financial obligations, state regulations guarantee payment—up to specified limits—for certain policies, including annuities. These payments are provided by each state's **guaranty association**, which is an agency composed of all life insurance companies operating in the state. To fund payments to customers of companies that go out of business, each state's guaranty association imposes mandatory assessments on all association member companies in the state. Each insurer's share of the total assessment is based on the company's share of total premiums written in that state. The state specifies the maximum amount that an insurer is required to contribute in any given year.

Beginning in 2003, publicly traded companies also will be required to satisfy federal financial disclosure requirements included in the Sarbanes-Oxley Act of 2002. One of the most important of these requirements is mandatory certification of the accuracy of a company's financial statements by the company's chief executive officer and chief financial

solvency.
The ability of an insurer to make specified payments to contract owners and to meet other financial obligations on time.

Annual Statement.
A financial report containing detailed accounting and statistical data about a U.S. insurance company; insurers must file an Annual Statement each year with the state insurance department(s) and the NAIC.

guaranty association.
A state agency composed of all life insurance companies operating in the state that funds payments to customers of companies that go out of business.

officer. Although the rules set out in the Sarbanes-Oxley Act apply only to publicly traded companies that are under the jurisdiction of the SEC, the NAIC is expected to apply many of the rules to all insurers.[1]

Market Conduct Regulation

Market conduct regulation governs a variety of insurance company activities related to annuity sales and operations. The most important areas of market conduct regulation that apply to annuities include (1) company and producer licensing, (2) contract approval, (3) advertising and disclosure, and (4) product suitability.

State Licensing Requirements

State laws require that both the companies that issue insurance and annuity products and the individuals and agencies that sell those products obtain a license from the state's insurance department before conducting insurance business in the state. In the case of insurance companies, this license—which is referred to as a **certificate of authority**—identifies the lines of insurance the company is authorized to issue. Generally, insurers are required to obtain a certificate of authority from each state in which they perform any of the following activities:

- Solicit applications for insurance and annuity products
- Issue and deliver insurance and annuity contracts
- Collect premiums for insurance and annuity contracts
- Maintain an office that transacts insurance business

Insurers also must satisfy a variety of state-mandated licensing requirements designed to ensure that only reputable and financially stable companies are selling insurance products in the state.

Because annuities are considered to be insurance products for regulatory purposes, an insurer that is licensed to offer ordinary life insurance in a state generally is authorized to offer fixed annuities in that state. Most states require insurers to obtain specific authority to offer variable life insurance and variable annuity products.

States also require that each **insurance producer**—an individual who sells insurance and annuity products to consumers and organizations—be licensed. The specific requirements producers must satisfy to sell insurance are intended to help ensure that producers are reputable and knowledgeable about the products they sell.

Most states require producers to be licensed to sell life insurance before they can sell annuity products. Some states require a separate license to sell annuities. Producers typically must renew their licenses every

certificate of authority. The state license an insurance company must obtain to conduct insurance business in that state.

insurance producer. An individual who is licensed to sell insurance and annuity products to consumers and organizations.

year. A state may revoke a producer's license if the producer engages in illegal or unethical practices.

Although producer licensing requirements vary from state to state, efforts have been made to streamline and simplify the producer licensing process and to make licensing requirements more uniform. For example, the Gramm-Leach-Bliley (GLB) Act of 1999 required the states to enact uniform or reciprocal producer licensing requirements or submit to federal uniform licensing requirements. In response to this federal mandate, the NAIC developed a **Producer Licensing Model Act**, which specifies requirements an individual must satisfy to be licensed as an insurance producer. The majority of states have now enacted laws based on the model act or other legislation designed to comply with the GLB Act's requirements.

Producer Licensing Model Act. A model act developed by the NAIC that specifies requirements an individual must satisfy to be licensed as an insurance producer.

State laws patterned after the Producer Licensing Model Act require individuals seeking a producer's license to

- Submit a written application that provides identifying information about the applicant and the lines of insurance the applicant intends to sell
- Be at least 18 years of age
- Pay any applicable licensing fees
- Pass a written examination on each line of insurance described in the application

Because of the complexity of insurance and annuity products, most states require licensed producers to participate in continuing education programs to maintain their licenses. The NAIC Agents Continuing Education Model Regulation recommends that resident producers complete a specified number of hours each year in courses or seminars approved by the state insurance department. In addition, licensed producers typically are required to notify the state insurance department of any changes in their home or business addresses and any administrative action or criminal prosecution taken against them by any state.

Contract Form Requirements

If an insurer intends to offer a new or modified insurance product in a state, the insurer must obtain approval from the state insurance department for the contract form describing that product. This contract filing requirement applies to all types of insurance products, including ordinary and variable insurance and fixed and variable annuities. The insurance department reviews contract forms to make sure that they (1) satisfy state readability requirements and (2) include all required provisions.

*readability requirements.
State-mandated requirements that limit the amount of technical jargon and legal language included in insurance and annuity contracts.*

State **readability requirements** limit sentence length, word length, and the amount of technical jargon and legal language included in insurance and annuity contracts. They are intended to make contracts easier to read and help ensure that consumers understand the terms of the contract. A contract form that does not meet a state's readability requirements will not be approved for use in that state.

State insurance laws require that all individual annuity contracts contain specified provisions. These required provisions—most of which were discussed in Chapter 2—are summarized in Figure 8.2.

Advertising and Disclosure Requirements

In addition to regulating the issue and sale of annuity products, most states regulate advertisements and other materials used in the sales process. Such regulation is designed to ensure that annuity buyers' purchase decisions are based on fair and accurate information about insurance companies and their products.

Because annuities are classified as insurance products, annuity advertising generally is subject to the same laws that govern insurance advertising. In many states, these laws are based on the NAIC **Advertisements of Life Insurance and Annuities Model Regulation**, which (1) defines the types of materials that constitute advertising and (2) describes the steps insurers must follow when preparing materials for use in the sales process.

*Advertisements of Life Insurance and Annuities Model Regulation.
A model law developed by the NAIC that (1) defines the types of materials that constitute advertising and (2) describes the steps insurers should follow when preparing materials for use in the sales process.*

The NAIC advertising rules define the following materials as advertisements:

- Promotional materials, including direct mail, radio, television, and print advertisements

- Sales aids, including brochures, pamphlets, letters, and sales illustrations

- Materials used to recruit or train producers

- Prepared sales talks, presentations, and other materials used by producers in the sales process

All materials classified as advertisements must clearly identify the product being sold and the insurer issuing the contract. Further, no advertisement may contain any false or misleading information or include unfair or incomplete comparisons to other products, producers, or insurers. For example, the model regulation prohibits the use of terms such as "investment," "investment plan," "deposit," "profits," "profit sharing," "interest plan," "savings," or "savings plan" when they have the capacity to mislead prospective customers into believing that they are purchasing something other than a life insurance policy or annuity contract.

FIGURE 8.2

Examples of Required Individual Annuity Contract Provisions

Provision	Description
Entire Contract Provision	Specifies that only those documents attached to or appearing in the annuity contract are part of the contract.
Free-Look Provision	Gives the contract owner a specified period within which to return the annuity contract and receive a refund of all premiums paid or the account value.
Incontestability Provision	States that the insurer, in most instances, cannot contest the validity of the annuity contract after it becomes effective.
Misstatement of Age or Sex Provision	States that, if the annuitant's age is misstated, then the annuity benefits payable will be those that the premiums paid would have purchased for the correct age. Most contracts allow insurers to make similar benefit adjustments for misstatements of the annuitant's sex.
Payout Options Provision (Settlement Options Provision)	Describes the contract owner's right to select how periodic payments will be paid and the payout options available.
Nonforfeiture Provision	States the benefit amounts that the insurer will pay under a deferred annuity contract if premium payments stop or the contract is surrendered during the accumulation period. If the contract provides for a lump-sum payout, the insurer must pay the contract owner a lump sum on surrender of the contract in lieu of an annuity benefit.
Conformity with State Statutes Provision (Conformity with Law Provision)	States that any policy provision that is in conflict with the laws of the state that governs the contract is amended to conform to the minimum requirements of such laws.

In addition to its advertising rules, the NAIC has adopted a ***Life Insurance Illustrations Model Regulation*** that provides formats, standards for use, and disclosure requirements for sales illustrations. Insurers and producers using illustrations must provide detailed documentation of their compliance with these requirements. The model regulation also describes activities that are not allowed. For example, under the model regulation, insurers and producers are prohibited from

Life Insurance Illustrations Model Regulation.
A model regulation developed by the NAIC that provides formats, standards for use, and disclosure requirements for sales illustrations.

- Representing a life insurance policy (or annuity contract) as anything other than a life insurance policy (or annuity contract)
- Using or describing nonguaranteed elements in a way that misleads or has the potential to mislead customers
- Suggesting that premium payments will not be due each year to maintain the policy, unless this is true

Some states impose additional disclosure requirements specific to annuities. Many of these requirements are based on the NAIC *Annuity Disclosure Model Regulation*, which requires insurers to provide prospective buyers of specific types of annuities with information to help them select an annuity that is appropriate for their needs. Under the terms of the model disclosure regulation, insurers must provide fixed annuity purchasers with the following documents at or before the time an application is taken:

- A *Buyer's Guide to Fixed Deferred Annuities*, which describes the various types of annuities available and some of the annuity features that consumers should consider before purchasing an annuity
- A *disclosure document*, which contains relevant contract and benefit information for the specific annuity that a consumer is considering purchasing

The model disclosure regulation applies to most individual fixed deferred annuities and group annuities; it does not apply to individual immediate annuities. Annuities that are subject to other disclosure laws and regulations—such as variable annuities—also are exempt from model regulation requirements.

Suitability Requirements

Another important goal of state regulation is to ensure that customers buying ordinary life insurance and fixed annuity products are making a suitable purchase. To achieve this goal, a few states have established a regulatory requirement, often referred to as a *suitability requirement*, which imposes a duty on producers and/or insurers to have reasonable grounds on which to recommend a specific product as appropriate for a customer's needs. The suitability of variable products is governed by federal regulations and will be discussed later in this chapter.

State suitability requirements typically require producers to have a basic understanding of a customer's current financial condition and future financial needs before making any product recommendation. Producers, therefore, are expected to make reasonable efforts to obtain certain customer information during the sales process. In the case of fixed annuity sales, this information includes

---

Annuity Disclosure Model Regulation.
A model regulation developed by the NAIC that requires insurers to provide prospective buyers of specific types of annuities with information to help them select an annuity that is appropriate for their needs.

Buyer's Guide to Fixed Deferred Annuities.
A document that describes the various types of annuities available and some of the annuity features that consumers should consider before purchasing an annuity.

disclosure document.
A document that contains relevant contract and benefit information for the specific annuity that a consumer is considering purchasing.

suitability requirement.
A requirement that imposes a duty on producers and/or insurers to have reasonable grounds on which to recommend a specific product as appropriate for a customer's needs.

- The customer's financial resources
- The customer's anticipated future financial obligations
- Any additional information that can be considered reasonable in making product recommendations

In an effort to expand the use of suitability guidelines among the states, the NAIC is proposing additional model laws and regulations. For example, in 2003, the NAIC drafted a new Senior Protection in Annuity Transactions Model Regulation and Model Act. The purpose of these models is to establish minimum standards and procedures for insurers and producers to follow when making recommendations to prospective customers age 65 or older regarding the sale, surrender, replacement, or other disposition of annuity products. The NAIC also is drafting a new Life Insurance and Annuities Suitability Model Law and Model Regulation. When completed, these models will define what constitutes a recommendation, what products will be covered by suitability requirements, and what actions insurers and producers must take to comply with regulatory requirements.

Suitability is a concern for replacements as well as initial purchases of life insurance and annuity products. A **replacement** is a transaction in which an existing individual life insurance or annuity contract is surrendered or otherwise terminated and the proceeds used to purchase another contract.

Most states have established regulations governing the replacement of insurance policies and annuity contracts. Many of these regulations are based on the NAIC **Replacement of Life Insurance and Annuities Model Regulation**, which specifies procedures that producers and insurers must follow when a new contract will replace an existing contract. To comply with these regulations, a producer typically must provide an annuity applicant with a state-approved "Notice Regarding Replacement" such as the one included in Figure 8.3. Both the applicant and the producer must sign the form.

If the new contract is a replacement, the producer must provide the applicant with information about the annuity being purchased and the potential effects of replacement. In addition, the producer must obtain a list of all existing contracts that will be replaced, including the name of the insurer, the name of the insured, and the policy number for each contract. The producer must submit this list, along with a copy of the signed notice of replacement form, to the replacing insurer. The replacing insurer must (1) send written notice to the original insurer that the original contract may be replaced and (2) provide a free-look period during which the contract owner can cancel the new contract and receive a full refund of premiums paid. The NAIC has proposed a new replacement model regulation that imposes additional requirements.

replacement.
A transaction in which an existing individual life insurance or annuity contract is surrendered or otherwise terminated in order to purchase another contract.

Replacement of Life Insurance and Annuities Model Regulation.
A model regulation developed by the NAIC which specifies procedures that producers and insurers must follow when a new contract will replace an existing contract.

FIGURE 8.3

Notice of Replacement[2]

Replacement of Life Insurance or Annuities

You are contemplating the purchase of a life insurance policy or annuity contract. In some cases, this purchase may involve discontinuing or changing an existing policy or contract. If so, a replacement is occurring.

We want you to understand the effects of replacements before you make your purchase decision and ask that you answer the following questions:

1. Are you considering discontinuing making premium payments, surrendering, forfeiting, assigning to the insurer, or otherwise terminating your existing policy or contract?

2. Are you considering using funds from your existing policies or contracts to pay premiums due on the new policy or contract?

If you answered "yes" to either of these questions, list each existing policy or contract you are contemplating replacing.

Make sure you know the facts. Contact your existing company or its agent for information about the old policy or contract. Ask for and retain all sales material used by the agent in the sales presentation. Be sure that you are making an informed decision.

I certify that the responses herein are, to the best of my knowledge, accurate:

_____   _____   _____
Applicant's Signature   Date   Agent's Signature

U.S. Federal Regulation

As we mentioned earlier, the states have primary authority to regulate most insurance company and insurance producer activities. States also have primary authority to regulate insurance and annuity products as long as those products meet the following three requirements:

- The contract must be issued by a corporation subject to the supervision of a state insurance commissioner, bank commissioner, or similar state regulator

- The contract's investment risk must be borne primarily by the issuer of the contract
- The product must not be marketed primarily as an investment

Ordinary life insurance products and fixed annuities clearly satisfy these requirements and are governed by state insurance laws. At present, equity-indexed annuities and most types of market value adjusted (MVA) annuities that offer specified investment and interest rate guarantees also are governed at the state level. However, marketing these products without emphasizing their investment features is difficult. As a result, state and federal regulators are reviewing these hybrid products to determine their regulatory status.

Variable life insurance, variable annuity products, and some MVA annuities are subject to many of the state insurance laws we discussed in the previous sections of this chapter. However, because these products have an investment component and require the contract owner to assume some or all of the risk associated with securities held in a separate account, they are subject to federal securities laws as well.

Securities Regulation

Most of the regulations governing securities are contained in the following four pieces of federal legislation:

- The **Securities Act of 1933**, which protects investors by requiring that they receive specified types of information about securities being offered for sale to the public. The Act also prohibits misrepresentation and fraud in the sale of securities.
- The **Securities Exchange Act of 1934**, which created the Securities and Exchange Commission (SEC) and granted it broad authority to enforce the Securities Act of 1933 and to regulate the securities industry.
- The **Investment Company Act of 1940**, which regulates the conduct of investment companies. The Act defines an **investment company** as a company that issues securities and engages primarily in investing and trading securities.
- The **Investment Advisor's Act of 1940**, which regulates the conduct of investment advisors. An **investment advisor** is a company or person that is compensated for providing advice to investors about the value of securities and the potential advantages and disadvantages of buying and selling securities.

In 1983, the SEC established the **National Association of Securities Dealers (NASD)**—a nonprofit organization of securities dealers—to regulate the market conduct of member companies and their

---

Securities Act of 1933.
A U.S. federal law that protects investors by requiring that they receive specified types of information about securities being offered for sale to the public.

Securities Exchange Act of 1934.
A U.S. federal law that created the Securities and Exchange Commission (SEC) and granted it broad authority to enforce the Securities Act of 1933 and to regulate the securities industry.

Investment Company Act of 1940.
A U.S. federal law that regulates the conduct of investment companies.

investment company.
A company that issues securities and engages primarily in investing and trading securities.

Investment Advisor's Act of 1940.
A U.S. federal law that regulates the conduct of investment advisors.

investment advisor.
A company or person that is compensated for providing advice to investors about the value of securities and the potential advantages and disadvantages of buying and selling securities.

National Association of Securities Dealers (NASD). A nonprofit organization of securities dealers that regulates the market conduct of member companies and their representatives; individuals and companies that are subject to SEC regulation are subject to NASD regulation.

representatives. All individuals and companies that are subject to SEC regulation also are subject to oversight by the NASD.

SEC and NASD authority over variable annuities is similar to the states' authority over fixed annuities and covers four primary operational and marketing activities: (1) company and producer registration, (2) product registration, (3) advertising and disclosure, and (4) suitability.

Company and Producer Registration

Under federal law, all investment companies must register with the SEC. Insurance companies that engage primarily in the business of insurance are not considered investment companies; however, the separate accounts that support variable annuities are classified as investment companies and must be registered with the SEC.

NASD registration also is required for investment advisors, producers who sell variable insurance and annuity products, and certain sales support and customer service personnel—such as call center representatives and new business and transaction processors—who facilitate the deposit, transfer, or withdrawal of funds from a variable annuity or other federally regulated securities product. As part of the registration process, individuals must disclose certain background information, comply with all NASD licensing requirements and codes of conduct, and take special examinations provided by the NASD. Producers who sell variable annuities also must be licensed as insurance producers at the state level.

registered representative. An investment advisor, a producer, or an insurance company employee who satisfies NASD registration requirements.

principal. An officer and/or manager of an NASD member company who is involved in the day-to-day operation of a securities business, has qualified as a registered representative, and has passed additional examinations.

Model Variable Annuity Regulation. A model regulation developed by the NAIC that establishes requirements for insurers that issue variable annuities and for variable annuity products.

An investment advisor, a producer, or an insurance company employee who satisfies NASD registration requirements is known as a ***registered representative.*** An officer and/or manager of an NASD member company who is involved in the day-to-day operation of a securities business, has qualified as a registered representative, and has passed additional examinations is classified as a ***principal.*** Figure 8.4 describes the types of registration categories that most often are required for registered representatives and principals.

Product Registration

In our discussion of U.S. state regulation, we noted that before an insurance company can offer a variable annuity product for sale in a state, it must submit the contract form to that state's insurance department for approval. As a result, variable contract forms must satisfy state-mandated requirements and include specific provisions designed to ensure that contract owners are treated fairly. State laws describing the provisions that must be included in variable annuity contracts generally are based on the NAIC ***Model Variable Annuity Regulation***, which establishes requirements for insurers that issue variable annuities and for variable annuity products.

FIGURE 8.4

NASD Registration Categories

Registration	Title	Description
Series 6	Investment Company/Variable Contract Representative	Required to sell mutual funds and variable annuities. May be required for sales support and customer service staff.
Series 26	Investment Company/Variable Contract Principal	Required to supervise registered representatives selling mutual funds and variable annuities.
Series 7	General Securities Representative	Required to sell bonds and stocks. Can be used in place of Series 6 to sell mutual funds and variable annuities. May be required for sales support and customer service staff.
Series 24	General Securities Principal	Required to supervise registered representatives selling bonds and stocks. Can be used in place of Series 26 to supervise registered representatives selling mutual funds and variable annuities.
Series 63	Uniform Securities Representative	Required to sell securities products, with emphasis on regulations and compliance.

In addition, investment companies must register all securities they intend to offer with the SEC. The SEC reviews registration statements to determine whether the information provided by the issuing company is complete and accurate. Although insurers must submit a registration statement to the SEC before a variable annuity can be offered, SEC acceptance of an insurer's registration statement does not indicate that the SEC approves of or acknowledges the merits of the product.

Advertising and Disclosure Requirements

Earlier in this chapter, we described state regulations governing annuity advertisements and sales materials that apply to both fixed and variable annuities. The SEC and NASD also impose requirements on advertisements and sales materials used to promote securities products, including variable annuities. For example, federal regulations require that advertisements for variable annuities must

- Include the name of the registered representative who is selling the annuity

- Not include any promises of specific investment results, including predictions and projections

- Not imply that any state or federal regulatory body has approved of or endorsed the product or the registered representative selling the product

These federal requirements generally represent the minimum standards that companies must satisfy. If state advertising laws include more stringent standards, those standards also must be met.

The SEC also requires insurers to disclose pertinent information about the investment features of variable annuity products. For example, insurers must provide prospective buyers with a **prospectus**, which is a written document describing specific aspects of the security being offered for sale. The prospectus must contain information explaining the investment philosophy and objectives of the separate account, any fund expenses and fees, and past performance of subaccounts within the separate account. Neither the prospectus nor any contract illustration used in the sales process can project future subaccount values based on past investment experience. However, the use of hypothetical assumed rates of return to illustrate possible subaccount values is allowed.

In addition, insurers must provide variable annuity contract owners with semi-annual and annual reports of separate account activity. These reports must detail (1) fund expenses and fees for the period covered, (2) investment performance and account values for all subaccounts in which the contract owner has funds invested, and (3) any changes in a subaccount's investment strategy or major holdings.

Suitability Requirements

As we mentioned earlier in this chapter, state regulations attempt to ensure that customers purchasing fixed annuities are making a suitable purchase. NASD rules require insurers to follow similar suitability assessment procedures when selling variable annuities. Registered representatives who sell variable annuities must have reasonable grounds for believing each recommendation they make to a customer is suitable based on the customer's financial situation and objectives. Thus, before making any product recommendations, a representative must obtain a basic understanding of the customer's current and future financial needs.

---

prospectus.
A written document describing specific aspects of a security being offered for sale.

FIGURE 8.5

Assessing the Suitability of Variable Annuities

Before recommending the purchase of a variable annuity product, a registered representative should consider the following issues:

- **The customer's investment objectives.** Is the customer interested in short-term earnings or long-term accumulation of funds? How much financial protection does the customer need? How important is liquidity to the customer?

- **The customer's current financial situation.** What is the customer's current income? What is the customer's tax status? What investment products does the customer own? How is the customer currently setting aside funds for the future? Does the customer currently own life insurance? Is the customer willing and/or able to invest a specified amount each year?

- **The customer's future financial needs.** Does the customer have a need for financial protection beyond that provided by life insurance? Does the customer need a way to provide retirement income?

- **The customer's tolerance for risk.** Does the customer understand the risk-return trade-off? How much security does the customer expect from an investment?

- **The customer's understanding of investments.** What is the customer's investment experience? Does the customer understand how variable annuities work? Does the customer fully understand how fees are assessed and how they affect premium payments? Can the customer monitor the performance of the separate account?

- **The customer's personal characteristics.** What is the customer's age? What is the customer's family situation? What is the customer's employment status?

NASD rules also require the representative to complete a suitability statement at the time of the sale. Information included in this statement is intended to enable the registered representative to provide sound and informed financial advice to the buyer regarding the variable annuity. Figure 8.5 lists some of the suitability issues and questions a registered representative should consider when recommending a variable annuity product to a customer.

Canadian Provincial Regulation

In Canada, both the federal government and provincial governments develop and enforce legislation to regulate insurance and annuity sales and insurance company operations. Provincial governments and the federal government share the authority to regulate the financial soundness of insurance companies. Provincial governments alone are responsible for regulating the market conduct of companies operating within their borders.

Each province has established an administrative agency to enforce the province's insurance laws and regulations. Typically, this agency is known as the **Office of the Superintendent of Insurance** and operates under the direction of a Superintendent of Insurance. The various provincial superintendents of insurance have voluntarily formed a collective body known as the **Canadian Council of Insurance Regulators (CCIR)** to discuss insurance issues and recommend uniform insurance legislation to the provinces. The CCIR is similar to the NAIC. Because most provinces have enacted laws based on model legislation recommended by the CCIR, provincial regulation of life insurance and annuity contracts is fairly uniform.

Office of the Superintendent of Insurance.
A Canadian provincial agency that operates under the direction of a Superintendent of Insurance to enforce the province's insurance laws and regulations.

Canadian Council of Insurance Regulators (CCIR).
An organization that consists of provincial superintendents of insurance that discusses insurance issues and recommends uniform insurance legislation to the provinces; similar to the NAIC in the United States.

Solvency Regulation

In Canada, an insurance company can be incorporated under the authority of one of the provincial governments or the federal government. To avoid duplication of solvency regulations, each province's Office of the Superintendent of Insurance supervises companies that were incorporated by the province and examines those companies periodically to ensure that they are able to meet their financial obligations. The provinces rely on the federal government to supervise federally incorporated companies.

Market Conduct Regulation

Provincial market conduct regulation, like state market conduct regulation in the United States, is designed to protect contract owners and to ensure that insurance companies conduct business fairly and ethically. The two primary areas of market conduct regulation in Canada are licensing and contract approval.

Licensing Requirements

Companies that wish to operate an insurance business in Canada must obtain a license from each province in which they intend to offer insurance and annuity products. Producers also must obtain the appropriate licenses from each province in which they intend to sell life insurance and annuity products. Licensing requirements and standards of conduct for Canadian insurance companies and insurance producers are similar to those governing U.S. companies and producers.

Contract Approval

Like state laws in the United States, Canadian provincial laws govern the contract forms that are used within each province. Unlike state laws, however, Canadian provincial regulations do not require that contract forms for all new and modified products be filed before they are issued. Instead, insurers are required to file contract forms in only two situations: (1) as a condition of obtaining a license to conduct an insurance business within the province and (2) before marketing a variable life insurance or annuity contract in the province. In spite of this flexibility, most insurers regularly file all their contract forms with the provincial superintendent of insurance.

Provincial regulations also require annuity contracts issued in the province to include certain provisions. These required provisions are similar to the provisions required by state regulators in the United States.

Canadian Federal Regulation

The **Insurance Companies Act** is the primary federal law that governs insurance companies operating in Canada. The Act includes a number of provisions that address the need for insurance companies to be financially stable and capable of paying debts and disbursing life insurance benefits and annuity proceeds when they come due. The Act applies to all (1) federally incorporated insurers, (2) foreign insurers, and (3) provincially incorporated insurers that conduct business outside their province of incorporation. Although companies have the option of incorporating through either the provincial governments or the federal government, most insurers are federally incorporated.

The **Office of the Superintendent of Financial Institutions (OSFI)**, a federal agency under the direction of the Superintendent of Financial Institutions, is responsible for monitoring the operations of all financial institutions in Canada, including life insurance companies, other than those incorporated in Quebec. The Inspector General of Financial Institutions monitors the operations of insurance companies incorporated in Quebec.

Every insurance company that is subject to federal regulation must prepare an Annual Return each year and file it with the appropriate regulatory agency. The **Annual Return** is a financial report that contains detailed accounting and statistical data about the insurer—similar to the data provided on the Annual Statement filed by insurers in the United States. The Insurance Companies Act also requires each

Insurance Companies Act.
The primary Canadian federal law that governs insurance companies operating in Canada.

Office of the Superintendent of Financial Institutions (OSFI).
A Canadian federal agency under the direction of the Superintendent of Financial Institutions that is responsible for monitoring the operations of all financial institutions in Canada.

Annual Return.
A document Canadian insurers must file each year that includes detailed accounting and statistical data about the insurer; similar to the Annual Statement required for insurers in the United States.

federally regulated insurer to undergo a periodic examination of its financial condition. Examinations are required at least every three years, but more frequent examinations can be conducted if necessary.

Key Terms

McCarran-Ferguson Act

state insurance department

National Association of Insurance Commissioners (NAIC)

model law

solvency

Annual Statement

guaranty association

certificate of authority

insurance producer

Producer Licensing Model Act

readability requirements

Advertisements of Life Insurance and Annuities Model Regulation

Life Insurance Illustrations Model Regulation

Annuity Disclosure Model Regulation

Buyer's Guide to Fixed Deferred Annuities

disclosure document

suitability requirement

replacement

Replacement of Life Insurance and Annuities Model Regulation

Securities Act of 1933

Securities Exchange Act of 1934

Investment Company Act of 1940

investment company

Investment Advisors Act of 1940

investment advisor

National Association of Securities Dealers (NASD)

registered representative

principal

Model Variable Annuity Regulation

prospectus

Office of the Superintendent of Insurance

Canadian Council of Insurance Regulators (CCIR)

Insurance Companies Act

Office of the Superintendent of Financial Institutions (OSFI)

Annual Return

Endnote

1. A.M. Best, "New SEC Rules Will Challenge Insurers in 2003," *Best's News* via NewsEdge Corporation, http://www.newsedge.com (4 March 2003).

2. Information adapted from National Association of Insurance Commissioners, *Life Insurance and Annuities Replacement Model Regulation*, Appendix A.

Annuity Principles and Products

Marketing and Distributing Annuities

After studying this chapter, you should be able to

- Define *marketing* and identify the elements of the marketing mix

- Describe the methods insurance companies use to identify their actual and potential customers

- Discuss the five core stages of the product development process

- Describe the methods insurance companies use to promote annuity products

- Explain what a distribution system is and discuss the different types of distribution systems insurers use to sell annuity products

OUTLINE

Market Selection

Product Development
Product Planning
Comprehensive Business Analysis
Product Technical Design
Product Implementation
Sales Monitoring and Product Review

Financial Design

Product Promotion
Personal Selling
Advertising
Sales Promotion and Marketing Materials
Publicity

Product Distribution
Personal Selling Distribution Systems
Financial Institutions Distribution Systems
Direct Response Distribution Systems

Marketing is the process of developing, pricing, promoting, and distributing ideas, goods, or services to create exchanges that satisfy the needs of both buyers and sellers. An *exchange* occurs when one party—a buyer—gives something of value to another party—a seller—and receives something of value in return.

Chapter 9 — Marketing and Distributing Annuities

In this chapter, we describe the activities involved in marketing annuities.

Because an insurance company cannot provide a product that meets customers' needs without first knowing who the customers are and what they need, we begin our discussion with an overview of the steps insurers take to define their market. We then describe the major factors a company considers when determining how it can best meet customer needs. These factors, which are known as the **marketing mix**, or the "Four Ps" of marketing, include

- *Product*—a good, service, or idea that a company offers to customers in order to satisfy their needs.
- *Price*—the item of value (usually an amount of money) that a customer gives to a company in exchange for a product.
- *Promotion*—the methods a company uses to communicate with customers and influence them to buy a product.
- *Distribution*—the methods a company uses to make products available for customers to buy. (Packaged goods companies refer to this element as "place.")

Market Selection

Ideally, before companies develop products and market them to potential customers, they conduct extensive research to determine the size and characteristics of the market. A **market** is a group of people who, either as individuals or as members of organizations, are the actual or potential buyers of a product.

Because a company's marketing efforts generally are more effective when they are focused on customers with similar needs than they are when directed toward customers whose needs are not as closely aligned, most companies divide the total market into smaller groups with similar characteristics and product needs. The process that companies use to divide large, heterogeneous markets into smaller, more homogeneous submarkets is known as **market segmentation**. Companies usually base market segmentation on characteristics such as age, gender, geographic location, education, occupation, income, and spending patterns. Each submarket, or group of customers with similar needs and preferences, identified through market segmentation is referred to as a **market segment**.

---

marketing.
The process of developing, pricing, promoting, and distributing ideas, goods, or services to create exchanges that satisfy the needs of both buyers and sellers.

exchange.
A transaction that occurs when one party—a buyer—gives something of value to another party—a seller—and receives something of value in return.

marketing mix.
The factors that a company considers when determining how it can best meet customer needs; includes product, price, promotion, and distribution.

product.
A good, service, or idea that a company offers to customers in order to satisfy their needs.

price.
The item of value (usually an amount of money) that a customer gives to a company in exchange for a product.

promotion.
The methods a company uses to communicate with customers and influence them to buy a product.

distribution.
The methods a company uses to make products available for customers to buy.

market.
A group of people who, either as individuals or as members of organizations, are the actual or potential buyers of a product.

market segmentation.
The process companies use to divide large, heterogeneous markets into smaller, more homogeneous submarkets.

market segment.
A submarket, or group of customers with similar needs and preferences, that is identified through market segmentation.

target marketing.
The process of evaluating various market segments and then selecting one or more of those segments to be the focus of a company's marketing activities.

target market.
A clearly defined market segment on which a company focuses its marketing activities.

Market segmentation often produces more segments than a company can effectively serve. Therefore, companies need to evaluate each segment in terms of its size, location, accessibility, and sales potential, and then select the market or markets that align best with company goals and objectives. To accomplish this task, companies engage in ***target marketing***, which is the process of evaluating various market segments and then selecting one or more of those segments to be the focus of the company's marketing activities. Each of the segments a company selects is called a ***target market***. Focusing on clearly defined target markets helps companies develop and market products and services that will be attractive to potential customers. Insight 9.1 illustrates how an insurance company might use market research, market segmentation, and target marketing to identify potential annuity customers.

Having identified its potential customers, a company can then begin the process of developing, pricing, promoting, and distributing products that satisfy customers' needs.

Product Development

For an insurance company, developing a product typically requires the expertise of staff from many functional areas, including marketing, sales, actuarial, investments, information systems, customer service, law, and accounting. Personnel from each of these areas must work together to ensure that the company's products (1) satisfy customer needs, (2) meet company objectives, (3) comply with applicable state and federal regulations, and (4) can be supported by the company's human, financial, and technological resources.

Although the product development process varies from company to company, most companies perform a core set of planning, analysis, design, implementation, and review activities, as shown in Figure 9.1. Our discussion in this section will cover each of these stages.

Product Planning

For most companies, product planning begins with an idea. The idea could be for a new product or line of products that the company has never offered, a new product to add to an existing product line, or a modification of an existing product or group of products. The idea may come from a special committee established by the company to generate new product ideas or it may come from an employee, a consumer group, members of the sales force, or some other source inside or outside the company.

Many insurance companies establish product development teams composed of staff from various departments who meet on a regular basis to review the insurer's overall product development strategy and to

INSIGHT 9.1

Identifying Annuity Customers

Before developing a new line of annuities, the Birchmore Insurance Company engaged in a series of marketing activities designed to identify potential customers for the company's proposed new products.

Market Research

As a first step, Birchmore conducted market research to determine the number, location, and characteristics of its potential and actual customers. This research indicated that the total market for annuity products includes men and women age 21 or older with annual incomes of $30,000 or more.

Market Segmentation

Because the market identified by its research was so diverse, Birchmore segmented the total market into smaller groups with similar characteristics and product needs. This process produced several possible market segments.

Target Marketing

Birchmore evaluated each of the identified segments in terms of its size, accessibility, and sales potential and selected the following segments as its target markets:

- Segment A: Affluent men and women age 40–51 with total household assets of $100,000 or more. Research showed that people in this segment are concerned with preserving wealth and protecting assets from excessive taxation. In addition, people in this group generally are willing to accept risk and are interested in financial products that offer long-term growth potential. Birchmore targeted this segment for its variable annuity products.

- Segment B: Married women age 45–54 with annual incomes of $75,000 or less. Research indicated that people in this segment are focused on saving for retirement and want a product that will provide a steady source of retirement income. They are not comfortable with risk and tend to be interested in financial products that offer investment guarantees. Birchmore targeted this segment for its fixed annuity products.

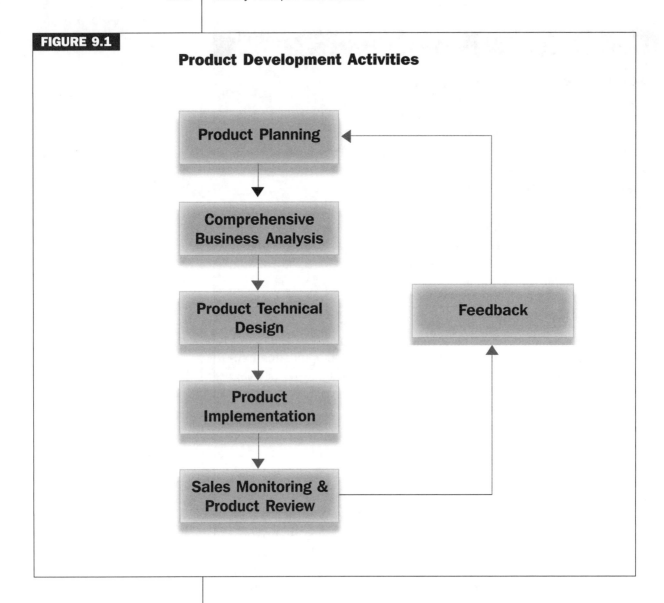

FIGURE 9.1 Product Development Activities

idea generation.
The process of searching for new product ideas that are consistent with overall company objectives and customer needs.

screening.
The process of quickly evaluating proposed product ideas to determine which ones merit further investigation and development.

generate and screen ideas for new or enhanced products. ***Idea generation*** involves searching for new product ideas that are consistent with overall company objectives and customer needs. As they generate ideas, development team members focus on creativity and utility rather than evaluation of the practical aspects of proposed products. During ***screening,*** the product development team quickly evaluates proposed product ideas to determine which ones merit further investigation and development. The team eliminates ideas that are not consistent with the insurer's current or future marketing plans or that cannot be supported by the insurer's current resources. The team then submits remaining ideas for a comprehensive business analysis.

Comprehensive Business Analysis

A *comprehensive business analysis* is a preliminary review of market conditions and other factors that affect the feasibility of new product ideas. During this stage of the product development process, the product development team

- Conducts a *market analysis*, which is a study of all the environmental factors that might affect sales of the product. A typical market analysis for a new annuity product includes an examination of the company's target markets, customers' needs, competitors' activities, current distribution systems, and field sales force requirements.

- Creates *product design objectives,* which specify—in broad terms—a product's basic features and benefits and the manner in which the benefits will be provided. For an annuity, design objectives include basic product characteristics such as contract charges and fees, interest guarantees and interest crediting frequency, investment options, surrender provisions, death benefits, living benefits, and annuity payout provisions.

- Evaluates the company's operational and technical resources to determine whether the company can produce, market, and support the proposed product. The team also evaluates the potential impact of the new product on the company's existing products.

- Develops a *marketing plan,* which is a document that specifies the company's overall marketing objectives for the product, the strategies needed to achieve those objectives, and the specific sales goals for the product.

- Estimates the product's financial requirements, sales, revenues, costs, and profits. These preliminary estimates are revised as more information becomes available.

All of the data gathered during the comprehensive business analysis is combined into a product proposal that the product development team submits to management. Company executives evaluate the proposal and determine whether to accept it, reject it, or send it back to the product development team for further analysis.

Product Technical Design

After the executives at an insurance company approve a product proposal, the product moves on to the technical design stage. During this stage, the team reviews and refines the product design objectives described in the proposal. Because of the varied and complex tasks involved in designing a new annuity product or enhancement, virtually every functional area of an insurance company can become involved at

---

comprehensive business analysis. A preliminary review of market conditions and other factors designed to determine the feasibility of any product ideas that appear to meet customer needs and company objectives.

market analysis. A study of all the environmental factors that might affect sales of a proposed product.

product design objectives. A description of a proposed product's basic features and benefits and the manner in which the benefits will be provided.

marketing plan. A document that specifies the company's overall marketing objectives for a product, the strategies needed to achieve those objectives, and the specific sales goals for the product.

FIGURE 9.2

Product Technical Design Activities

Marketing and sales personnel review the product to determine its potential appeal to consumers and the ease with which the company can promote, distribute, and sell the product.

Actuaries scrutinize the product's rate structure and other product features to ensure that it is financially sound.

Representatives from the investment area determine what types of investments are necessary to make the product successful.

The accounting department determines what, if any, special accounting procedures must be developed to manage accounts for the product.

The information systems department identifies the type of computer systems and technological support the company needs to administer the product.

The company's lawyers or compliance department staff review product specifications to ensure that they comply with all applicable state and federal regulations.

Customer service and administrative staff determine what resources and procedures are needed to support the product.

---

this stage. Figure 9.2 describes some of the typical activities performed during the technical design stage for a new product or product enhancement.

At the end of the technical design stage, the company finalizes the product's features, benefits, provisions, and financial design and drafts contract forms.

Product Implementation

During product implementation, a company performs all of the activities necessary to introduce and market a new product. These activities are shown in Figure 9.3.

FIGURE 9.3

Product Implementation Activities

Insurance companies perform the following activities during product implementation for an annuity product:

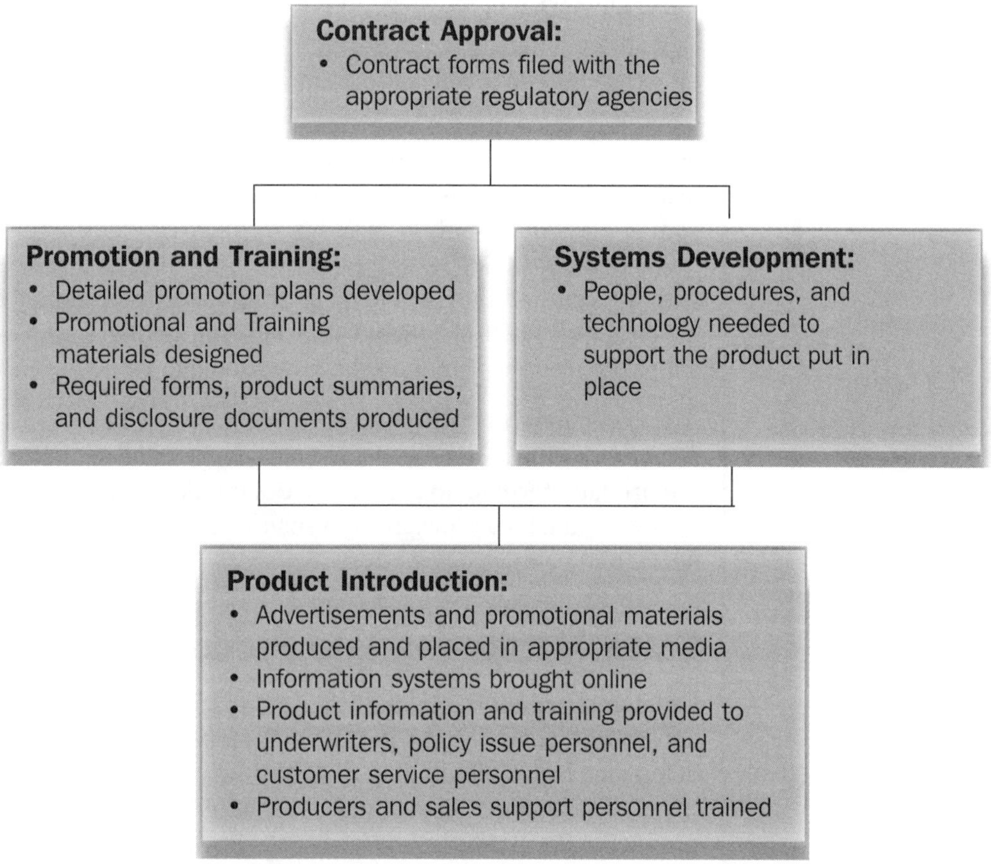

Contract Approval:
- Contract forms filed with the appropriate regulatory agencies

Promotion and Training:
- Detailed promotion plans developed
- Promotional and Training materials designed
- Required forms, product summaries, and disclosure documents produced

Systems Development:
- People, procedures, and technology needed to support the product put in place

Product Introduction:
- Advertisements and promotional materials produced and placed in appropriate media
- Information systems brought online
- Product information and training provided to underwriters, policy issue personnel, and customer service personnel
- Producers and sales support personnel trained

The implementation of a new annuity product generally begins when the company files contract forms with the appropriate state, provincial, and federal regulatory agencies to obtain permission to market the product. Reviewers may approve the form as submitted, or they may recommend changes to ensure that the contract complies with regulatory requirements.

The company's marketing department (1) develops detailed plans to promote the product, (2) designs promotional and training materials for the company's sales and administrative personnel, and (3) produces paper and electronic versions of all required forms, product summaries, and disclosure documents. At the same time, employees throughout the company begin to put into place the people, procedures, and technology needed to support the product. The amount of time spent on these activities and the number of employees involved depend on the product's technical design and any changes that might result from the contract approval process. Development of product information is often the critical path in any new product launch.

The final step in product implementation is introduction of the product to the market. The company focus during this step is to ensure that all necessary marketing and product support elements are in place. For example, the marketing department places advertisements and other promotional materials in the appropriate media. Technical support personnel bring information systems on line. Product managers provide underwriters, policy issue personnel, and customer service personnel with information they will need to administer the product. Wholesalers educate and train producers and internal trainers educate and train sales support personnel on the new product.

Although product introduction represents the culmination of a company's efforts to create a new product, it does not signal the end of the product development process. Companies must continuously evaluate the product's performance to ensure that it actually meets customers' needs and company objectives.

Sales Monitoring and Product Review

Following product introduction, companies review sales results to determine whether product development and budget objectives are being met. Sales monitoring and product review helps companies identify potential weaknesses and determine what, if any, changes in the product or its marketing activities are needed. For example, a company that discovers a weakness in a product's performance may add new features, riders, or investment options as a way to keep the product competitive. Because most insurers use sales and marketing data to generate ideas for new products or product enhancements, information gathered during ongoing sales monitoring and product review also provides valuable feedback to the product development process. Such feedback improves the likelihood that the company will produce successful products in the future.

Financial Design

pricing.
The process of determining the amount to charge a customer for a product.

For most consumer products, **pricing** is the process of determining the amount to charge a customer for a product. For financial services products, this process is referred to as financial design. The elements of financial design vary according to the type of product. For example, the key element in the financial design of life insurance products is the premium. The key element in the financial design of annuity products is typically the interest rate.

Most of a company's financial design decisions are made during the technical design stage. After a product is launched, activities focus on monitoring performance and setting interest crediting rates.

Although the actual process insurers use to determine the financial design of annuity products is extremely complex—and therefore beyond the scope of this text—the ultimate goal of a new annuity product's financial design is to allow the product to generate enough revenue to (1) cover the costs of producing, marketing, and administering the product and (2) provide the company with a reasonable profit. From a marketing perspective, the financial design for annuity products depends on the following factors:

- **Company objectives.** Is the product's financial design intended to keep pace with or beat the competition? Is it intended to generate profits quickly, or to build customer interest and loyalty?

- **Product costs.** What costs has the company incurred in developing the product? What are its ongoing marketing, administrative, and distribution costs?

- **Distribution requirements.** What distribution channels will be used to market the product? Do career agents receive compensation based on established contracts? What is required to gain acceptance of the product by broker-dealers?

- **Market demand.** How many potential customers are in the market? Do they consider the product important? Necessary? How is demand affected by the product's financial design?

- **Customers' purchasing power.** How much income do customers have? How much are they willing to pay for the product?

- **Investment options.** How much income is each investment option intended to produce relative to client returns?

- **Competition.** How many similar products are already on the market? Is the product's proposed financial design likely to create a reaction among competitors?

- **Regulatory requirements.** Does the proposed financial design meet state and federal guidelines? Is the product's financial design subject to legal or regulatory restrictions?

- **Other marketing mix variables.** How large a promotion budget will be required to launch the product? Can the product be distributed through existing distribution systems? Will the product's financial design affect the sales of other company products?

Product Promotion

Before any sales can take place, companies must generate customer interest in and demand for a product. Most companies accomplish this goal through one of the following forms of promotion: personal selling, advertising, sales promotion, and publicity.

Personal Selling

personal selling.
A form of promotion in which salespeople present product information during face-to-face meetings between a sales person and one or more prospective customers.

Personal selling is a form of promotion in which salespeople present product information directly to prospective customers. Usually, personal selling takes place during face-to-face meetings between a sales person and one or more customers. However, it can be conducted via telephone, e-mail, or other remote contacts as well. Figure 9.4 lists the typical elements of a personal sales presentation. Keep in mind, however, that the process may require more than one contact with a prospective buyer to generate a sale.

Personal selling is a primary form of promotion for insurers because it is one of the best means of communicating information about complex financial products such as annuities. However, personal selling can be expensive, and insurers may choose not to use it when they want to reach large numbers of potential customers.

Advertising

advertising.
A form of nonpersonal promotion in which information about a company or its products and services is generated by an identified sponsor and transmitted, for a fee, by the media.

Advertising is a form of nonpersonal promotion in which information about a company or its products and services is generated by an identified sponsor and transmitted, for a fee, by the media. Companies can advertise their products through the mass media—television, radio, direct mail, newspapers, and magazines—or outdoor media—billboards, signs, and posters. The Internet also is a prime location for product advertising. Advertising is more economical than personal selling for reaching large numbers of potential customers because it allows the insurer to reach customers at a much lower cost per person. However, insurers must choose advertising media carefully to ensure that advertisements appear in media that will be seen by customers in the insurer's target markets.

Sales Promotion and Marketing Materials

sales promotion.
A form of promotion designed to encourage salespeople to sell a product or customers to buy a product.

Sales promotion is a form of promotion designed to encourage salespeople to sell a product or customers to buy a product. Most sales promotion efforts are short-term and intended to spur sales during a defined period. They are especially effective in connection with the release of new or revised products.

FIGURE 9.4

Personal Sales Presentation for an Annuity

1 — Identify a prospect—a potential buyer for an annuity product.

2 — Contact the prospect and gather personal and financial information.

3 — Complete an initial needs analysis—an assessment of the prospect's financial needs—based on the data supplied by the prospect.

4 — Educate the prospect about the differences between fixed annuity contracts and variable annuity contracts. Begin educating the prospect on the concepts of asset allocation, dollar cost averaging, and investment strategies. If a variable annuity is being considered, provide the prospect with a prospectus and any other NASD required supporting materials.

5 — Propose an annuity product or products that will meet the prospect's identified financial needs. Explain significant product features, benefits, risks, and expenses.

6 — Implement the proposal with a completed and signed application for the proposed annuity product

---

Insurers direct most of their sales promotion efforts toward producers. Some insurers sponsor sales contests offering cash prizes or merchandise to producers who sell its products. Other insurers offer attendance at conferences or sales meetings. In some cases, the specific types of sales promotion an insurer uses are governed by state or federal regulation. For example, New York limits the type and amount of incentives offered to producers. The NASD and SEC also limit the use of incentives for sales of variable products.

Although sales promotions directed toward customers are common among other types of companies, insurers generally do not offer monetary incentives to customers. Instead, they frequently use a form of promotion known as specialty advertising. **Specialty advertising**

specialty advertising. A form of promotion that consists of articles imprinted with a company name or logo, address, phone number, and sometimes a sales message promoting a company, its producers, or its products.

consists of articles imprinted with a company name or logo, address, phone number, and sometimes a sales message promoting a company, its producers, or its products. These imprinted articles typically include items such as calendars, coffee mugs, and pens. Producers also use specialty advertising as a means of promoting products to customers. Unlike other forms of sales promotion, specialty advertising generally is used to build product awareness rather than to generate immediate sales.

In addition to sales promotion, insurers use marketing materials, such as brochures, sales illustrations, and informative guides, to help promote interest in annuity products, educate consumers, and encourage sales. Most marketing materials focus on the appropriate uses of annuities, how annuities work, and the specific features contained in various types of annuity products. Figure 9.5 lists some of the annuity uses and product features that insurers include in sales promotions and marketing materials.

Publicity

publicity.
A form of promotion in which information about a company or its products and services is transmitted in a news format by the mass media.

Publicity is a form of promotion in which information about a company or its products and services is transmitted in a news format by the mass media. Publicity information can appear in the format of a news conference, a public service announcement on television or radio, or a magazine or newspaper article. The message itself can be positive or negative. Although companies provide publicity information to the media—usually in the form of news releases—they do not pay the media to present the information.

Because an insurer does not pay the media to deliver information, and therefore incurs no direct promotion costs, publicity is one of the most economical means of getting company and product information to customers and distributors. In addition, because information is presented in a news format, customers often consider publicity more credible than company-sponsored, paid advertisements. However, the insurer has no control over how much, if any, information is presented or the way in which information is presented. Figure 9.6 summarizes the strengths and weaknesses of each of the promotional tools described in this section.

Product Distribution

distribution system.
A network of companies, agencies, and people that performs all the marketing activities needed to deliver products to customers. Also known as a distribution channel.

A *distribution system* is a network of companies, agencies, and people that perform all the marketing activities needed to deliver products to customers. The type of distribution system a company uses for its products depends on the characteristics of the

FIGURE 9.5
Annuity Uses and Product Features

Annuity Uses

Retirement savings
— Individual annuities
— Group annuities

Education savings

Managing lump-sum cash distributions from
— Pensions
— Insurance settlements
— Gifts (charitable gifting)

Estate planning
— Life insurance funded by annuity payout

Product Features

Tax-deferred wealth accumulation (in nonqualified markets)

Variety of annuity payout options

Potential for a guaranteed lifetime income on either a fixed or variable payment plan basis

Death benefit guarantees

Fixed annuity interest rate guarantees

Variable annuity investment options

Guaranteed interest funds within variable annuities

- **Customers in the target market**, including their number, type, location, preferred ways of purchasing the products offered, and product needs

- **Product the company intends to market,** including its complexity and level of familiarity among potential customers

- **Marketing environment in which the company operates**, including current and projected economic conditions, technological advances, competitive forces, legal rulings, and social conditions

- **Company**, including its human, technological, and financial resources; its mission, culture, goals, objectives, and marketing philosophy; and its existing distribution channels

- **Proposed distribution system**, including the degree of control it offers and its start-up and maintenance costs

Distribution systems vary widely from company to company, and providing a description that applies in all situations is difficult. However,

FIGURE 9.6

Strengths and Weaknesses of Promotional Tools

Promotional Tool	Strengths	Weaknesses
Personal Selling	Interactive Message can be tailored to specific buyer needs Can deliver complex messages Allows immediate response to customer objections Effective for products that are likely to be "sold" rather than "bought"	High cost Risk of losing account if producer leaves company Limited to one-to-one or one-to-few interactions
Advertising	Economical for reaching large audiences Company maintains control over message	Generally not effective in reaching narrowly targeted audiences Cannot deliver complex messages
Sales Promotion and Marketing Materials	Effective in educating customers and producers, generating interest, and encouraging product trial and sales Can produce measurable short-term results Company maintains control over message	Little impact on long-term sales or profitability Tends to encourage product-oriented rather than needs-oriented marketing
Publicity	Fast Economical High degree of credibility	Company has no control over exposure or message Company is vulnerable to negative coverage

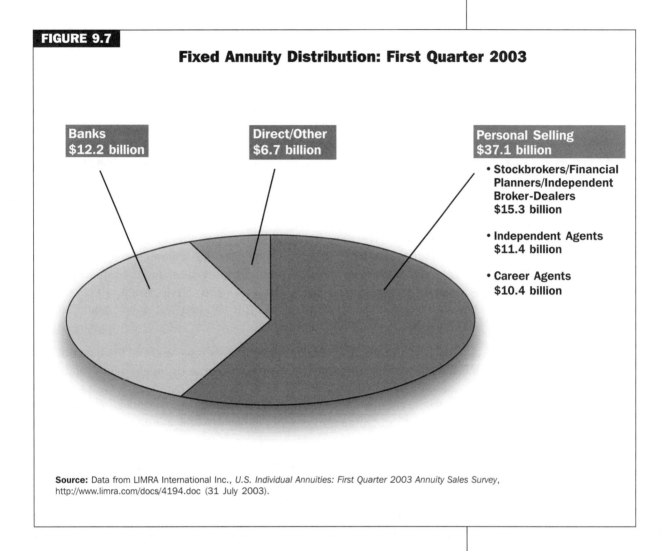

distribution systems generally fall into one of the following three categories: (1) personal selling distribution systems, (2) financial institutions distribution systems, and (3) direct response distribution systems. Figure 9.7 shows fixed annuity sales for the first quarter of 2003, broken down by distribution system.

Personal Selling Distribution Systems

A *personal selling distribution system* is a distribution system in which commissioned or salaried salespeople sell products through oral and written presentations made to prospective customers. Because annuities are complex financial products, insurance companies traditionally have relied on personal selling by salespeople who explain the appropriate uses, provisions, and tax advantages of annuities to prospects.

personal selling distribution system.
A distribution system in which commissioned or salaried salespeople sell products through oral and written presentations made to prospective customers.

agency contract.
An agreement between a principal and an agent that defines the agent's role and responsibilities, describes the agent's compensation, and specifically determines the agent's right to act for the principal.

agent.
A salesperson or producer who is authorized to act on behalf of an insurance company.

principal.
An insurance company that grants authority to agents or producers to act on the company's behalf.

agency-building system.
A personal selling distribution system in which an insurance company recruits and trains producers and provides them with financial support and office facilities.

nonagency-building system.
A personal selling distribution system in which an insurance company recruits producers who require little training, are financially self-supporting, and work out of independent offices.

career agent.
An insurance producer who is under contract to at least one insurance company.

exclusive agent.
A career agent who is under contract to only one insurance company and is not permitted to sell the products of other insurers.

To justify the time and expense necessary to educate and train their sales force, insurers generally require salespeople to enter into an agency contract. An ***agency contract*** is an agreement between a principal and an agent that defines the agent's role and responsibilities, describes the agent's compensation, and specifically determines the agent's right to act for the principal. Under the terms of an agency contract, the salesperson or producer who is authorized to act on behalf of the insurer is the ***agent*** and the insurer who grants authority to the agent is the ***principal***.

Insurers use a wide variety of personal selling distribution systems for annuity products. In some of these systems, the insurance company recruits and trains producers and provides them with financial support and office facilities. This type of distribution system is referred to as an ***agency-building system.*** Agency-building distribution systems provide the insurer with maximum control over the activities of producers. However, agency-building systems typically are the most expensive for insurers to establish and maintain.

In other personal selling distribution systems, most of the costs of setting up and maintaining the system are borne by independent producers or agencies. A system in which the insurance company recruits producers who require little training, are financially self-supporting, and work out of independent offices is referred to as a ***nonagency-building system.***

Most of the producers who sell insurance products are career agents. A ***career agent*** is a producer who is under contract to at least one insurance company. An ***exclusive agent*** is a career agent who is under contract to only one insurance company and is not permitted to sell the products of other insurers. An ***agent-broker*** is a career agent who holds an agency contract with one insurance company but who can place business with companies other than the primary company. Most career agents are considered to be independent contractors, rather than employees of an insurance company.

Typically, compensation for agents is provided in the form of commissions. A ***commission*** is a type of payment for services that is based on a specified percentage of an agent's sales. Commissions for an insurance agent generally are based on a percentage of the premiums paid on each contract the agent sells. For variable annuities, commissions also can be linked to contract assets.

Figure 9.8 shows the personal selling distribution systems used most often for annuity products. We will describe each of these systems briefly in the following sections.

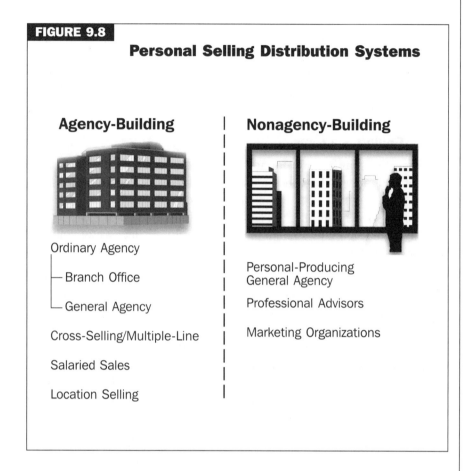

Ordinary Agency Systems

An ***ordinary agency system*** is an agency-building distribution system that uses full-time or part-time career agents to sell and service insurance products, including annuities. The ordinary agency system can be divided into two forms: the branch office system and the general agency system.

Under the ***branch office system***, an insurance company establishes and maintains a series of field sales offices, each headed by a ***branch manager*** who recruits, selects, and trains career agents and acts as the sales manager for the geographic area served by the sales office. Most branch managers receive a salary from the insurer and are not actively involved in selling the insurer's products. Producers who work in the branch office do not receive a salary from the insurer, but they are under contract to the insurer.

Under the ***general agency system***, each of the insurance company's individual field sales offices is established and maintained by a ***general agent***—an independent business person who is under contract to the insurer and has the authority to represent the company and to develop

agent-broker.
A career agent who holds an agency contract with one insurance company but who can place business with companies other than the primary company.

commission.
A type of payment for services that is based on a specified percentage of an agent's sales; in insurance, commissions typically are based on a percentage of the premiums paid on each contract the agent sells.

ordinary agency system.
An agency-building distribution system that uses full-time or part-time career agents to sell and service insurance products, including annuities; consists of the branch office system and the general agency system.

branch office system.
An agency-building distribution system in which an insurance company establishes and maintains a series of field sales offices, each headed by a branch manager.

branch manager.
The person who heads a field sales office in the branch office distribution system; the branch manager is responsible for recruiting, selecting, and training career agents and for managing sales in the geographic area served by the sales office.

general agency system.
An agency-building distribution system in which each of an insurance company's individual field sales offices is established and maintained by an independent general agent.

general agent.
An independent business person who is under contract to an insurer and has the authority to represent the company and to develop new business.

cross-selling.
The process of identifying a customer's needs for additional products while selling a primary product.

cross-selling distribution system.
A distribution system that uses career agents to market all of the insurance, annuity, and other financial services products of financially interrelated or commonly managed financial services companies.

salaried sales distribution system.
An agency-building distribution system that relies on the use of a company's salaried sales representatives to sell and service all types of insurance and annuity products; most often used for group insurance and annuity products.

salaried sales representative.
An employee of an insurer who is paid on a salaried basis.

new business. General agents do not receive a salary from the insurer; instead, they receive a commission on all sales generated by the sales office and often are actively involved in product sales. Producers in the sales office may be under contract to the general agent or to the insurance company.

Cross-Selling Systems

Insurance companies have found that as agents provide service to their current customers, they become aware of those customers' additional needs. Thus, agents with established customer relationships are in a position to cross sell other products. ***Cross-selling*** is the process of identifying a customer's needs for additional products while selling a primary product.

To take advantage of the marketing opportunities available through cross-selling, insurance companies have developed a ***cross-selling distribution system*** that uses career agents to market all of the insurance, annuity, and other financial services products of financially interrelated or commonly managed financial services companies. The multiple-line agency (MLA) distribution system used by insurance companies to sell the life, health, and property/casualty insurance products of an interrelated group of insurance companies is an example of a cross-selling distribution system.

Cross-selling systems increase marketing efficiency because one agent can address most or all of a customer's financial needs. Because customer satisfaction often is greater when multiple products and services are provided by a single agent rather than by separate agents, cross-selling systems also tend to increase the number of customers who stay with the company and the length of time they keep their contracts in force.

Salaried Sales Distribution Systems

A ***salaried sales distribution system*** is an agency-building distribution system that relies on the use of a company's salaried sales representatives to sell and service insurance and annuity products. A ***salaried sales representative*** is an employee of the insurer and is paid on a salary basis. Most often, the salaried sales distribution system is used for group products.

Salaried sales representatives also are an important component of call centers and contact centers. A ***call center*** is a facility where telephone calls are made or received to support activities such as customer service, sales, technical support, and other specialized business functions. A ***contact center*** is a facility that provides a variety of remote channels for communicating with customers, including phone, e-mail, regular mail, Internet, and facsimile. Although call centers and contact centers initially were used as a means of providing customer service, their role has expanded to include sales and retention. Because these centers are accessible to all of the company's customers, they are an important method of cross-selling the company's products.

Location Selling Distribution Systems

A *location selling distribution system* is an agency-building distribution system wherein an insurer sets up an office or installs an information kiosk in a retail store, shopping mall, bank, or other financial institution to attract insurance and annuity customers. To market annuity products through location selling distribution systems, insurers usually establish a formal distribution agreement with a participating store, bank, or financial institution.

Personal-Producing General Agency Distribution Systems

A *personal-producing general agency (PPGA) system* is a nonagency-building distribution system that relies on personal-producing general agents to sell and service insurance and annuity products. A *personal-producing general agent* is a commissioned sales agent who typically works alone, is not housed in an insurance company field office, and engages primarily in personal selling. Typically, a personal-producing general agent is an experienced agent who holds agency contracts with several insurance companies.

The primary advantage of the PPGA distribution system to an insurer is its relatively low cost. Because an insurer using this system typically incurs minimal recruiting and training costs and pays nothing to personal-producing general agents until they make a sale, the company has few up-front expenses and development costs.

Professional Advisors Distribution Systems

A *professional advisors distribution system* is a nonagency-building distribution system wherein professional advisors who are licensed to sell insurance—including financial planners, certified public accountants, and attorneys—enter into sales agreements with one or more insurance companies to distribute their products. A *financial planner* is a professional who analyzes a customer's personal financial circumstances and goals and prepares a program, usually in writing, to meet the customer's financial goals.

Professional advisors assist customers with activities such as insurance planning, investment management, asset accumulation, estate planning, tax planning, and retirement planning. Annuity sales typically are incidental to providing these professional services. Laws and ethical codes specific to each profession dictate how professional advisors can operate outside their stated profession.

---

call center.
A facility where telephone calls are made or received to support marketing activities such as customer service, sales, technical support, and other specialized business functions.

contact center.
A facility that provides a variety of remote channels for communicating with customers, including phone, e-mail, regular mail, Internet, and facsimile.

location selling distribution system.
An agency-building distribution system wherein an insurer sets up an office or installs an information kiosk in a retail store, shopping mall, bank, or other financial institution to attract customers for insurance and annuity products.

personal-producing general agency (PPGA) system.
A nonagency-building distribution system that relies on personal-producing general agents to sell and service insurance and annuity products.

personal-producing general agent.
A commissioned sales agent who typically works alone, is not housed in an insurance company field office, and engages primarily in personal selling; the agent typically is experienced and holds agency contracts with several insurance companies.

Marketing Organizations Distribution Systems

Some insurers use outside marketing organizations, such as independent marketing organizations or agency marketing organizations, to distribute their products. An **independent marketing organization (IMO)** is a non-company affiliated marketing organization that contracts with an insurance company to distribute one or more of the company's products or product lines. An **agency marketing organization (AMO)** is an independent sales agency that contracts with an insurance company to distribute the insurer's products or product lines. In some cases, insurers contract with marketing organizations to perform other marketing functions as well.

Marketing organizations usually focus on specific market niches and certain types of products. They operate by locating a product that fits the organization's market, developing a method to help agents reach the market, and recruiting and training agents to deliver uncomplicated, single-need sales presentations. IMOs and AMOs usually recruit and contract with their own agents, supervise their activities, and provide them with marketing support and service.

One of the marketing services IMOs and AMOs provide to their agents is lead generation. Many marketing organizations use telemarketing, seminars, direct mail, and third-party mail to qualify prospects and set appointments. Because agents associated with marketing organizations do not need to spend time prospecting, they often make more sales presentations per week than do career agents. To offset the organization's prospecting costs, agents often receive lower commissions on policies sold than do career agents.

Financial Institutions Distribution Systems

Although only insurance companies are allowed to issue annuity products, laws in the United States allow other financial institutions to distribute insurance products. Insurers generally distribute products through three types of institutional distributors: (1) broker-dealers, (2) banks, and (3) other insurance companies.

Broker-Dealer Distribution

Because variable annuity products are considered securities in the United States, insurers can sell these products only through broker-dealer firms. A **broker-dealer** is a firm that (1) provides information or advice to its customers regarding the sale and/or purchase of securities, (2) serves as a financial intermediary between buyers and sellers by underwriting or acquiring securities to market to its customers, and (3) supervises the sales process to make sure that sales agents comply with applicable SEC and NASD regulations.

---

professional advisors distribution system.
A nonagency-building distribution system wherein professional advisors who are licensed to sell insurance—including financial planners, certified public accountants, and attorneys—enter into sales agreements with one or more insurance companies to distribute their products.

financial planner.
A professional who analyzes a customer's personal financial circumstances and goals and prepares a program, usually in writing, to meet the customer's financial goals.

independent marketing organization (IMO).
A non-company affiliated marketing organization that contracts with an insurance company to distribute one or more of the company's products or product lines.

agency marketing organization (AMO).
An independent sales agency that contracts with an insurance company to distribute the insurer's products or product lines.

An insurance company can sell variable products directly by registering with the SEC and NASD as a broker-dealer. Alternatively, insurers can establish their own broker-dealer subsidiaries, or they can enter into relationships with existing broker-dealer firms. Broker-dealers distribute variable products through their registered representatives and principals—who are located primarily in retail branch offices—and via the Internet.

In Canada, variable life insurance and variable annuities are considered insurance products and not securities. Therefore insurers and producers do not need to satisfy special securities requirements. Canadian insurers, however, generally use broker-dealers to distribute variable products.

Bank Distribution

The distribution of insurance products to bank customers through a bank-affiliated insurer or insurance agency is referred to as **bank insurance.** Largely because of the **Gramm-Leach-Bliley (GLB) Act**—a U.S. federal law enacted in 1999 that removed many of the regulatory barriers between various sectors of the financial services industry—bank insurance has gained considerable momentum in the United States. In some cases, banks serve only as intermediaries in the distribution system; in other cases, they have formed partnerships with insurers through joint ventures or mergers; in still other cases, banks have acquired insurers and insurance agencies, and insurers have acquired savings banks and trust companies. Banks typically distribute insurance products through producers, direct mail, telemarketing, and the Internet.

In Canada, banks are allowed to own insurance companies and operate in life and property/casualty insurance through their own insurance subsidiaries. However, Canadian banks are prohibited from selling most kinds of insurance through their branches. In addition, the use of bank customer data by insurance companies, including those affiliated with the bank, is limited.

Insurance Company Distribution

Some insurers have become distribution channels for certain **nonproprietary products**, that is, products issued by other insurers. By serving as a distribution channel for other insurers, companies can provide their producers with a full portfolio of insurance products to offer customers and increase both producer and customer satisfaction.

Insurers can use one of the following three arrangements to distribute nonproprietary products:

- A **home-office-to-home-office arrangement**, in which an insurance company that does not offer a particular product or product line

---

broker-dealer.
A firm that (1) provides information or advice to customers regarding the sale and/or purchase of securities, (2) serves as a financial intermediary between buyers and sellers by underwriting or acquiring securities in order to market them to its customers, and (3) supervises the sales process to make sure that sales agents comply with applicable SEC and NASD regulations.

bank insurance.
The distribution of insurance products to bank customers through a bank-affiliated insurer or insurance agency.

Gramm-Leach-Bliley (GLB) Act.
A U.S. federal law enacted in 1999 that removed many of the regulatory barriers between various sectors of the financial services industry.

nonproprietary products.
Products issued by one insurer and sold by a different insurer.

home-office-to-home-office arrangement.
An insurance company distribution system in which an insurer that chooses not to offer a particular product or product line agrees to distribute specific products or product lines issued by another insurer.

agrees to distribute specific products or product lines issued by another insurer.

- A ***brokerage general agency arrangement***, in which a company that does not offer a particular product or product line arranges for its agents to broker certain business through an agency operated by a brokerage general agent who is under contract to a number of insurers. Because brokerage general agents have access to several companies' products, they can provide a wider product choice than can be provided under a home-office-to-home-office arrangement.

- An ***in-house brokerage agency arrangement***, in which a company that does not offer a particular product or product line uses its own agent-brokers, rather than outside brokers or agencies, to solicit distribution agreements with other insurers to sell the issuing companies' products.

Direct Response Distribution Systems

Under direct response distribution systems, insurance companies sell products through direct appeals to customers using a variety of advertising media, including television, radio, newspapers, magazines, direct mail, and Internet Web sites. Two of the most important forms of direct response distribution for annuity products are direct mail and Internet sales.

Unlike the other types of distribution we have discussed in this chapter, direct response distribution does not involve face-to-face contact between producers and customers. Product advertisements and other forms of solicitation generally contain all the information the customer needs to make a purchase decision and to apply for the product. Historically, direct response distribution has been best suited for relatively simple products that require little explanation, such as term life insurance or fixed annuities. However, changes in the market, increased customer sophistication, and innovative methods of explaining products without the use of face-to-face meetings have made direct response distribution popular for variable products as well. In fact, in 1998, nearly 95 percent of direct response annuity sales were for variable annuities.

Direct Mail

Direct mail is a method of distributing marketing messages to customers, usually in print form, through a mail service. Insurers using direct mail systems send an information package, known as a ***mail kit***, to prospective customers on a mailing list. Mail kits typically include an introductory letter, a product brochure, a response form, such as an insurance application or a request for more information, and a return envelope.

---

brokerage general agency arrangement.
An insurance company distribution system in which a company that does not offer a particular product or product line arranges for its agents to broker certain business through an agency operated by a brokerage general agent who is under contract to a number of insurers.

in-house brokerage agency arrangement.
An insurance company distribution system in which a company that does not offer a product or product line uses its own agent-brokers, rather than outside brokers or agencies, to solicit distribution agreements with other insurers to sell the issuing companies' products.

direct mail.
A method of distributing marketing messages to customers, usually in print form, through a mail service.

mail kit.
An information package, consisting of an introductory letter, a product brochure, a response form, and a return envelope, that is sent to a mailing list of prospective customers.

Because mailing lists can be built to reflect specific geographic, demographic, or psychographic characteristics, direct mail solicitations can be narrowly targeted and highly personalized. Moderate development and production costs also make direct mail a cost-effective distribution system. However, response rates typically are low and companies cannot guarantee that customers who receive mail kits will actually open them and read the product information.

Internet Sales

Most insurers today have sites on the Internet that provide customers with product information and allow them to ask questions. These Web sites generally allow customers to perform the following types of tasks online:

- Request premium quotes
- Apply for insurance or annuity products
- Purchase insurance or annuity products
- Make address changes, changes to asset allocations within variable annuities, and loan requests
- Request change of beneficiary forms and other forms
- Locate a local producer

Conducting business over the Internet offers benefits to both customers and companies. For customers, the Internet offers easy access, convenience, personalized service, and timeliness. For companies, the Internet offers increased accuracy, operational efficiency, integrated communication, unlimited time and space to present information, and a variety of text, graphics, and video options.

Although some insurance companies are hesitant to sell products online because of unclear regulatory implications and imperfect security measures, the demand for Internet sales is growing. In fact, researchers expect financial services to become the single largest service sold online. Online stock trades and online banking are already well-established, and more and more online insurance products, including annuities, are introduced each year.

Key Terms

marketing
exchange
marketing mix
product
price
promotion
distribution
market
market segmentation
market segment
target marketing
target market
idea generation
screening
comprehensive business analysis
market analysis
product design objectives
marketing plan
pricing
personal selling
advertising
sales promotion
specialty advertising
publicity
distribution system
personal selling distribution system
agency contract
agent
principal
agency-building system
nonagency-building system
career agent
exclusive agent
agent-broker
commission
ordinary agency system
branch office system
branch manager
general agency system
general agent
cross-selling
cross-selling distribution system
salaried sales distribution system
salaried sales representative
call center
contact center
location selling distribution system

personal-producing general agency (PPGA) system

personal-producing general agent

professional advisors distribution system

financial planner

independent marketing organization (IMO)

agency marketing organization (AMO)

broker-dealer

bank insurance

Gramm-Leach-Bliley (GLB) Act

nonproprietary products

home-office-to-home-office arrangement

brokerage general agency arrangement

in-house brokerage agency arrangement

direct mail

mail kit

Annuity Principles and Products

CHAPTER 10

The Future of Annuities

After studying this chapter, you should be able to

- Discuss the economic, demographic, and regulatory changes that affect the annuities industry

- Describe the methods that have been proposed to reform the Social Security System

- Discuss how insurers are responding to changes in the retirement savings environment

OUTLINE

Economic Changes
Market Volatility
Corporate Changes

Demographic Changes
Aging of the Population
Changing Employment Profile
Slower Wage and Earnings Growth

Regulatory Changes
Industry Consolidation
Tax Reforms
Reclassification of Annuities

Social Security Changes
Tax Increases
Benefit Reductions
Program Privatization

Industry Response
New Fixed Annuity Products
New Equity-Indexed Annuity Products
New Variable Annuity Products
Financial Services

Americans historically have relied on employer-sponsored retirement plans, Social Security, and personal savings to provide retirement income. Recent changes in economic, social, and regulatory conditions and the increasing financial instability of the Social Security system have caused many Americans to explore alternative approaches.

In this chapter, we describe some of the factors that affect retirement savings and the demand for annuities. These factors are outlined in Figure 10.1. We also describe how the insurance industry is responding to changing conditions with new annuity products and services.

Economic Changes

During the 1980s and 1990s, the U.S. economy prospered as new companies—especially technology-based companies—entered the market, existing companies expanded their operations domestically and globally, more and more people joined the work force, and stock market values rose to all-time highs. Many observers expected this "new economy," fueled by advances in technology, to bring decades of continued growth. So far, that has not been the case. Instead of growing, the U.S. economy slowed, leading to market volatility and extensive corporate changes.

Market Volatility

Over the last two decades, the U.S. stock market has proved to be far more volatile than expected. In the late 1990s, the market was booming. With this boom came an increased demand for market-based investments, especially variable annuities and mutual funds. Between 1990 and 2000, sales of variable annuities rose from $12 billion to $137.5 billion. By the end of 2000, market values had plummeted. Much of this market decline may have been the inevitable result of market values rising to what some analysts contended were artificially high—and unsustainable—levels. Other factors, such as the political uncertainty created by terrorist attacks on the United States and the collapse of several high-profile corporations also contributed to stock market volatility.

Like the bull market of the 1990s, the bear market has affected annuity product development and sales. Although low to negative market returns have slowed sales of variable annuities, they have increased the demand for fixed annuities and products that offer investment guarantees. Sales of fixed annuities increased from $17.2 billion at the end of the second quarter of 2001 to $29.5 billion at the end of the second quarter of 2002, bringing fixed annuity sales to the same level as variable annuity sales for the first time in nearly a decade.

FIGURE 10.1

Factors Affecting Annuity Sales

CHANGE	EFFECT
Economic changes ■ Stock market volatility ■ Corporate changes (mergers/acquisitions, restructuring)	Reduction in corporate-sponsored retirement plans Increased need for personal retirement plans, including annuities
Demographic changes ■ Aging of the population ■ Changing employment profile ■ Slowing wage growth	Lengthening of retirement periods Reduction in amounts in retirement accounts Decreased emphasis on retirement savings
Regulatory changes ■ Industry consolidation ■ Tax reforms ■ Reclassification of annuities	Change in product development and marketing strategies Establishment of incentives for employer-sponsored retirement plans Reduction of tax advantages of annuities
Social Security Changes ■ Tax increases ■ Benefit reductions ■ Program privatization	Responsibility for providing retirement income shifted from Social Security system to retirees Elimination of tax and savings advantages of annuities

Corporate Changes

The trend toward corporate expansion also has slowed. Although the decline has been most noticeable among "dot.com" companies, which seemed to appear overnight and disappear almost as quickly, nearly all industries have been affected, including the financial services industry.

Mergers, acquisitions, and spin-offs have become common as companies attempt to position themselves in an increasingly competitive environment. Consolidation and reorganization also have become common. In addition to the "dot.com" companies, several airlines declared bankruptcy or filed for reorganization during 2001 and 2002. Most other carriers have reduced the number of flights they offer, and thousands of employees have been laid off. Major manufacturers have reduced their work forces through layoffs and early retirement offers. In the financial services industry, a number of companies have been abandoning peripheral lines of business and focusing on core products and services. Regulatory changes, which we will discuss later in this chapter, have accelerated corporate restructuring and other strategic initiatives.

Corporate changes have had a significant effect on company sponsorship of employee retirement plans and on employee participation in those plans. Because of declining profits and economic uncertainty, an increasing number of companies have switched existing plans from defined benefit to defined contribution plans. In addition, companies that were considering establishing retirement plans are shelving their efforts, at least for the short term. These reductions in corporate-sponsored retirement plans are likely to increase the need for personal retirement and savings programs.

Demographic Changes

Three demographic factors are likely to affect annuity product development and sales in the future: (1) continued aging of the population, (2) changing employment profile, and (3) slower wage and earnings growth.

Aging of the Population

The most important demographic factor affecting the annuity industry in the future will be the continued aging of a large percentage of the population. As you recall from Chapter 1, census figures for 2000 showed that over 34 million people were retirees age 65 or older. An additional 15 million people—those age 55–64—will reach retirement age in the next 10 years.[1] By the year 2030, the number of retirees in the United States will double.

American men and women also are living longer. As we noted in Chapter 1, the median age in the United States increased by 5.5 years between 1980 and 2000. Projections indicate that Americans will be living even longer in the next century. In fact, a recent study prepared for the Social Security Advisory Board recommended that longevity assumptions for the year 2070 be increased by as much as 3.7 years.[2]

The impact of an aging population and longer life expectancies on the future of annuities and other retirement savings products will be dramatic. In the past, people who retired at age 65 could expect to spend 5 to 10 years in retirement. Today, retirement periods commonly last 20 years or more. Those people who retire before age 65 may well spend as many years in retirement as they spent working.

Changing Employment Profile

The economic conditions we described earlier have changed the profile of the U.S. workforce. Perhaps the most noticeable change has been an increase in unemployment. For example, between 2000 and 2001 the number of unemployed people in the United States increased by nearly 1 million.[3] A significant portion of this increase can be attributed to employees leaving the workforce involuntarily as a result of layoffs. Other employees, concerned about the possibility of future layoffs and benefit reductions, have accepted early retirement offers.

Another change has been a reduction in the number of full-time, year-round employees as (1) employers attempt to reduce costs by reducing employees' hours, (2) older employees who have suffered significant losses in the market attempt to postpone retirement to maintain an income stream, and (3) retirees exploring ways to supplement their retirement income re-enter the workforce. Together, these changes are redefining retirement and driving people to reassess their retirement income needs.

Slower Wage and Earnings Growth

As employment conditions change, earnings and savings also change. According to an AARP (American Association of Retired Persons) study, median net worth and median family income for Americans age 50 or older rose to record highs between 1983 and 1998. After 1998, these rates slowed, largely because of the poor market performance and extensive corporate downsizing we described earlier in this chapter. As Figure 10.2 shows, median income rose 2 percent or less between 2000 and 2001 for retirees and those facing retirement. As levels of discretionary income go down, people tend to spend more on daily living expenses and less on retirement savings.

Regulatory Changes

A number of important changes in the regulatory environment in the United States have occurred over the last few years. Additional changes are under consideration. In this section, we will describe some of the

FIGURE 10.2

Median Income in the United States: 2000 and 2001

Age	Median Income 2000	Median Income 2001
45–54	$57,642	$58,045
55–64	$44,853	$45,864
65–74	$28,151	$28,172
75 +	$18,814	$19,174

Source: Data from U.S. Census Bureau, "Income 2001," http://www.census.gov/hhes/income/income01/inctab1.html (3 February 2003).

recent and proposed changes that have the greatest impact on the way insurance companies develop and market annuity products.

Industry Consolidation

As you recall from Chapter 9, the Gramm-Leach-Bliley (GLB) Act of 1999 removed many of the regulatory barriers between various sectors of the financial services industry. As a result, some financial services companies have begun to enter into each other's traditional business, thereby changing the structure of the financial services industry and redefining business categories.

Initially, market analysts predicted that the GLB Act would lead many financial services companies to focus on three major business categories:

- **Employee benefits**, which provides employers with insurance products and retirement plans for their employees
- **Protection/retirement savings**, which provides basic insurance and retirement savings products to the general population
- **Wealth management**, which provides products and services that allow the affluent/high-net-worth market to accumulate, protect, and transfer wealth

However, a recent report prepared by Deloitte & Touche suggests that to succeed in today's economic environment, companies should focus on their core business and divest lines of business that don't support their core strategy.[4] Either of these strategies is likely to impact the way insurers develop and market annuity products.

Tax Reforms

The past decade has produced a wide range of tax reform proposals. The most important of these proposals from an annuity perspective are (1) the Economic Growth and Tax Relief Reconciliation Act, (2) changes in the tax treatment of investment earnings, and (3) proposed changes in the tax treatment of 1035 exchanges.

Economic Growth and Tax Relief Reconciliation Act

Although the majority of large companies in the United States offer some sort of retirement savings plan to employees, small companies typically do not. In fact, only 34 percent of employees in small companies are covered by retirement plans. The Economic Growth and Tax Relief Reconciliation Act (EGTRRA) of 2001 attempted to close the "pension gap" and encourage small businesses to sponsor employment-based retirement plans.

EGTRRA calls for a variety of tax reductions and changes in the tax treatment of retirement plans. For example, EGTRRA allows employees to increase the amount they contribute to retirement plans and to roll over assets, including after-tax amounts, into other plans. EGTRRA also increases benefit limits. We discussed the specifics of these provisions in Chapter 6. For employers, the primary feature of EGTRRA is a federal tax credit for up to 50 percent of start-up costs for SIMPLE plans. EGTRRA provisions are scheduled to expire in 2011 unless extended by Congress.

So far, EGTRRA has generated less response among small employers than expected. According to the 2002 Small Employer Retirement Survey (SERS), the majority of small employers had no knowledge of EGTRRA's tax advantages. In fact, 68 percent of companies that sponsor retirement plans and 87 percent of nonsponsoring companies were not aware that the tax law allows them to take a tax credit for the costs of establishing and administering a retirement plan. When told of the tax credit, 68 percent of nonsponsoring companies said it would make sponsorship more appealing.[5]

Employees also appear to be unaware of the benefits of plan participation. According to the 2002 SERS, 22 percent of nonsponsoring companies reported that the "most important" reason they did not offer a retirement plan was that "employees prefer wages and/or other benefits."[6] Unless officials can increase awareness and understanding of the benefits offered under EGTTRA, plan sponsorship and plan participation in small companies is likely to remain a public policy issue.

Tax Treatment of Investment Earnings

In 1997, Congress enacted legislation that lowered the taxes on capital gains. In 2003, President Bush signed a new tax law that reduces tax rates applied to dividend income and capital gains. Industry analysts believe that these reforms will put variable annuities at a disadvantage when compared to mutual funds and other personal investments.

Currently, mutual funds are subject to two types of taxes: taxes on earnings and capital gains taxes. Earnings—which include dividends, interest, and short- and long-term gains—are taxed at the shareholder's individual tax rate in the year they are generated. These annual taxes on dividends are payable even if the dividends are left in the fund for reinvestment. Capital gains, which represent the difference between the purchase price and the selling price of the shares, are taxed when the shareholder sells shares or changes funds.

Earnings on variable annuity investments are taxed as ordinary income. However, taxes on these earnings are deferred until funds are withdrawn from the account, and are payable only if the account actually increases in value. No tax is imposed when the contract owner transfers funds among variable subaccounts. In addition, variable annuity contract owners can, under Section 1035 of the U.S. tax code, exchange an existing contract for another contract without paying taxes on any accumulated income or investment gains in the original account.

The 2003 tax law lessens or even eliminates the tax advantages variable annuities have over other investments. For example, the advantage of tax-deferral already is tempered by the fact that capital gains are taxed at a lower rate than ordinary income. Lowering the top rates on capital gains taxes from 20 percent to 15 percent and reducing the top rates on dividend income from 38.6 percent to 15 percent—as called for under this law—will narrow the advantage even more.

Efforts are underway in the annuities industry to level the playing field by educating lawmakers of the advantages of lifetime annuity payments. One result of these efforts is proposed Lifetime Annuity Payout (LAP) legislation that would tax lifetime annuity payments from individual nonqualified annuities as capital gains rather than ordinary income. If passed, this legislation would provide a lower tax rate for most recipients and encourage individuals to purchase annuities.

Tax Treatment of 1035 Exchanges

Another reform initiative under consideration, but not yet approved, is modification of the section of the Internal Revenue Code governing 1035 exchanges. The proposed change would require annuity contract owners to pay taxes on annuity earnings if an annuity contract is replaced by another annuity contract. Insurers and retirement planning experts argue that eliminating tax-free exchanges would make already poor savings habits in the United States worse.

Reclassification of Annuities

As we mentioned in Chapter 8, the regulatory status of equity-indexed and market value adjusted (MVA) annuities is being debated. Under current law, as long as these products provide certain principal and interest rate guarantees, they can be marketed as fixed annuities. Critics argue that, because it is difficult to market these products without emphasizing their exposure to investment results, they should be classified as securities and regulated by the SEC. Some states already have enacted legislation requiring insurers to market these hybrid products as securities.

Social Security Changes

As we mentioned in Chapter 1, the question of whether the Social Security system should be modified, supplemented, or replaced has been debated for several years. To date, nothing has been done. Unfortunately, the problems plaguing Social Security are worsening.

In 1995, analysts predicted that the Social Security trust fund, which already depends on current payroll tax revenues to support current retirement benefits, would become insolvent by the year 2030. More recent studies predict that, with increasing numbers of people entering retirement and retirement periods growing longer, the current system will be able to pay 100 percent of promised benefits only until 2017. Existing mechanisms for collecting additional revenues may be able to extend full benefits until 2041, but after 2041 benefit levels will decrease until the fund is exhausted.

Because of the widespread support for Social Security among all age groups, it is unlikely that the system will be eliminated. However, it is almost certain that the system will be modified. Most of the proposals submitted to date recommend reforming Social Security in one of three ways: (1) raising taxes, (2) decreasing total benefits, or (3) privatizing the system.

Tax Increases

Currently, the Social Security tax for workers in the United States is 12.4 percent of income. Employees pay half of this amount through payroll deductions and the other half comes from mandatory employer contributions. Early reform proposals called for an increase in payroll taxes of about 2 percent. More recent proposals call for an increase of 3 percent until 2020 and additional increases thereafter. Under these proposals, Social Security taxes could be as high as 19 percent by 2060. Although increasing taxes is considered to be a quick and easy way to prevent the predicted solvency crisis, this approach currently has very little public or political support.

Benefit Reductions

Another way to ease the strain on Social Security is to reduce overall benefit payments. These reductions can be achieved by (1) reducing current benefits, (2) reducing future benefits, and/or (3) changing benefit structures.

Reducing Current Benefits

In 2001, the average benefit payment to new retirees was $878 per month. Reform proposals advocating immediate benefit reductions call for a direct, one-time cut in this amount for all new retirees entering the system. Some proposals call for cuts of $200 per month or more; other proposals call for more modest reductions.

On the surface, such an approach appears equitable, because the same reductions would apply to all new retirees. In fact, reductions are likely to affect lower-income employees far more than they would affect higher-income employees, because lower-income workers rely almost entirely on Social Security for retirement income. As is the case with tax increases, direct benefit reductions would reduce the strain on Social Security immediately, but they lack public and political appeal.

Reducing Future Benefits

Another approach to reducing benefit payments is to reduce cost of living adjustments (COLAs). Currently, Social Security benefits increase with increases in the Consumer Price Index (CPI). Reform advocates argue that the CPI overestimates inflation and call for the link between benefits and the CPI to be modified or eliminated. Although reducing COLAs generally is more politically acceptable than other approaches to benefit reduction, it is unacceptable to many elderly Social Security recipients who rely on COLAs to cover increases in health care and other expenses.

Changing Benefit Structures

As an alternative to direct cuts in benefit payments, some reform proposals call for new formulas for translating contributions into benefits. Unlike direct cuts, these new formulas would produce a wide range of payment reductions and allow for progressive changes in funding.

Other proposals recommend raising the qualifying age for Social Security benefits or making eligibility dependent on financial need.

Proponents of raising the retirement age argue that postponing retirement until age 67 or 68 would reduce total benefits, increase fund revenues, and overcome the effects of longer life expectancies. In periods of economic growth, proposals to raise the retirement age generally are popular. During economic downturns, when lay-offs and early retirement offers increase, these proposals become less appealing.

Proponents of linking eligibility to financial need argue that Social Security benefits should be a means of guaranteeing a minimum income, or a "safety net," for retirees rather than a means of supplementing existing sources of income. Under these proposals, the more income a person has from personal sources, such as savings accounts, IRAs, investments, and annuities, the less the person would receive from Social Security. People whose income from personal sources is above an established limit would be ineligible to receive Social Security benefits.

Critics argue that tying benefits to income is likely to further reduce the incentive for people to save for retirement. Another drawback of this approach is the need to establish an eligibility limit. If the limit is set too high, most people would remain eligible and program savings would be minimal. If the limit is set too low, many low- and moderate-income people who rely on Social Security for retirement income would no longer qualify.

Program Privatization

In 2003, the Bush administration added another plan to a growing list of proposals to privatize Social Security. Privatization plans would allow each eligible employee to establish a **personal retirement account (PRA)** into which the employee would deposit a percentage of current Social Security payroll taxes. Funds in the PRA would be used to purchase shares in various investment vehicles—such as stocks and bonds—or annuities. Upon retirement, the individual would receive monthly payments from both the PRA and Social Security to bring the total benefit up to an established guaranteed minimum amount.

The benefits of privatization of Social Security are unclear. For example, the amounts employees can contribute to PRAs under most proposals are relatively small—typically one to two percent of Social Security payroll taxes. At these rates, building up sufficient value in a PRA to generate adequate lifetime benefits is likely to take several decades. Such a scenario is unlikely to provide an incentive for people to save or to reduce the strain on current programs.

---

personal retirement account (PRA).
A savings account into which an employee would deposit a percentage of current Social Security payroll taxes; accounts would be used to replace or supplement Social Security payments at retirement.

Industry Response

Economic uncertainty and the prospect of diminished Social Security funding have increased the demand for financial products and services that can help consumers reduce risk and protect assets. Insurers have responded to this demand with a variety of new products and new services.

New Fixed Annuity Products

When market values began to decline, sales of fixed annuities, which offer a guaranteed return regardless of market performance, increased. Fixed deferred annuity sales showed the greatest increase—a 76 percent increase in sales between the second quarter of 2001 and the second quarter of 2002.[7]

However, regulatory changes are likely to slow this trend. In March 2002, the NAIC adopted proposed revisions of the law that sets the minimum guarantee and submitted them to the states for legislative approval. These revisions replace the current 3 percent minimum with a variable rate linked to the yield of a five-year, constant-maturity treasury note. The new rate can vary from a low of 1 percent to a high of 3 percent. In May 2003, the American Council of Life Insurers (ACLI) reported that 28 states and the District of Columbia had already adopted the proposed legislation and another 20 states had similar legislation pending.[8] The rate included in these laws currently is 1.5 percent.

To maintain consumer interest in fixed annuities, insurers are focusing on new products. One of the most successful new annuity products is a CD-type annuity that offers a contract duration period equal to the surrender penalty period. Unlike traditional fixed annuities, under which the insurer guarantees a current interest rate for one, three, or five years and then adjusts the rate at renewal to reflect market conditions, CD-type annuities extend the guarantee period for as long as seven years. Many customers consider this approach both safer and more equitable.

New Equity-Indexed Annuity Products

Insurers have used a variety of approaches to make equity-indexed annuities more attractive to customers. These approaches include

- **Year-round averaging.** Instead of crediting excess interest yearly or once during the specified contract period, some insurers are offering products that shorten the contract period and credit interest throughout the period. For example, a one-year-by-one-year product would be averaged twelve times per year. These products appeal to customers because continuous averaging offers increased earnings potential and allows contract owners to lock in gains more frequently.

- **Greater use of spreads.** As you recall from Chapter 3, insurers can use spreads or participation rates to calculate excess interest on equity-indexed annuities. A spread is a specified percentage that is deducted from the index gain; a participation rate is a specified percentage of the index gain. Although spreads typically produce lower earnings than participation rates when market performance is low, they produce noticeably higher earnings when market performance rises. Figure 10.3 shows a sample comparison of the earnings produced by a spread and a participation rate.

- **Split participation rates.** Under traditional equity-indexed annuities, the same participation rate is used throughout the life of the contract. Under some new products, insurers offer a higher participation rate for returns up to a specified level and a lower rate for returns above that level. For example, a contract might offer 100 percent participation between 0 percent and 10 percent growth in the index and 40 percent participation on anything above 10 percent

---

FIGURE 10.3

Earnings from Spreads vs. Participation Rates

The following table shows the differences in earnings generated by a 4 percent spread and a 60 percent participation rate:

Market Return	4% Spread	60% Participation Rate
5% return	1% earnings (5% - 4%)	3% earnings (5% × .60)
10% return	6% earnings (10% - 4%)	6% earnings (10% × .60)
20% return	16% earnings (20% - 4%)	12% earnings (20% × .60)
40% return	36% earnings (40% - 4%)	24% earnings (40% × .60)

growth. Although participation goes down when the index performs exceptionally well, earnings potential remains high because participation is calculated on a greater amount of earnings.

- **Multi-strategy products.** These new products offer stock option funds as well as traditional bond option and money market funds. These multiple strategies allow customers to allocate their investments to match their risk preferences.

New Variable Annuity Products

To adjust to uncertain market conditions, insurers also are modifying variable products. In Chapter 4, we described some of the guaranteed living benefits and death benefit guarantees that have been added to variable annuities. Two additional innovations are bonus annuities and unbundled annuities.

A **bonus annuity** is an annuity under which the insurer credits a stated amount to the initial purchase payment or subsequent purchase payments as a bonus for the contract owner's purchase of the annuity. These bonuses, which are typically between 1 percent and 5 percent of the premium paid, give customers extra cash in their annuity account. For example, if an investor purchases a bonus annuity with a $50,000 lump-sum payment and the insurer offers a 4 percent sign-up bonus, then the amount of the bonus will be $2,000 ($50,000 × 0.04) and the account value at the time of purchase will be $52,000 ($50,000 + $2,000). Some insurers offer similar bonuses on fixed annuities.

For investors, the extra value generated by sign-up bonuses can be significant, especially for large investments. The disadvantage of bonus annuities is increased cost. Insurers typically add additional expense and surrender charges to the contract and extend the contract's surrender period—usually from 7 years to 9 years. The minimum premium amount typically increases as well. In some cases, the total of these additional charges is almost the same as the bonus amount.

An **unbundled annuity** is a variable annuity that is broken down into two parts: (1) a simple base product with relatively low asset fees and relatively standard features and (2) a set of enhanced benefits that the customer can purchase at an additional cost. Figure 10.4 lists some of the add-on benefits insurers typically offer in unbundled annuities.

Almost half of all variable annuities now offer at least one benefit rider. Some offer as many as 20 add-on benefits. For customers, unbundling offers a way to customize products to meet individual needs. For insurers, administering these highly complex products can be a challenging, but necessary part of doing business in an increasingly competitive environment.

bonus annuity.
A type of annuity under which the insurer credits a stated amount to the initial purchase payment or subsequent purchase payments as a bonus for the contract owner's purchase of the annuity.

unbundled annuity.
A variable annuity that is broken down into two parts: (1) a simple base product with relatively low asset fees and relatively standard features and (2) a set of enhanced benefits that the customer can purchase at an additional cost.

FIGURE 10.4

Examples of Unbundled Annuity Benefits

Add-on benefits offered as part of unbundled annuities include:

- Bonuses
- Reduced minimum payments
- Guaranteed minimum income benefits
- Guaranteed death benefits linked to earnings
- Beneficiary protection
- Shorter contingent deferred sales charge (CDSC) periods
- Additional free withdrawals
- Hardship and disability waivers

Financial Services

According to a recent report, Baby-Boomers entering retirement in the next five years will generate nearly $2.7 trillion in rollover money from IRAs and employer-sponsored retirement plans.[9] Few of these investors understand the basics of income management or have formal financial plans in place to manage fund distribution and allocation. Even fewer appear to be aware of recent changes in tax laws that affect rollovers and minimum required distributions. To help manage funds effectively during retirement, these individuals need financial information and advice.

Business owners also need financial planning services, for themselves and their employees. For example, business owners need information and advice about establishing and maintaining employee retirement savings plans. Choosing and monitoring plan investments and complying with complex legal and regulatory requirements requires considerable time and expertise. Companies with extensive resources often can handle the process internally. Companies with fewer resources typically need help from external advisors. Business owners also need advice on how to manage assets as their companies move through the business life cycle from start-up and growth to sale or transfer to another owner or family member. The more successful the business, the greater the need for ongoing financial planning.

FIGURE 10.5

Financial Services Offered by Insurance Companies

Services Available to		
Consumers	**Business Owners**	**Financial Advisors**
■ Retirement education and planning	■ Business continuation planning	■ Client surveys
■ Long-range estate planning	■ Disaster recovery planning	■ Business valuation tools
■ Tax planning	■ Employee risk tolerance assessments	■ Asset allocation modeling tools
■ Rollovers and fund allocation	■ Work-force profiling	■ Specialty consulting services
■ Investment planning	■ Investment research, selection, and monitoring tools	■ Tactical and technical support programs

Insurers are taking steps to meet the financial planning needs of individual customers, business owners, and financial advisors. Figure 10.5 lists some of the educational, planning, and support services insurance companies are offering to their customers. Some companies are delivering these services through face-to-face meetings with clients; others are focusing on online programs, seminars offered in the workplace, and even direct mail campaigns.

Insurers also have repositioned their producers as financial advisors and are promoting them as an integral part of a client's total financial planning team. Insight 10.1 illustrates how financial services companies are exploring new opportunities to provide consumers with retirement education and planning.

INSIGHT 10.1

Save for Retirement and Get Wisdom, Too

Since the beginning of 2000, Dr. James L. McCoy has watched his 401(k) account lose half its value. But he hasn't altered his investment strategy. "I didn't adjust; I just rode it out," he said. ...

[In January 2003], he will be receiving some help. Along with other employees of the Holston Medical Group in Kingsport, Tennessee, he will be among the first Americans to delegate active management of their 401(k)s to the financial professionals who run their retirement accounts.

In a pilot program offered by AIG, the financial services giant, Dr. McCoy's 401(k) portfolio will be tailored for him, factoring in his age, risk tolerance, savings level, and retirement goals, as well as current market conditions and forecasts. For a fee of up to 1.25 percent of his account's value, his portfolio will be rebalanced each quarter.

The program was made possible by an advisory opinion in December 2001 by the Labor Department that gave AIG's SunAmerica subsidiary an exemption from conflict-of-interest regulations that had prohibited 401(k) providers from directly advising their investors. Under the ruling, 401(k) providers are required to hire independent firms to do the calculations for portfolio recommendations. AIG has hired Ibbotson Associates, a consulting firm in Chicago.

The ruling allows all 401(k) providers to start offering advice, according to Ann L. Combs, assistant labor secretary for pension and welfare benefits. "As more people are relying on 401(k)-type plans for their retirement, they've been given more responsibility to make investment decisions, and we wanted to make sure they're equipped to handle those decisions," she said. "It gives them access to specific investment advice. Previously, employers were offering them education, but this takes the next step."

[Beginning in February 2003], Merrill Lynch will...offer a similar service, also using calculations by Ibbotson, according to Mark Feuer, chief operating officer of Merrill's retirement group. Merrill will start by handling the accounts of the 600 employees of BMI, the music-licensing company in New York, and plans to offer the service nationwide in April, Mr. Feuer said. He said Merrill had not determined its fees for the service.

CitiStreet, a joint venture of Citigroup and State Street of Boston, has offered advice and active management of individual accounts since July [2002], Ms. Combs said, but 401(k) participants retain more control over their accounts. CitiStreet uses calculations by Financial Engines to make investment recommendations. Annual fees range from 0.01 percent to 0.75 percent of an account's balance. Corporations that use the service for all of their employees pay lower fees.

Other financial services companies are also preparing to enter the field. T. Rowe Price, for example, intends to announce its plans shortly, said John J. Doyle, vice president and director for marketing and communications. Mr. Doyle said his company had not acted until now because it had been waiting for Congress to enact legislation that might broaden its options. "A lot of us are moving slower than we might have because we know there could be another shoe to drop," he said.

Representative John A. Boehner, Republican of Ohio, is sponsoring a bill that would allow employers and 401(k) providers to offer advice to employees without requiring them to hire outside firms to create investment models, as is now necessary. It would also remove the fiduciary responsibility for such advice from employers and place it with the financial services companies that give the advice. The House passed the bill last April, but it stalled in the Senate. Mr. Boehner plans to reintroduce it.

There is considerable evidence that 401(k) investors want additional advice. "We certainly have seen a larger volume of questions as more Americans are concerned about their future and retirement goals because many of their accounts have vanished," said Mr. Feuer at Merrill.

A survey released last year by Hewitt Associates showed that 80.5 percent of 401(k) participants didn't make any changes in their investment allocations in 2001. Most financial advisors recommend that investors review and rebalance accounts at least once a year. Many investors say they don't know enough about finance to make these decisions on their own.

The new services will provide investors with the kind of financial advice and information that is routinely available to traditional pension plans, said Joshua D. Dietch, associate director of Cerulli Associates, a research firm in Boston. "Essentially, [this is] pension-plan quality advice," he said. "Instead of a trustee that manages the assets of the total population, they're managing the assets for one."

Richard J. Lindsay, senior vice president for strategic planning at AIG VALIC, the part of AIG running the investment service, said that the failure of most 401(k) investors to manage their own accounts actively was largely "a behavioral issue." He added: "You have to overcome the inertia that has got the majority of participants not doing anything. They're throwing up their hands, not knowing what to do or focusing on the wrong decision."...

AIG uses Ibbotson's financial software to pick a mix of stock and bond mutual funds for the portfolio, using its own assessments of the market and of appropriate asset allocations for investors [with] varying risk levels. Ibbotson's computer programs will rebalance the account quarterly to make sure that it matches the allocation model. AIG will execute trades when needed.

Merrill will offer similar choices in its program, Mr. Feuer said. CitiStreet's program requires investors to provide extensive information about themselves before the company will create a mutual fund portfolio, according to Ray Martin, president of CitiStreet. ...

Even before the Labor Department ruling, many companies offered employees access to online financial planning programs provided by companies like Financial Engines, mPower, and Morningstar. But computer-based advice programs may not help those who do not have the interest, time, or aptitude to supply their investment information and act on the recommendations.

Dr. McCoy said he preferred to delegate responsibility. "I'm hoping that someone with expertise and timing can bird-dog the funds and transfer the money," he said.

Source: Excerpted from Elizabeth Harris, "Save for Retirement and Get Wisdom, Too," *The New York Times*, 19 January 2003. Copyright © 2003 by The New York Times Co. Reprinted with permission.

Key Terms

personal retirement account (PRA)

bonus annuity

unbundled annuity

Endnotes

1. U.S. Census Bureau, "Income 2001," http://www.census.gov/hhes/income/income01/inctab1.html (3 February 2003).

2. National Center for Policy Analysis, "Social Security: Assume Longer Life Expectancies, SSA Report Says," http://www.ncpa.org/pi/congress/pd120799d.html (3 February 2003).

3. U.S. Census Bureau.

4. Deloitte & Touche, "Insurers Need to Focus on Core Business," *National Underwriter Online News Service*, http://www.nationalunderwriter.com/lifeandhealth/hotnews/viewLHasp?article=2_12_03_9_8013.xml (12 February 2003).

5. Employee Benefit Research Institute, "2002 Small Employer Retirement Survey: Most Small Businesses Unaware of New Tax Law Incentives to Sponsor a Retirement Plan," 7 May 2002, http://www.ebri.org/prrel/pr596.pdf (29 July 2003).

6. Ibid.

7. Eric Sondergeld and Dan Q. Beatrice, "Fixed Annuity Sales in 2nd Quarter Match Variable Annuity Sales," *National Underwriter*, Life & Health/Financial Services ed. (7 October 2002): 8.

8. Thompson Media, "States Create Annuity-Rate-Floor Patchwork," *American Banker* via NewsEdge Corporation, http://newsedge.com (5 May 2003).

9. Marcella DeSimone, "Baby-Boom Retirees Want Advice on High-Balance IRA Rollovers," *National Underwriter*, Life & Health/Financial Services ed. (25 June 2001): 37.

Annuity Principles and Products

Glossary

401(k) plan.
An arrangement that allows both employers and employees to make contributions to a qualified tax-deferred retirement savings plan established for the benefit of employees. [6]

403(b) plan.
An arrangement that allows not-for-profit employers and their employees to make contributions to a qualified tax-deferred retirement savings plan established for the benefit of employees. [6]

457 plan.
An arrangement that allows state and local governments and their employees to make contributions to a qualified tax-deferred retirement plan established for the benefit of employees. [6]

529 program.
See **qualified tuition program**.

accumulated value.
The net amount paid for an annuity plus interest earned, less the amount of any withdrawals or fees. [1]

accumulation period.
The time period between the date the contract owner purchases a deferred annuity and the date that annuity benefit payments begin. [1]

accumulation units.
Ownership shares in selected subaccounts of an insurer's separate account that are purchased with premiums for a variable annuity. [2]

administrative fee.
A charge an insurer levies on an annuity contract to cover the costs of issuing the contract, making administrative changes to the contract, preparing the contract owner's statements, and performing other "maintenance" activities. [2]

Advertisements of Life Insurance and Annuities Model Regulation.
A model law developed by the NAIC that (1) defines the types of materials that constitute advertising and (2) describes the steps insurers should follow when preparing materials for use in the sales process. [8]

advertising.
A form of nonpersonal promotion in which information about a company or its products and services is generated by an identified sponsor and transmitted, for a fee, by the media. [9]

agency-building system.
A personal selling distribution system in which an insurance company recruits and trains producers and provides them with financial support and office facilities. [9]

agency contract.
An agreement between a principal and an agent that defines the agent's role and responsibilities, describes the agent's compensation, and specifically determines the agent's right to act for the principal. [9]

agency marketing organization (AMO).
An independent sales agency that contracts with an insurance company to distribute the insurer's products or product lines. [9]

agent.
A salesperson or producer who is authorized to act on behalf of an insurance company. [9]

agent-broker.
A career agent who holds an agency contract with one insurance company but who can place business with companies other than the primary company. [9]

AIR.
See **assumed investment rate**.

AMO.
See **agency marketing organization**.

annual reset method.
A method of calculating excess interest on an equity-indexed annuity that involves comparing the value of the index at the end of each contract year with the value at the start of that year. The ending value of each year is then used as the starting value for the next year. Also known as the *ratchet method*. [3]

Annual Return.
A document Canadian insurers must file each year that includes detailed accounting and statistical data about the insurer; similar to the Annual Statement required for insurers in the United States. [8]

Annual Statement.
A financial report containing detailed accounting and statistical data about a U.S. insurance company; insurers must file an Annual Statement each year with the state insurance department(s) and the NAIC. [8]

annuitant.
>The person whose lifetime is used to measure the length of time annuitized payments are payable under an annuity contract. [1]

annuity certain.
>An annuity that provides benefit payments for a stated period of time, regardless of whether the annuitant is living at the end of the period. [2]

annuity contract.
>A legally enforceable written agreement between an insurance company and a contract owner under which the insurer promises to make a series of periodic payments to a named person in exchange for a premium or a series of premiums. [1]

annuity date.
>*See* **maturity date**.

Annuity Disclosure Model Regulation.
>A model regulation developed by the NAIC that requires insurers to provide prospective buyers of specific types of annuities with information to help them select an annuity that is appropriate for their needs. [8]

annuity period.
>The time span between each of the payments in the series of periodic annuity payments. [1]

annuity unit.
>A share in an insurer's separate account that is obtained by converting accumulation units in various subaccounts before the first annuity payment is made. [2]

asset allocation.
>The process of investing premiums for variable annuities in fixed accounts, money markets, bonds, and stocks in predetermined proportions. [4]

asset allocation model.
>A tool that uses an investor's personal and financial data to generate options for strategically distributing assets among different types and classes of investments. [4]

asset class.
>A group of similar investment instruments linked by related risk and return features. [4]

asset management fee.
>A fee assessed by an investment fund manager to cover the fund management costs and operating expenses associated with a variable annuity's underlying investment funds. [2]

assignment provision.
A provision in a nonqualified annuity contract that grants the contract owner the right to temporarily or permanently transfer ownership of the contract. [2]

assumed investment rate (AIR).
The minimum rate of return that variable annuity subaccount investments are expected to earn. [2]

automatic dollar cost averaging provision.
A provision in a variable annuity contract that allows the contract owner to use a single premium payment to make periodic purchases of accumulation units in one or more variable subaccounts over a specified period of time. [4]

automatic rebalancing provision.
A provision in a variable annuity contract which states that values automatically will be transferred among specified subaccounts to maintain the allocation percentages designated by the contract owner. [4]

back-end loaded account.
An investment account that charges a fee when shares are sold. [1]

bailout provision.
A provision in an annuity contract that enables the contract owner to surrender the annuity, usually without a surrender charge, if renewal interest rates on a fixed annuity fall below a pre-established level. Also known as an *escape clause* or *cash-out provision*. [2]

bank insurance.
The distribution of insurance products to bank customers through a bank-affiliated insurer or insurance agency. [9]

beneficiary.
The person or legal entity who receives annuity death benefits, if applicable. [1]

bond.
A type of debt that reflects money an organization has borrowed and must repay to the bond-holder. [4]

bond subaccount.
A subaccount in an insurance company's separate account that consists of a variety of both short-term and long-term government and corporate bonds. [4]

bonus annuity.
    A type of annuity under which the insurer credits a stated amount to the initial purchase payment or subsequent purchase payments as a bonus for the contract owner's purchase of the annuity. [10]

branch manager.
    The person who heads a field sales office in the branch office distribution system; the branch manager is responsible for recruiting, selecting, and training career agents and for managing sales in the geographic area served by the sales office. [9]

branch office system.
    An agency-building distribution system in which an insurance company establishes and maintains a series of field sales offices, each headed by a branch manager. [9]

brokerage general agency arrangement.
    An insurance company distribution system in which a company that does not offer a particular product or product line arranges for its agents to broker certain business through an agency operated by a brokerage general agent who is under contract to a number of insurers. [9]

broker-dealer.
    A firm that (1) provides information or advice to customers regarding the sale and/or purchase of securities, (2) serves as a financial intermediary between buyers and sellers by underwriting or acquiring securities in order to market them to its customers, and (3) supervises the sales process to make sure that sales agents comply with applicable SEC and NASD regulations. [9]

Buyer's Guide to Fixed Deferred Annuities.
    A document that describes the various types of annuities available and some of the annuity features that consumers should consider before purchasing an annuity. [8]

call center.
    A facility where telephone calls are made or received to support marketing activities such as customer service, sales, technical support, and other specialized business functions. [9]

Canadian Council of Insurance Regulators (CCIR).
    An organization that consists of provincial superintendents of insurance that discusses insurance issues and recommends uniform insurance legislation to the provinces; similar to the NAIC in the United States. [8]

cap.
    The upper limit on the amount of excess interest that will be credited to an equity-indexed annuity contract. [3]

capital appreciation.
An increase in the market value of invested assets. [4]

capital gain.
The difference between the purchase price of a stock or mutual fund share and its selling price. [5]

career agent.
An insurance producer who is under contract to at least one insurance company. [9]

cash-out provision.
See **bailout provision**.

cash surrender value.
The amount available to a contract owner who surrenders the contract; equal to the accumulated value of the contract, less any charges. [2]

CCIR.
See **Canadian Council of Insurance Regulators**.

CD.
See **certificate of deposit**.

CDSC.
See **contingent deferred sales charge**.

certificate of authority.
The state license an insurance company must obtain to conduct insurance business in that state. [8]

certificate of deposit (CD).
A contractual agreement issued by a bank that returns the investor's principal, with interest, on a specified date. [5]

commission.
A type of payment for services that is based on a specified percentage of an agent's sales; in insurance, commissions typically are based on a percentage of the premiums paid on each contract the agent sells. [9]

comprehensive business analysis.
A preliminary review of market conditions and other factors designed to determine the feasibility of any product ideas that appear to meet customer needs and company objectives. [9]

compound interest.
Interest that is earned on both the principal and the accumulated interest. [5]

contact center.
A facility that provides a variety of remote channels for communicating with customers, including phone, e-mail, regular mail, Internet, and facsimile. [9]

contingent annuitant.
A person who becomes the annuitant of an annuity contract if the primary annuitant dies before annuity payments begin or during the payout period. [1]

contingent deferred sales charge (CDSC).
A charge imposed by an insurer when the owner of a share-based variable annuity withdraws funds from or surrenders the annuity. [2]

contract duration.
A specified time period during which the insurer will pay a specified interest rate on premiums for a fixed annuity. [2]

contract owner.
The person who applies for and purchases an annuity. [1]

cost recovery rule.
A tax calculation method which states that withdrawals from nonqualified annuity contracts are considered to be a return of the tax cost basis first and are therefore not taxable income; applies to annuity contracts established on or before August 13, 1982. [7]

Coverdell Education Savings Account.
A special form of IRA that allows the owner to make withdrawals at any time—without penalty—as long as the money is used to cover qualified education costs. Also known as an *education IRA*. [6]

cross-selling.
The process of identifying a customer's needs for additional products while selling a primary product. [9]

cross-selling distribution system.
A distribution system that uses career agents to market all of the insurance, annuity, and other financial services products of financially interrelated or commonly managed financial services companies. [9]

current interest rate.
The interest rate prevailing in the economy, generally offered for the contract duration of a fixed annuity. [2]

death benefit guarantee.
A provision in a variable annuity contract which states that if the contract owner dies before annuity payments begin, the beneficiary named by the contract owner will receive a benefit equal to the greater of (1) the total amount of premium payments made for the annuity, less any withdrawals made, or (2) the accumulated value at the time of the contract owner's death. [4]

deferred annuity.
An annuity contract under which periodic annuity payments generally begin more than one annuity period after the date on which the annuity is purchased. [1]

deferred profit sharing plan (DPSP).
A type of registered retirement plan in Canada that allows employers to make contributions on behalf of employees that are related to profits; similar to qualified profit sharing plans in the United States. [6]

defined benefit plan.
A type of pension plan that specifies the amount of benefit—based on the employee's income, years of service, or both income and years of service—a participant will receive at retirement. [6]

defined contribution plan.
A type of pension plan that specifies the annual contribution an employer will deposit into a pension plan on behalf of each plan participant. [6]

direct mail.
A method of distributing marketing messages to customers, usually in print form, through a mail service. [9]

distribution.
The methods a company uses to make products available for customers to buy. [9]

disclosure document.
A document that contains relevant contract and benefit information for the specific annuity that a consumer is considering purchasing. [8]

distribution channel.
See **distribution system**.

distribution system.
A network of companies, agencies, and people that performs all the marketing activities needed to deliver products to customers. Also known as a *distribution channel*. [9]

diversification.
The process of investing in a number of financial instruments to minimize the risk associated with any one investment or type of investment. [4]

dividend.
A share of a company's profits from its stock. [4]

dollar cost averaging.
The process of investing a fixed dollar amount in one or more financial instruments on a regular, periodic basis, regardless of the current values of the selected instruments. [4]

DPSP.
See **deferred profit sharing plan**.

education IRA.
See **Coverdell Education Savings Account**.

entire contract provision.
A provision in an annuity contract which states that only those documents attached to or appearing in the contract are part of the contract. [2]

equity-indexed annuity.
An annuity that offers certain principal and earnings guarantees, but also offers the possibility of additional earnings by linking the contract to a published index. [1]

escape clause.
See **bailout provision**.

exchange.
A transaction that occurs when one party—a buyer—gives something of value to another party—a seller—and receives something of value in return. [9]

exclusion ratio.
A formula used to calculate the amount of a fixed annuity benefit payment that is exempt from taxable income; equal to the investment in the contract as of the date annuity payments begin divided by the contract's expected return. [7]

exclusive agent.
A career agent who is under contract to only one insurance company and is not permitted to sell the products of other insurers. [9]

FDIC.
See **Federal Deposit Insurance Corporation**.

Federal Deposit Insurance Corporation (FDIC).
A U.S. federal agency that guarantees funds on deposit—up to a $100,000 limit—in member institutions. [5]

financial planner.
A professional who analyzes a customer's personal financial circumstances and goals and prepares a program, usually in writing, to meet the customer's financial goals. [9]

fixed account.
A variable annuity account that guarantees payment of a fixed rate of interest for a specified period of time. Also known as a *variable guaranteed account*. [4]

fixed amount option.
A form of nonannuitized payout in which the contract owner elects to receive payments of a designated minimum amount for as long a period as the contract's accumulated value will provide. [2]

fixed annuity.
An annuity contract under which the insurer guarantees the minimum interest rate that will be applied to premium payments and the minimum annuity payment that will be made for each dollar of the annuity's accumulated value at the end of the accumulation period. [1]

fixed payout.
A variable annuity payout option in which the insurer makes a series of payments to the payee that are of a fixed amount throughout the payout period. [2]

fixed period option.
A form of nonannuitized payout in which a contract owner elects to receive annuity payments for a designated period of time. [2]

fixed-premium annuity.
An annuity contract that requires the contract owner to pay premiums of a fixed amount at specified, regular intervals. [1]

flexible-premium annuity.
An annuity contract purchased with periodic premium payments in an amount that falls between a stated minimum and a stated maximum. [1]

free look provision.
A provision in an annuity contract which states that the contract owner has a period of time—usually 10 to 20 days after receiving the contract—to examine the contract with the option of returning it to the insurer during this time for a full refund of the premium paid or the current market value of the contract. [2]

free withdrawal provision.
A provision in an annuity contract that grants the contract owner the right to withdraw a portion (typically between 10 and 15 percent) of the contract's accumulated value during the accumulation period without a surrender charge. [2]

front-end loaded account.
An investment account that charges a fee for purchasing shares in the account and requires the entire amount of the charge to be paid up front. [1]

future value (FV).
The amount that an original sum is expected to be worth at the end of a specified period of time, if it is invested at a specified interest rate. [5]

FV.
See **future value**.

general account.
The general fund of assets invested to support an insurer's traditional, nonvariable insurance products. [1]

general agency system.
An agency-building distribution system in which each of an insurance company's individual field sales offices is established and maintained by an independent general agent. [9]

general agent.
An independent business person who is under contract to an insurer and has the authority to represent the company and to develop new business. [9]

GLB Act.
See **Gramm-Leach-Bliley Act**.

Gramm-Leach-Bliley (GLB) Act.
A U.S. federal law enacted in 1999 that removed many of the regulatory barriers between various sectors of the financial services industry. [9]

gross estate.
The total value of property subject to estate taxes. [7]

guaranteed interest rate.
The minimum rate an insurer will pay on a fixed annuity's accumulated value. [2]

guaranty association.
A state agency composed of all life insurance companies operating in the state that funds payments to customers of companies that go out of business. [8]

high water mark method.
A method of calculating excess interest on an equity-indexed annuity that involves comparing the value of the index at the beginning of the contract term with the highest value that the index reaches on any contract anniversary date during the term. [3]

home-office-to-home-office arrangement.
An insurance company distribution system in which an insurer that chooses not to offer a particular product or product line agrees to distribute specific products or product lines issued by another insurer. [9]

idea generation.
The process of searching for new product ideas that are consistent with overall company objectives and customer needs. [9]

immediate annuity.
An annuity contract under which annuity payments generally begin one annuity period after the date on which the annuity is purchased. [1]

IMO.
See **independent marketing organization.**

income tax.
A tax levied in the United States on compensation that a person or business receives for services rendered. [7]

incontestability provision.
A provision in an annuity contract which states that, after the contract becomes effective, the insurer generally cannot contest it. [2]

independent marketing organization (IMO).
A non-company affiliated marketing organization that contracts with an insurance company to distribute one or more of the company's products or product lines. [9]

index.
A statistical measurement system that tracks the performance of a group of similar investments. [1]

individual retirement account.
See **individual retirement arrangement.**

individual retirement arrangement (IRA).
A retirement savings plans that allows people with taxable compensation to deposit a portion of that income in a tax-deferred savings plan. Also known as an *individual retirement account*. [6]

inflation risk.
The risk that the average level of prices for goods and services during an investment period will increase at a higher rate than investment earnings. [5]

in-house brokerage agency arrangement.
An insurance company distribution system in which a company that does not offer a product or product line uses its own agent-brokers, rather than outside brokers or agencies, to solicit distribution agreements with other insurers to sell the issuing companies' products. [9]

Insurance Companies Act.
The primary Canadian federal law that governs insurance companies operating in Canada. [8]

insurance producer.
An individual who is licensed to sell insurance and annuity products to consumers and organizations. [8]

interest.
A fee that banks and other financial institutions pay for the use of borrowed money. [4]

interest first rule.
A tax calculation method which states that any amount a contract owner takes out of a nonqualified annuity will be considered a withdrawal of interest (which has not been taxed), until the contract owner has withdrawn all of the interest in the contract; applies to annuity contracts established after August 13, 1982. [7]

interest rate risk.
The chance that unpredictable fluctuations in interest rates will jeopardize the opportunity to maximize the return on an investment. [5]

investment advisor.
A company or person that is compensated for providing advice to investors about the value of securities and the potential advantages and disadvantages of buying and selling securities. [8]

Investment Advisor's Act of 1940.
A U.S. federal law that regulates the conduct of investment advisors. [8]

investment company.
A U.S. company that issues securities and engages primarily in investing and trading securities. [8]

Investment Company Act of 1940.
A U.S. federal law that regulates the conduct of investment companies. [8]

joint and survivor annuity.
A form of life only annuity that provides a series of periodic payments based upon the life expectancies of two or more annuitants, and those payments continue until the last annuitant dies. [2]

joint annuitant.
A second person, in addition to the primary annuitant, whose life is used to measure the length of time annuitized payments are payable. [1]

joint owner.
A person who shares ownership of an annuity with the contract owner. [1]

Keogh plan.
An arrangement that allows self-employed persons to deposit a portion of their income earned from self-employment in a tax-deferred savings plan. [6]

life annuity.
An annuity that provides periodic payments for at least the lifetime of the annuitant. [2]

life income with period certain annuity.
An annuity that guarantees that payments will be made throughout the annuitant's lifetime and that payments will continue for at least a specified period, even if the annuitant dies before the end of that period. [2]

life income with refund annuity.
An annuity that provides annuity payments throughout the lifetime of the annuitant and guarantees that at least the purchase price of the annuity will be paid out. Also known as a refund annuity. [2]

Life Insurance Illustrations Model Regulation.
A model regulation developed by the NAIC that provides formats, standards for use, and disclosure requirements for sales illustrations. [8]

life only annuity.
An annuity that provides periodic payments only for as long as the annuitant lives; upon the death of the annuitant, the insurer makes no further payments. Also known as *straight life annuity*. [2]

location selling distribution system.
An agency-building distribution system wherein an insurer sets up an office or installs an information kiosk in a retail store, shopping mall, bank, or other financial institution to attract customers for insurance and annuity products. [9]

lump-sum distribution.
A form of nonannuitized payout in which the accumulated value of an annuity contract is distributed in a single payment. [2]

mail kit.
An information package, consisting of an introductory letter, a product brochure, a response form, and a return envelope, that is sent to a mailing list of prospective customers. [9]

margin.
See **spread**.

market.
A group of people who, either as individuals or as members of organizations, are the actual or potential buyers of a product. [9]

market analysis.
A study of all the environmental factors that might affect sales of a proposed product. [9]

market risk.
The risk associated with fluctuations in stock prices. [5]

market segment.
A submarket, or group of customers with similar needs and preferences, that is identified through market segmentation. [9]

market segmentation.
The process companies use to divide large, heterogeneous markets into smaller, more homogeneous submarkets. [9]

market value adjusted (MVA) annuity.
An annuity that offers multiple guarantee periods and multiple fixed rates; market value adjusted annuities that meet certain regulatory guidelines can be issued as fixed annuities. [1]

marketing.
The process of developing, pricing, promoting, and distributing ideas, goods, or services to create exchanges that satisfy the needs of both buyers and sellers. [9]

marketing mix.
The factors that a company considers when determining how it can best meet customer needs; includes product, price, promotion, and distribution. [9]

marketing plan.
A document that specifies the company's overall marketing objectives for a product, the strategies needed to achieve those objectives, and the specific sales goals for the product. [9]

maturity date.
The date on which an insurer begins to make annuity payments, or distributions, under an annuity contract. Also known as the *annuity date*. [2]

McCarran-Ferguson Act.
A U.S. federal law that grants the authority to regulate the insurance industry to the states as long as Congress considers state regulation to be adequate. [8]

M&E charge.
See **mortality and expense risks charge**.

minimum distribution.
The minimum amount a contract owner is required to withdraw from an annuity contract at maturity. [7]

model law.
Sample legislation that is intended to serve as a guide for state lawmakers. [8]

Model Variable Annuity Regulation.
A model regulation developed by the NAIC that establishes requirements for insurers that issue variable annuities and for variable annuity products. [8]

money market subaccount.
A subaccount in an insurance company's separate account that consists of short-term money instruments or cash equivalents, such as U.S. Treasury bills. [4]

mortality and expense risks (M&E) charge.
A fee designed to compensate the insurer for risks under the contract and to reimburse the insurer for administrative and distribution costs associated with providing variable subaccount options. [2]

mutual fund.
An account established by an investment company that combines the money of many people and invests it in a variety of financial instruments. [1]

MVA annuity.
See **market value adjusted annuity**.

NAIC.
See **National Association of Insurance Commissioners**.

NASD.
See **National Association of Securities Dealers**.

National Association of Insurance Commissioners (NAIC).
A private, nonprofit organization made up of the insurance commissioners or state superintendents of insurance of each state, the District of Columbia, and the four U.S. territories that works to promote uniformity of state regulation. [8]

National Association of Securities Dealers (NASD).
A nonprofit organization of securities dealers that regulates the market conduct of member companies and their representatives; individuals and companies that are subject to SEC regulation are subject to NASD regulation. [8]

nonagency-building system.
A personal selling distribution system in which an insurance company recruits producers who require little training, are financially self-supporting, and work out of independent offices. [9]

non-natural owner.
An entity such as a trust, partnership, or corporation that owns an annuity contract. [1]

nonproprietary products.
Products issued by one insurer and sold by a different insurer. [9]

nonqualified annuity.
An annuity that does not qualify to receive favorable tax treatment. [1]

Office of the Superintendent of Financial Institutions (OSFI).
A Canadian federal agency under the direction of the Superintendent of Financial Institutions that is responsible for monitoring the operations of all financial institutions in Canada. [8]

Office of the Superintendent of Insurance.
A Canadian provincial agency that operates under the direction of a Superintendent of Insurance to enforce the province's insurance laws and regulations. [8]

ordinary agency system.
An agency-building distribution system that uses full-time or part-time career agents to sell and service insurance products, including annuities; consists of the branch office system and the general agency system. [9]

OSFI.
See **Office of the Superintendent of Financial Institutions**.

participation rate.
The percentage of the specified index's gain in value that an equity-indexed annuity contract will earn. [3]

payee.
The person or legal entity who receives the annuity payments. [1]

payout options provision.
A provision in an annuity contract which identifies and describes each of the options the contract owner may elect for the distribution of annuity benefits during the payout period. Also known as a *settlement options provision.* [2]

payout period.
The time during which annuity payments are made. [1]

pension plan.
A type of qualified employer-sponsored retirement plan under which an employer makes contributions on behalf of employees to provide those employees with a lifetime monthly income benefit that begins at retirement. [6]

Pension Benefits Act.
A Canadian federal law that governs the terms and operation of private retirement plans. [6]

period certain.
The specified period of time over which an insurer guarantees payments under an annuity certain. [2]

personal-producing general agency (PPGA) system.
A nonagency-building distribution system that relies on personal-producing general agents to sell and service insurance and annuity products. [9]

personal-producing general agent.
A commissioned sales agent who typically works alone, is not housed in an insurance company field office, and engages primarily in personal selling; the agent typically is experienced and holds agency contracts with several insurance companies. [9]

personal retirement account (PRA).
A savings account into which an employee would deposit a percentage of current Social Security payroll taxes; accounts would be used to replace or supplement Social Security payments at retirement. [10]

personal selling.
    A form of promotion in which salespeople present product information during face-to-face meetings between a sales person and one or more prospective customers. [9]

personal selling distribution system.
    A distribution system in which commissioned or salaried salespeople sell products through oral and written presentations made to prospective customers. [9]

plan participant.
    An employee who is covered by a private employer-sponsored retirement plan. [6]

plan sponsor.
    An employer that establishes a private retirement plan on behalf of its employees. [6]

plan trustee.
    A person, appointed by the sponsor of a qualified retirement plan, who holds legal title to the retirement plan assets on behalf of plan participants. [6]

point-to-point method.
    A method of calculating excess interest on an equity-indexed annuity that involves comparing the value of the index at the start of the annuity contract term to the value at the end of the term to determine what, if any, excess interest has accrued because of a change in the index. [3]

PPGA.
    See **personal-producing general agency system**.

PRA.
    See **personal retirement account**.

premature distribution.
    A withdrawal of earnings from an annuity made before the contract owner reaches age 59½. [7]

present value (PV).
    The amount that must be invested now, at a given rate of interest, to accumulate a specified amount by a certain future date. [5]

price.
    The item of value (usually an amount of money) that a customer gives to a company in exchange for a product. [9]

pricing.
    The process of determining the amount to charge a customer for a product. [9]

principal.
　The total amount of premiums paid into an annuity, exclusive of any investment returns. [3]

　An officer and/or manager of an NASD member company who is involved in the day-to-day operation of a securities business, has qualified as a registered representative, and has passed additional examinations. [8]

　An insurance company that grants authority to agents or producers to act on the company's behalf. [9]

Producer Licensing Model Act.
　A model act developed by the NAIC that specifies requirements an individual must satisfy to be licensed as an insurance producer. [8]

product.
　A good, service, or idea that a company offers to customers in order to satisfy their needs. [9]

product design objectives.
　A description of a proposed product's basic features and benefits and the manner in which the benefits will be provided. [9]

professional advisors distribution system.
　A nonagency-building distribution system wherein professional advisors who are licensed to sell insurance—including financial planners, certified public accountants, and attorneys—enter into sales agreements with one or more insurance companies to distribute their products. [9]

profit sharing plan.
　A type of qualified employer-sponsored retirement plan that is funded by employer contributions payable from, and usually based on, the employer's profits. [6]

promotion.
　The methods a company uses to communicate with customers and influence them to buy a product. [9]

prospectus.
　A written document describing specific aspects of a security being offered for sale. [8]

publicity.
　A form of promotion in which information about a company or its products and services is transmitted in a news format by the mass media.

PV.
See **present value**.

qualified annuity.
An annuity purchased to accumulate or distribute funds from a tax-qualified plan. [1]

qualified tuition program.
A form of prepaid tuition plan designed to help parents save for their children's college tuition. Also known as a *529 program*. [6]

ratchet method.
See **annual reset method**.

readability requirements.
State-mandated requirements that limit the amount of technical jargon and legal language included in insurance and annuity contracts. [8]

refund annuity.
See **life income with refund annuity**.

registered pension plan (RPP).
A type of registered retirement plan in Canada; equivalent to a qualified pension plan in the United States. [6]

registered representative.
An investment advisor, a producer, or an insurance company employee who satisfies NASD registration requirements. [8]

registered retirement savings plan (RRSP).
A type of registered retirement plan in Canada that allows people with earned income (not employers) to make tax-deductible contributions into a tax-deferred savings plan; equivalent to an individual retirement arrangement (IRA) in the United States. [6]

renewal rate.
The interest rate an insurer will pay for the next period of a fixed annuity; may be higher or lower than the current interest rate, depending on conditions in the general economy and how the insurer has invested the annuity funds. [2]

replacement.
A transaction in which an existing individual life insurance or annuity contract is surrendered or otherwise terminated in order to purchase another contract. [8]

Replacement of Life Insurance and Annuities Model Regulation.
A model regulation developed by the NAIC that specifies procedures that producers and insurers must follow when a new contract will replace an existing contract. [8]

return.
 The profit an investor earns on his investment. [4]

risk.
 The possibility that an investment will lose value. [4]

risk-return trade-off.
 The interplay between risks and returns offered by various investment options, in which higher risks usually generate higher returns and lower risks usually generate lower returns. [4]

rollover.
 A tax-free contribution of cash or other assets disbursed from one retirement plan into another retirement plan. [6]

RPP.
 See **registered pension plan**.

RRSP.
 See **registered retirement savings plan**.

salaried sales distribution system.
 An agency-building distribution system that relies on the use of a company's salaried sales representatives to sell and service all types of insurance and annuity products; most often used for group insurance and annuity products. [9]

salaried sales representative.
 An employee of an insurer who is paid on a salaried basis. [9]

sales promotion.
 A form of promotion designed to encourage salespeople to sell a product or customers to buy a product. [9]

Savings Incentive Match Plan for Employees (SIMPLE) 401(k).
 An arrangement whereby an employer with 100 or fewer employees can establish a simplified 401(k) retirement savings plan for employees. [6]

Savings Incentive Match Plan for Employees (SIMPLE) IRA.
 An arrangement whereby an employer with 100 or fewer employees can establish a simplified IRA for employees. [6]

screening.
 The process of quickly evaluating proposed product ideas to determine which ones merit further investigation and development. [9]

segregated account. *See* **separate account**.

Section 1035 exchange.
An arrangement under which an insurer transfers contract values, tax free, from an original life insurance or annuity contract to a new contract without any distribution passing through the hands of the contract owner. [7]

Securities Act of 1933.
A U.S. federal law that protects investors by requiring that they receive specified types of information about securities being offered for sale to the public. [8]

Securities Exchange Act of 1934.
A U.S. federal law that created the Securities and Exchange Commission (SEC) and granted it broad authority to enforce the Securities Act of 1933 and to regulate the securities industry. [8]

SEP plan.
See **simplified employee pension plan**.

separate account.
An investment account maintained apart from an insurer's general account to help manage the funds placed in variable insurance products such as variable annuities. In Canada, the separate account is known as a *segregated account*. [1]

settlement options provision.
See **payout options provision**.

SIMPLE IRA.
See **Savings Incentive Match Plan for Employees IRA**.

SIMPLE 401(k).
See **Savings Incentive Match Plan for Employees 401(k)**.

simplified employee pension (SEP) plan.
An arrangement under which an employer makes contributions to an IRA for each participating employee. [6]

single-premium annuity.
An annuity contract that is purchased by the payment of one lump-sum premium. [1]

single-premium deferred annuity (SPDA).
An annuity contract under which the lump-sum premium used to purchase the annuity is held by the insurer and payments are deferred until some future date specified by the contract owner. [1]

single-premium immediate annuity (SPIA).
An annuity contract purchased with a single premium payment that begins paying annuity benefits one annuity period after the annuity is purchased. [1]

solvency.
The ability of an insurer to make specified payments to contract owners and to meet other financial obligations on time. [8]

specialty advertising.
A form of promotion that consists of articles imprinted with a company name or logo, address, phone number, and sometimes a sales message promoting a company, its producers, or its products. [9]

SPDA.
See **single-premium deferred annuity**.

SPIA.
See **single-premium immediate annuity**.

spread.
A specified percentage that is deducted from the index gain to determine the amount of gain that an equity-indexed annuity contract will earn. Also known as a *margin*. [3]

stagnant market risk.
The risk that the stock market will experience neither a significant gain nor a significant loss. [5]

state department of insurance.
See **state insurance department**.

state insurance department.
A state agency charged with making sure that insurance companies operating within a state comply with all of that state's insurance laws and regulations. Also known as the *state department of insurance*. [8]

stock.
An ownership share in a company. [4]

stock subaccount.
A subaccount in an insurance company's separate account that consists of an array of domestic and foreign stocks. [4]

Straight life annuity.
See **life only annuity**.

subaccount.
One of several investment funds in an insurer's separate account; subaccounts offer a variety of risk and return options. [1]

suitability requirement.
A requirement that imposes a duty on producers and/or insurers to have reasonable grounds on which to recommend a specific product as appropriate for a customer's needs. [8]

surrender.
A transaction in which the contract owner receives the annuity contract's entire cash surrender value and thereby cancels the contract. [2]

surrender charge.
A penalty imposed by an insurer when a contract owner withdraws funds from or surrenders an annuity contract. [2]

target market.
A clearly defined market segment on which a company focuses its marketing activities. [9]

target marketing.
The process of evaluating various market segments and then selecting one or more of those segments to be the focus of a company's marketing activities. [9]

tax cost basis.
The amount of money contract owners pay into Roth IRAs and non-IRA individual nonqualified annuities. [7]

tax-qualified plan.
An employer-sponsored retirement plan that satisfies Internal Revenue Code and Employee Retirement Income Security Act (ERISA) requirements and, as a result, provides certain favorable tax treatments for both the employer and the participating employees. [1]

Tax Sheltered Annuity (TSA).
A retirement annuity sold only to public school teachers and employees of hospitals, colleges, and other organizations offering qualified retirement plans under section 403(b) of the U.S. Internal Revenue Code. [6]

term.
The length of time over which excess interest on an equity-indexed annuity is calculated. [3]

time value of money.
An investment principle which states that the value of a sum of money will change over time as a result of the effects of interest. [5]

transfer.
A special service that allows a contract owner to move assets among variable annuity subaccounts during the accumulation period or the payout period. [4]

trustee-to-trustee transfer.
A type of rollover transfer in which the entire account balance in one qualified retirement savings plan is transferred directly to a new qualified plan, without any part of the distribution going to the plan participant. [7]

TSA.
See **Tax Sheltered Annuity**.

unbundled annuity.
A variable annuity that is broken down into two parts: (1) a simple base product with relatively low asset fees and relatively standard features and (2) a set of enhanced benefits that the customer can purchase at an additional cost. [10]

variable annuity.
An annuity contract under which the amount of the contract's accumulated value and the amount of the periodic annuity benefit payments fluctuate in accordance with the performance of a specified pool of investments. [1]

variable guaranteed account.
See **fixed account**.

variable payout.
A variable annuity payout option in which the insurer makes a series of payments to the annuitant that vary throughout the payout period according to the performance of subaccount values. [2]

vesting schedule.
A timetable that specifies how much a contract owner can withdraw—before the end of the contract term—of the excess interest that has been credited to an equity-indexed annuity. [3]

waiver of premium for disability rider.
A rider included in annuity contracts which allows contract owners to stop making premium payments in the event that they become disabled. [2]

waiver of surrender charge provision.
A provision in an annuity contract which states that no surrender charge will be assessed on surrenders or withdrawals in excess of specified levels under certain conditions, such as disability, poor medical condition, terminal illness, unemployment, and confinement in a nursing home or hospital. [2]

window premiums.
Additional premiums paid during the first contract year of a single-premium deferred annuity. [1]

withdrawal.
A transaction in which the owner of an annuity removes a portion of the annuity's accumulated value from the contract account, but does not cancel the contract. [2]

Annuity Principles and Products

INDEX

Aa

access to funds 83
accumulated value 10
accumulation period 8
accumulation units 27
administrative fee 28
advertising 160
Advertisements of Life Insurance and Annuities Model Regulation 136
advertising and disclosure requirements 136, 143–144
agency contract 166
agency marketing organization 170
agency-building system 166
agent 166
agent-broker 166, 167
AIR. *See* assumed investment rate
AMO. *See* agency marketing organization
annual reset method 49
Annual Return 147
Annual Statement 133
annuitant 4, 5
annuities, types of 7–12
annuitized payout options 35–38
annuity certain 34
annuity contract 2, 3, 21–41
annuity contract provisions 137
annuity date. *See* maturity date
Annuity Disclosure Model Regulation 138
annuity period 7
annuity unit 37
asset allocation 63, 82
asset allocation model 64
asset allocation model options 65
asset class 61
asset management fee 29
assignment provision 25
assumed investment rate 40
automatic dollar cost averaging provision 68
automatic rebalancing provision 70

Bb

back-end loaded account 11, 12
bailout provision 32
bank distribution 171
bank insurance 171
beneficiary 4, 6
beneficiary provision 24
bond 61
bond subaccount 61
bonus annuity 191
branch manager 167
branch office system 167
broker-dealer 170, 171
broker-dealer distribution 170
brokerage general agency arrangement 172
Buyer's Guide to Fixed Deferred Annuities 138

Cc

calculating annuity benefit payments 39–41
calculating excess interest 49–50
calculating market value adjustments 53–54
call center 168, 169
Canadian Council of Insurance Regulators 146
Canadian federal regulation 147
Canadian provincial regulation 146–147
cap 51
capital appreciation 60, 61
capital gain 87
career agent 166
cash surrender value 29
cash-out provision. *See* bailout provision
CCIR. *See* Canadian Council of Insurance Regulators
CD. *See* certificate of deposit

CDSC. *See* contingent deferred sales charge
certificate of authority 134
certificate of deposit 75
commission 166, 167
compound interest 80
comprehensive business analysis 155
conformity with law provision. *See* conformity with state statutes provision
conformity with state statutes provision 137
contact center 168, 169
contingent annuitant 6
contingent deferred sales charge 30
contract duration 23
contract form requirements 135–136
contract options 22–23
contract owner 3–5
contract provisions 23, 137
contract values 66, 67
corporate changes 180–181
cost recovery rule 120
Coverdell Education Savings Account 99
crediting earnings 26–27
cross-selling 168
cross-selling distribution system 168
current interest rate 26

Dd

death benefit guarantee 71
deferred annuity 8
deferred fixed annuity 47
deferred profit sharing plan 110
defined benefit plan 102
defined contribution plan 104
demographic changes 12–15, 181–182
direct mail 172
direct response distribution systems 172–173

disclosure document 138
distribution 102, 151
distribution system 162
distributions 33
diversification 64, 82
dividend 60
dollar cost averaging 68, 81
DPSP. *See* deferred profit sharing plan

Ee

Economic Growth and Tax Relief Reconciliation Act 100, 184
education IRA. *See* Coverdell Education Savings Account
EGTRRA. *See* Economic Growth and Tax Relief Reconciliation Act
Employee Retirement Income Security Act 101
employee stock option plans 104
entire contract provision 23, 137
equity-indexed annuities 10, 48–52
ERISA. *See* Employee Retirement Income Security Act
escape clause. *See* bailout provision
estate taxes 125–126
exchange 151
exchange of contract(s) 126
exclusion ratio 118–119
exclusive agent 166

Ff

FDIC. *See* Federal Deposit Insurance Corporation
Federal Deposit Insurance Corporation 75
federal regulations 140–145, 171
fees and charges 28–32

financial institutions distribution systems 170–172
financial planner 169, 170
529 program. *See* qualified tuition program
fixed account 61
fixed amount option 34
fixed annuities 10, 43–54
fixed payout 37, 40
fixed period option 34
fixed-premium annuity 10
flexible-premium annuity 10
401(k) 104, 105, 107
403(b) 106
403(b) plan 106
457 plan 106
free look provision 25, 137
free withdrawal provision 31
front-end loaded account 11, 12
future of annuities 177–195
   demographic changes 181–182
   economic changes 179–181
   industry response 189–193
   regulatory changes 182–186
   Social Security changes 186–188
future of the fixed annuity market 54
future value 80
FV. *See* future value

Gg

general account 10
general agency system 167, 168
general agent 167, 168
GLB. *See* Gramm-Leach-Bliley Act
GMAB. *See* Guaranteed Minimum Accumulation Benefit
GMIB. *See* Guaranteed Minimum Income Benefit
GMWB. *See* Guaranteed Minimum Withdrawal Benefit
grace period provision 24
Gramm-Leach-Bliley Act 171
gross estate 125
group annuities 11, 91, 100–109
guaranteed interest rate 26
Guaranteed Minimum Accumulation Benefit 71
Guaranteed Minimum Income Benefit 70
Guaranteed Minimum Withdrawal Benefit 70
guaranty association 133

Hh

high water mark method 50
home-office-to-home-office arrangement 171

Ii

idea generation 154
immediate annuity 7
IMO. *See* independent marketing organization
in-house brokerage agency arrangement 172
income taxes 116–123
   annuity benefit payments 117–120
   annuity earnings 117
   annuity premiums 116–117
   loans 121
   United States 116–123
   withdrawals 120
incontestability provision 25, 137
independent marketing organization 170
index 10
individual annuities 11, 93–100
individual retirement account. *See* individual retirement arrangement
individual retirement arrangement 93–96
industry response to changes 189–193
inflation erosion 48
inflation risk 79

initial premium 23
Insurance Companies Act 147
insurance company distribution 171–172
insurance producers 134
insurer 3, 5
interest 60
interest first rule 121
interest rate guarantees 45, 49–51
interest rate risk 79
Internet sales 173
investment advisor 141
Investment Advisor's Act of 1940 141
investment company 141
Investment Company Act of 1940 141
investment features of various financial products 83–87
investment options 53
investment principles 75–82
Investment Risk Strategy Quiz 76-77
investment security 83
investments 102
IRA. *See* individual retirement arrangement
IRA-based annuities 94–96
    Roth IRAs 95–96
    traditional IRAs 94–95

Jj

joint and survivor annuity 36
joint annuitant 6
joint owner 4

Kk

Keogh plans 103, 109

Ll

life annuity 35
life income with period certain annuity 36
life income with refund annuity 37
Life Insurance Illustrations Model Regulation 137
life only annuity 35
loans 32, 121–123
    individual nonqualified annuities 122
    qualified annuities 32, 122
location selling distribution system 169
Long Term Care Benefit 71
lump-sum distribution 33, 96–98

Mm

M&E charge. *See* mortality and expense risks charge
mail kit 172
margin. *See* spread
market 151, 152
market analysis 155
market conduct regulation 134–139
market risk 79
market segment 151, 152
market segmentation 151, 152
market selection 151–152
market value adjusted annuity 10, 11, 52–54
market value adjustments 53
market volatility 179
marketing 149–175
marketing mix 151
marketing plan 155
maturity date 33
McCarran-Ferguson Act 131
minimum distribution 125
misstatement of age or sex provision 24, 137
model law 131
Model Variable Annuity Regulation 142
money market subaccount 61
money-purchase plans 104
mortality and expense risks charge 29

multi-strategy products 191
mutual fund 11
MVA. *See* market value adjusted annuity

Nn

NAIC 142. *See* National Association of Insurance Commissioners
NAIC Model Laws 132
   Advertisements of Life Insurance and Annuities Model Regulation 132
   Annuity Disclosure Model Regulation 132
   Life and Health Insurance Policy Language Simplification Model Act 132
   Model Variable Annuity Regulation 132
   New Annuity Mortality Table Model Rule 132
   Producer Licensing Model Act 132
   Replacement of Life Insurance and Annuities Model Regulation 132
   Standard Nonforfeiture Law for Individual Deferred Annuities 132
NASD. *See* National Association of Securities Dealers
National Association of Insurance Commissioners 131
National Association of Securities Dealers 141, 142
non-natural owner 4
nonagency-building system 166
nonannuitized payouts 33–35
nondiscrimination 102
nonforfeiture provision 24, 137
nonproprietary products 171
nonqualified annuities 12, 93–94, 118–120, 122
nonqualified retirement plans 110

Nursing Home Care Benefit 71

Oo

Office of the Superintendent of Financial Institutions 147
Office of the Superintendent of Insurance 146
ordinary agency system 167
OSFI. *See* Office of the Superintendent of Financial Institutions

Pp

participation 102
participation rate 51
payee 4, 6
payment of death benefits 32–33
payout guarantees 46–47
payout options 37–41, 88
payout options provision 26, 137
payout period 8
penalty taxes 123–125
Pension Benefits Act 109
pension plans 101, 103
period certain 34
personal retirement accounts 188
personal selling 160
personal selling distribution system 165–170
personal-producing general agency system 169
personal-producing general agent 169
plan participant 100
plan sponsor 100
plan trustee 101
point-to-point method 50
PPGA. *See* personal-producing general agency system
PRA. *See* personal retirement accounts
premature distribution 124
present value 80

price 151
pricing 158–159
principal 45, 142, 166
principal guarantees 45, 48
Producer Licensing Model Act 135
product 151
product design objectives 155
product development 152–155
product distribution 162–171
product implementation 156–158
product planning 152
product pricing 158–159
product promotion 160–162
product review 158
product technical design 155–156
professional advisors distribution system 169, 170
profit sharing plans 103, 104
promotion 151
prospectus 144
publicity 162
PV. *See* present value

Qq

qualified annuities 12, 120, 122
qualified retirement plans 101–109
qualified retirement savings plans 103
qualified tuition program 100

Rr

ratchet method. *See* annual reset method
readability requirements 136
refund annuity. *See* life income with refund annuity
registered pension plan 109
registered representative 142
registered retirement plans in Canada 109–110, 127
regulatory changes 182–186

reinstatement provision 24
renewal rate 27
replacement 139–140
Replacement of Life Insurance and Annuities Model Regulation 139
reporting 102
retirement savings plans 103, 105–109
return 59, 75
risk 59, 75–79
  risk tolerance 76–79
  risk-return trade-off 59
  types of risk 78–79
rollovers 96–99, 127
  types of 98
Roth IRAs 95–96
RPP. *See* registered pension plan
RRSP. *See* registered retirement savings plan

Ss

salaried sales distribution system 168–169
salaried sales representative 168
sales monitoring 158
sales promotion 160–162
Savings Incentive Match Plans for Employees 103, 108
screening 154
SEC. *See* Securities and Exchange Commission
Section 1035 exchange 126, 185
Securities Act of 1933 141
Securities and Exchange Commission 141–144
Securities Exchange Act of 1934 141
securities regulation 141–145
segregated account 11
SEP. *See* simplified employee pension plans
separate account 11

SERS. *See* Small Employer Retirement Survey
settlement options provision. *See also* payout options provision
SIMPLE 103, 107, 184. *See* Savings Incentive Match Plan for Employees
simple interest 80
simplified employee pension plans 103, 106
single-premium annuity 9
single-premium deferred annuity 9
single-premium immediate annuity 9
Small Employer Retirement Survey 184
Social Security Changes 186–188
solvency 133
solvency regulation 133
SPDA. *See* single-premium deferred annuity
specialty advertising 161–162
SPIA. *See* single-premium immediate annuity
split participation rates 190
spread 51, 190
stagnant market risk 79
state department of insurance. *See also* state insurance department
state insurance department 131
stock 61
stock bonus plans 104
stock subaccount 61
straight life annuity 35
subaccount 11, 61–63
   bond 61
   money market 61
   stock 61
   variable annuity 62
subaccount investments 59–66
subaccount values 64–66
suitability requirement 138
surrender 29
surrender charge 29–32
surrender provision 24, 30

Tt

target benefit plans 104
target market 152
target marketing 152
tax advantages of investments 85–88, 116–117
tax cost basis 116
tax laws 98, 100, 105, 106
tax reforms 184–185
Tax Sheltered Annuity 106
tax-qualified plan 12
taxation of annuities 113–127
   Canada 127
   United States 116–123
1035 exchanges 126, 185
term 49
time value of money 80
traditional fixed annuities 45–48
traditional IRAs 94–95, 120
transfer 69
trustee-to-trustee transfer 127
TSA. *See* Tax Sheltered Annuity

Uu

U.S. estate taxes 125–126
U.S. income taxes 116–123
U.S. penalty taxes 123–125
unbundled annuity 191

Vv

variable annuities 11, 37–39, 57–72
variable annuity subaccounts 62
variable guaranteed account. *See also* fixed account 61
variable payout 37, 41
vesting 102
vesting rights 52
vesting schedule 52

Ww

waiver of premium for disability
    rider 25
waiver of surrender charge
    provision 32
window premiums 9
withdrawal 29
withdrawal provision 24

Yy

year-round averaging 189